Biblical Ethics &
HOMOSEXUALITY

Listening to Scripture

Robert L. Brawley
Editor

Westminster John Knox Press
Louisville, Kentucky

© 1996 Westminster John Knox Press

Scripture quotations from the New Revised Standard Version of the Bible are copyright © 1989 by the Division of Christian Education of the National Council of the Churches of Christ in the U.S.A. and are used by permission.

Excerpt from "An die Nachgeborenen" in *Selected Poems* by Bertolt Brecht, English trans. by H. R. Hayes, copyright 1947 by Bertolt Brecht and H. R. Hayes, and renewed 1975 by Stefan S. Brecht and H. R. Hayes. Reprinted by permission of Harcourt Brace & Company.

Book design by Jennifer K. Cox

Cover design by Kevin Darst

First edition

Published by Westminster John Knox Press
Louisville, Kentucky

This book is printed on acid-free paper that meets the American National Standards Institute Z39.48 standard. ∞

PRINTED IN THE UNITED STATES OF AMERICA

96 97 98 99 00 01 02 03 04 05 — 10 9 8 7 6 5 4 3 2 1

Library of Congress Cataloging-in-Publication Data

Biblical ethics and homosexuality : listening to scripture / Robert L. Brawley, editor. — 1st ed.
    p.   cm.
   Includes bibliographical references.
   ISBN 0-664-25638-4 (alk. paper)
   1. Homosexuality—Biblical teaching.   2. Sex—Biblical teaching.
3. Ethics in the Bible.   4. Christian ethics—Biblical teaching.
5. Homosexuality—Religious aspects—Christianity.   I. Brawley, Robert L. (Robert Lawson)
BS680.H67B52   1996
241'.66—dc20   95-46243

Biblical Ethics &
HOMOSEXUALITY

Contents

Preface

To begin on a personal note, my initial sex education in the home was integrally related to listening to scripture. My parents responded to my earliest questions about the mysteries of human sexuality with scientific and anatomically correct candor, but they also repeatedly linked their answers to Ps. 139:14: "I will praise you [God], for I am fearfully and wonderfully made." Henceforth, sex could never be either abhorrent or banal for me. Meanwhile, much of my culture has inclined either to make sex an abomination or to make it cheap. My childhood peers called it nasty, and modern cinematic portrayals often diminish sex to an animalistic titillation. But my parents had interpreted sexuality in mystery and wonder as a part of my relationship with God—nothing less than a relationship of praise to the God who searches me and knows me.

The dominant Christian tradition has tried to reduce sexuality in its mystery, wonder, and divine praise to heterosexual monogamous marriage. On the one hand, the guidance of the church to reserve sex for such marriage has preserved it from abomination and banality and conferred on it the role of mediating intimacy and love. In the church's effort to reserve sex for marriage and preserve it from abomination, the Christian tradition has recognized that human sexuality has enormous potential for the fulfillment of human beings—enough for them to praise God for their being fearfully and wonderfully made. The church has recognized as well the enormous potential of sexuality for disaster—wounded lives and broken hearts. This potential of sex for bane and blessing has made it a matter of Christian morality. So the church has generally stamped sexuality with a theological "handle with care" and has not left sexual behavior merely to personal discretion. The Christian community has guided its members to practice something that goes far beyond "safe sex."

On the other hand, sexuality does not always come in the single form of heterosexual monogamous marriage that the dominant tradition has endorsed. Sexual desire does not wait for marriage or even puberty. Monogamy has come upon hard times in the last half of the twentieth century, and a new social tolerance of and empathy with divorce and remarriage has made a version of serial polygamy a strong competitor with heterosexual monogomous marriage. Celibacy is also a time-honored alternative, and celibates do not cease to be sexual subjects in their celibacy. Further, sexual desire can be felt for members of one's own sex rather than for members of the opposite sex.

With the revision of the cultural landscape in the so-called sexual revolution of the 1970s, the Presbyterian Church brought issues of people engaged in same-sex relationships out of the closet. In 1976, the Presbytery of New York City and the Presbytery of the Palisades overtured the General Assembly of the United Presbyterian Church, U.S.A., to request "definitive guidance" on the ordination of self-acknowledged practicing homosexuals. The General Assembly appointed a Task Force to Study Homosexuality, and the task force submitted its report to the General Assembly in 1978. A majority of the task force recommended that the definitive guidance state that there is no prohibition of the ordination of self-affirming practicing homosexual persons. But a minority report recommended that the definitive guidance state that unrepentant homosexual practice is contrary to the requirements for ordination.

The minority report was adopted by the General Assembly and continues to be the position of the Presbyterian Church (U.S.A.). But two decades of debate in the Presbyterian Church have not produced harmonious consent. In 1993, the General Assembly urged its constituents to study and dialogue on issues of human sexual behavior and orientation with a view toward a review of the findings in 1996.

This volume is in response to the recommendation of the General Assembly for such study and dialogue. Twenty-four Bible scholars—primarily Presbyterians from Presbyterian seminaries—convened at McCormick Theological Seminary in Chicago, August 25–27, 1995, in a Consultation on Biblical Ethics and Human Sexuality. One of the basic warrants for convening a group of Bible scholars has to do with our efforts to determine what the Bible has to say in a normative way for Christians and the Christian church today. Another has to do with power plays among groups with different perspectives and agendas on human sexuality. Especially among Presbyterians with a heritage of *sola scriptura*, the Bible plays a major role in the power plays. Readers of this volume will encounter both examples of interpretation to determine the sense in which the Bible is normative for us today and examples of using the Bible to persuade others to accept different perspectives and agendas on human sexuality.

The chapters in this volume formed the core of the study and dialogue of the 1995 Consultation on Biblical Ethics and Human Sexuality in

Chicago. One of the concerns of the Consultation was methodology in biblical ethics. How do we use the Bible in determining human behavior? Ulrich Mauser appeals to use of the Old Testament creation stories of Genesis 1—2 in the New Testament, and he builds the case that in a number of instances the New Testament relies on God's creation of one human form of life in the polarity of male and female as the measure of human sexual behavior. In the present discussion on homosexuality Choon-Leong Seow attempts to broaden the use of the Bible beyond texts that explicitly deal with same-sex relationships. He contends particularly that wisdom literature warrants reflecting on human sexuality "from below," that is, reflecting on human sexuality from nature, human experience, reason, and science. My own contribution emphasizes a contrasting methodology that begins with God, and it advocates Christian behavior as the fruit of being led by the Spirit of God. But all the other chapters, explicitly or implicitly, have to do with how we use the Bible in determining human behavior.

In keeping with the recommendation of the General Assembly, the Consultation on Biblical Ethics and Human Sexuality had two additional foci. One has to do with human sexual behavior in general. In this category, Andrew Dearman's chapter, "Marriage in the Old Testament," develops the thesis that in the Old Testament human beings draw their social identity from their membership in families, and he contrasts that with modern perspectives on individual rights and self-fulfillment. Elizabeth Edwards's study of Paul's use of "flesh" first argues that developing Christian tradition interpreted Paul's concept negatively with detrimental consequences for an understanding of our sexuality. Then she suggests that Paul's patriarchal perspectives already contributed to that detrimental understanding. Sarah Melcher's contribution, "The Holiness Code and Human Sexuality," proposes that the Old Testament laws about sexuality in Leviticus 17—26 have to do with ensuring Israel's existence as a distinctive group both materially and culturally.

Three other chapters place more particular concern on the status of gays and lesbians in the modern church. Herman Waetjen attempts to explain the phenomenon of same-sex relationships in the cultural context of the New Testament and then to show the incongruity of modern categories of sexual orientation with the first-century cultural repertoire. But he turns back to the New Testament for a paradigm of overthrowing systems that divide human beings into clean (acceptable) and unclean (unacceptable). Dale Martin's detailed study of the Greek terms *arsenokoitês* and *malakos*—frequently understood as designations for homosexual persons—concludes that we have no way of knowing the meaning of the first term and that the second means "effeminate" in such a way as to reflect a negative social construct of females (and therefore of effeminate people). So he maintains that fundamentalist approaches that interpret 1 Cor. 6:9 and 1 Tim. 1:10 as against gays and lesbians are fallacious. He points instead to the double command of love of God and love of neighbor. Jeffrey Siker appropriates images from the parable of the wheat and the tares and the early church's inclusion of Gentiles among the people of God in order to support open Christian affirmation of committed, monogamous, same-sex unions.

Though aimed at a general audience, the entries contain notes that document sources and suggest additional resources. Abbreviations of biblical books, ancient Jewish literature, classical literature, and commonly used periodicals, reference works, and serials follow the conventions used in the *Society of Biblical Literature Handbook for Editors and Authors*.

Any reader expecting a group of Bible scholars to reach consensus on questions of human sexuality will be surprised by this volume. Twenty-four Bible scholars in study and dialogue did not reach unanimity in interpreting the Bible. But this lack of consensus devalues neither the Bible nor the study and dialogue on human sexuality. Rather, when Christians want to listen to scripture in connection with human sexuality, they enter a labyrinth. A labyrinth is not a dead end, but the way out is often complicated. Multiplicity in interpretation means that ethical understanding of human sexuality involves an intricate interplay of perspectives that reinforce, redirect, and correct one other. One outcome is that vistas are widened. We may see what we have not seen before and discern what we have not discerned before. But another outcome is that the interplay of perspectives undergirds the mystery of Ps. 139:14—we are "fearfully and wonderfully made." Some aspects of our human sexuality and our relationship to God do lie beyond our grasp, and we can live in fearful and wonderful awe of that divine mystery beyond our comprehension.

This volume is possible only through the collaboration of a number of people. I have stated that the Consultation involved the cooperation of twenty-four Bible scholars. Some of the participants have been engaged in similar study and dialogue on other fronts. Choon-Leong Seow is editing another volume with Westminster John Knox Press (*Homosexuality and Christian Community*), and readers of this volume may follow both his work and the work of Ulrich Mauser in that volume. The administration and staff of McCormick Theological Seminary contributed time, effort, and support—both moral and material—for hosting the Consultation. McCormick graduate Douglas Chial handled arrangements. Twenty-six private donors provided funds for the consultation. Jon Berquist of Westminster John Knox Press participated in the consultation and nursed the volume through the publication process. This volume itself is a token of gratitude to all whose collaboration made it possible.

Part 1

Methods: How We Use
the Bible in Christian Ethics

1

Creation and Human Sexuality in the New Testament

Ulrich W. Mauser

In several New Testament passages dealing with aspects of the relationship between men and women, we find an appeal to the Old Testament creation stories in Genesis 1 and 2. These passages are fundamental for New Testament perceptions of human sexuality. It is true that issues of sexual attitudes and conduct can also, in other New Testament traditions, be discussed without reference to the creation narratives. Jesus' teaching on adultery and on divorce in the Sermon on the Mount (Matt. 5:27–32) does not refer to the Genesis accounts, and the apostle Paul can write a long section of his correspondence with the Christian community in Corinth about marriage questions (1 Corinthians 7) without mentioning the primal history of the Old Testament. There are, however, five passages in the New Testament that consider some basic problems of human sexuality in which the evocation of the creation stories is essential to the argument. These five passages are (1) Mark 10:2–9 and its parallel, Matt. 19:3–9; (2) Rom. 1:18–32, specifically verses 24–27; (3) 1 Cor. 6:12–20; (4) 1 Cor. 11:2–16; and (5) Eph. 5:21–33.[1] We shall deal with Rom. 1:18–32 last because it is the only passage that contains no direct citation of Genesis 1 or 2. The space allotted does not permit consideration of Eph. 5:21–33.

The New Testament passages just cited have in common an appeal to the Genesis story of creation for the purpose of giving guidance about sexual attitudes and conduct. We shall now look more closely at the linkage between the creation stories and the specific issues raised in each of the four passages under consideration. Other critical issues will be mentioned only in passing. The dominant question will be, throughout, What are the reasons, the purpose, and the result of the authors' practice to address questions of sexual behavior in the earliest Christian communities by connecting them with the creation stories of Genesis 1 and 2?

Mark 10:2–9 and Matt. 19:3–9

Jesus' teaching against divorce is preserved in the New Testament in five different wordings, none of which agrees verbatim with the others (Matt. 5:32; 19:9; Mark 10:11–12; Luke 16:18; 1 Cor. 7:10–11). The modifying clause "except for unchastity" in Matt. 5:32 and 19:9 is a secondary addition to the teaching, since it is not found in Mark, Luke, or Paul. In Mark 10:2–9 and Matt. 19:3–9, Jesus' words against divorce are built into the setting of a debate about issues of Jewish law. The passages both in Mark and in Matthew cannot reflect a genuine origin in Jesus' life; rather, they are the work of early formations of traditions in Christian communities: The question put in the Pharisees' mouths, "Is it lawful for a man to divorce his wife?" (Mark 10:2), is unthinkable from teachers of Jewish law because that issue was not controversial, having been settled by Deut. 24:1–4; and the quotations from Gen. 2:24 in Matt. 19:5 and Mark 10:7 depend on the Septuagint.

The two accounts in Mark and Matthew vary considerably. Omitting details, we note that the introduction of the argument from creation is put at the beginning of the exchanges of questions and answers in Matthew (19:4–6), whereas in Mark the citation concludes the flow of the debate (10:6–9). In Matthew the Pharisees understand the legislation of Deut. 24:1–4 to be a command, and Jesus interprets it as permission (19:7, 8), but Mark states the reverse (10:3, 4). The appeal to the primal order of sexuality is made once in Mark (10:6); in Matthew it is repeated and thus underscored (19:4, 8). In spite of these and other differences, the reference to Gen. 1:27 and 2:24 in relation to Jesus' sayings about divorce is the same in both accounts. What is expressed in the appeal to creation?

The Mosaic law permitting and regulating divorce is superseded by an older, more original order of sexuality.[2] Appeal is made to an order of things prevailing "at [or from] the beginning" (Matt. 19:4; Mark 10:6). Moses' law opens the door to a possibility that, at the beginning in God's creation, was not given. The appeal to creation against Moses' Torah presupposes the restoration of a state of human sexuality in which adjustments to sick and destroyed relationships between husbands and wives are no longer necessary. The idea of the correspondence of primal time and final time (protology and eschatology) is introduced into the concept of human sexuality:[3] with the coming of the kingdom of God a restored condition of the husband–wife relation has arrived that confirms God's good, pristine order.

Genesis 1 and 2 were in New Testament times read as a single continuous narrative. Thus the statement about the creation of male and female (Gen. 1:27) and the sentence about the leaving of the parental home by the husband to cling to his wife, forming a new oneness out of two (Gen. 2:24), are welded into a single statement in which the former sentence becomes the reason for the second: "God made them male and female. *For this rea-*

son a man shall leave his father and mother and be joined to his wife, and the two shall become one flesh" (Mark 10:6–8; Matt. 19:4–5, with negligible differences). The drive that causes a man to abandon his family's unit to form with his wife a new union of life is grounded in an antecedent act of divine creation, the calling into being of the single human species (Gen. 1:27, septuagint *anthrōpon*) in the actual differentiation of male and female (*arsen kai thēly epoiēsen autous*). As God's creation there is only one human being existing in two separate, distinct, and different forms of male and female; and vice versa, they are in their separateness, distinction, and difference one single human being. In this simultaneous oneness and duality male and female together are in the image of God, receive the blessing of God, and have the unrestricted approval of their Creator to be "very good" (Gen. 1:28, 31).

The drift of the debate about divorce in Mark 10 and Matthew 19 leads to ethical conclusions and to moral imperatives: "What God has joined together, let no one separate" (Mark 10:9; Matt. 19:6). But the imperatives are laid, through their connection with the creation stories, on the foundation of a primal facticity that is neither subject to nor dependent on human decision and conduct. Jesus' judgment against divorce is not pegged to a superior morality but to the divine verdict of creation. Perhaps it is necessary to use philosophical terminology to establish the point most clearly: The words of the creation stories uncover a level of existence prior to morality and law; they are ontologically oriented, not morally directed. Exactly in that ontological grounding they receive their true moral potency.

The truth or falsehood of this vision of the nature of the male–female relationship does not depend on the human ability, or inability, to live up to its demands. The Matthean version of the debate on divorce is, significantly enough, followed by the disillusioned statement of the disciples: "If such is the case of a man with his wife, it is better not to marry" (19:10). Jesus' words were, then, experienced as a provocation, an unwelcome revelation, a jolting out of natural complacency. The condition of our moral sensibilities and the range of what our life experiences dictate as achievable are not the measure with which human sexuality is discovered as God's creation.

1 Corinthians 6:12–20

The passage fights against the view that the affirmation "all things are lawful for me" (6:12) be misused as permission for members of the Christian community in Corinth to hire the services of prostitutes. Manifestly, there was a group among the Corinthian Christians who advocated this practice, and their support of it seems to have appealed to the notion of Christian freedom. The outlines of their argument appear to be fairly clear from 1 Cor. 6:12–20. They must have reasoned that sexual activity is a purely biological function comparable to the need for food and drink

(6:13). As the stomach requires periodic intake of nourishment causing a constant cycle of hunger, satisfaction, and renewed hunger, so sexual activity is governed by the similar cycle of desire, satisfaction, and newly awakened desire. It is probable that this purely biological view of sexual activity was coupled, for the group in question, with a low esteem of matters that were bound to human corporeality; possibly the conviction that God will destroy both the stomach and the food reflects not only Paul's judgment but that of the Corinthian group as well. Be this as it may, Paul's turn against the apology for prostitution is clear: "Shun prostitution" (6:18). Prostitution is not an exercise of Christian freedom but a form of being dominated, not only for the female prostitute but equally for the male who engages her service (6:12).

Woven into the argument against prostitution is a direct citation of a part of Gen. 2:24 and a play with words used in the same verse. A male using a prostitute clings to her (6:16) as a believer clings to the Lord (6:17). The Greek word employed in both verses (*kollōmai*) is the same as the one used in Gen. 2:24 for the union of man and woman. A part of Gen. 2:24 is quoted verbatim in 1 Cor. 6:16, "the two shall be one flesh." The Genesis word is pivotal in the context because it states an act in which two persons distinct from each other become a unity of life. There is, in this respect, an exact parallel between the unity established by a man and a prostitute and the unity achieved between the believer and the Lord: "Whoever clings to a prostitute becomes one body with her" and "anyone who clings to the Lord becomes one spirit with him" (6:16–17, my trans.).

Is Gen. 2:24 quoted in 1 Cor. 6:16 merely to give scriptural authority to an argument that would have been just as compelling without the reference? I do not think so. In distinction to the fuller quotation of Gen. 2:24 in Matt. 19:5 and Mark 10:7–8, Paul concentrates the Genesis word completely into the event in which two become one; the leaving of the parental home is omitted and the clinging together of husband and wife is reduced to the mere echo of the word *kollōmai*. In this way the whole question is reduced to the single point of two becoming one. This becoming one out of two is the devastating analogy between the act of prostitution and the act of Christian faith. In the sentence from the creation story "the two shall be one flesh," Paul heard the affirmation that the sexual union between a man and a woman establishes intrinsically a union in which their selves, their personhoods, come together so that each belongs to the other. "Flesh" is not distinct from "body" in this case, as is shown by the parallel between becoming "one body" with the prostitute and becoming "one flesh" of husband and wife in 6:16. The sexual act involves the body, not merely the stomach, because it involves the total self, which, in its corporeality, is in dependency and communion with the other,[4] be it the legitimate or the illegitimate sexual partner, or be it the Christian community with which the believer is "one body," or the Lord with whom the Christian is one spirit. This union of two selves in the sexual act can be in harmony with the union of the believer and the Lord. But it becomes, in Paul's reading of Gen. 2:24, a contradiction in terms if it involves intercourse with a prostitute. "Christ is the faithfulness of God in person, whereas the harlot personifies human unfaithfulness toward other humans."[5] Union with the prostitute, therefore, is not an expression of Christian freedom but its destruction, its perversion into slavery.

By establishing the analogy between the Christians' unity in the Lord and the unity of two human selves in the sexual act, Paul also imputed a meaning to Gen. 2:24 that this verse had never before achieved. Prostitution was not outlawed in the Mosaic Torah. No Jewish interpreter has ever, to my knowledge, drawn consequences from this sentence in the biblical creation story leading to the verdict that prostitution was intrinsically and essentially a contradiction to being a member of the community of God. The intensity of Paul's understanding of belonging to Christ, of sharing a new life with him beyond the destructive realities of sin and death, seems to have intensified also his sensibilities for the dimensions of sexuality. He incorporated the creation story at the very core of his stand against prostitution, but he also read the Genesis narrative as one who had passed from death to life in his becoming one with Christ. Creation including human sexuality remained for him a key to understanding the new creation. But the reverse is also true: It is the belonging to Christ that unlocks depths in the understanding of sexuality unfathomed before.

1 Corinthians 11:2–16

References to Genesis 1 and 2 are integrated into this passage to an extent that has caused some interpreters to say the section is a midrash on key sentences of the biblical creation account.[6] The quotes and allusions to the first two chapters of Genesis are applied to a specific problem in the Christian community at Corinth whose precise reconstruction causes extreme difficulties. A good half dozen words are clearly linked to a special situation. The specific words employed, and the social circumstances to which they belong, defy certainty of analysis.

Our purpose is limited to the assessment of the role played by the Genesis quotations in the discussion of a problem in Corinth that is clearly related to gender questions. In order to weigh the contribution of the scriptural echoes, some hypothesis needs to be stated about the nature of the tensions addressed in 1 Cor. 11:2–16. Although the hypothesis will be restricted to very general terms, it is supported by evidence that is not beyond legitimate dispute.

It is our assumption that the tension to which Paul addresses himself in this passage arises in the public worship of the community. In view is not a dress code for private gatherings, or for the streets of Corinth, but a regulation about headdress and hairstyle when the community meets for worship. In this act of worship women pray aloud and prophesy, along with the men, and no criticism of this custom is implied (vv. 4–5). What is controversial, however, is the way some women cut their hair and discard certain pieces of clothing covering their head during public worship (vv. 5–6, 13–15). Men's hairstyles are mentioned, but only by way of contrast (v. 4). The women's appearance is given far more space; it is their problem that sets Paul off on a long and involved discourse.

We adopt a background for the tension reflected in 1 Cor. 11:2–16, which while certainly hypothetical has some solid evidence to support it. A group of spirit-filled enthusiasts in Corinth interpreted Paul's own teaching as the arrival of a freedom in which material limitations of human life were eliminated. Marriage was to be shunned because it necessitated a bondage to physical realities that the perfect Christian is to transcend (1 Cor. 7:1, to be read as a slogan of the Corinthian enthusiasts). The spiritual Christian is already now empowered to speak in tongues: that is, in the language spoken by angels in heaven (13:1; cf. Luke 20:34–36). The possession of the spirit transports the higher class of Christians into an experience of liberation from physical bonds, together with forms of conduct enforced by obligations to communal life in the family, so that already existing marriages are dissolved to leave the partners free for ecstatic experiences of their true selves (7:10–11). This search for freedom led some women in Corinth to manifest their liberation in ways that were meant to demonstrate the annulment of the differences between men and women. There is evidence from Jewish groups, but also from Greco-Roman backgrounds, that women cut their hair short and dressed like men because they wanted to display their refusal to be confined and defined by the characteristics of gender.[7] In Christ there is no longer male and female (cf. Gal. 3:28), and therefore worship was the appropriate place to show in public that being a man or a woman was inconsequential, even detrimental, to Christian freedom. The problem Paul is addressing in 1 Cor. 11:2–16 is, therefore, not primarily an issue of dress or haircut but the claim of an enthusiastic group that the distinction between men and women had to be abrogated, that the natural polarity of human existence in the differentiation of the sexes was inferior to life in the spirit, and that the arrival of the new age canceled out the reality of nature.

Some particularly telling evidence for this orientation can be found in the Gospel of Thomas. Logion 22 of the Gospel of Thomas preserves a version of Jesus' saying that one has to be like a child to enter the kingdom of God: "Jesus said to them, 'When you make the two one, and when you make the inside like the outside and the outside like the inside, and the above like the below, and when you make the male and the female one and the same, so that the male not be male nor the female female . . . then you will enter (the kingdom).' " Similar is logion 114 of the Gospel of Thomas: "Simon Peter said to them, 'Let Mary leave us, for women are not worthy of life.' Jesus said, 'I myself shall lead her in order to make her male, so that she too may become a living spirit resembling you males. For every woman who will make herself male will enter the kingdom of heaven.' "[8]

We assume, then, that Paul responded in 1 Cor. 11:2–16 to a situation in which a group of Christian women took the gathering for worship as an occasion to demonstrate their conviction that life in the spirit of God provided freedom from the natural differentiation of male and female. The external sign of this conviction was the decision of this group to remove from their head a customary cover and to cut their hair in a fashion to exhibit that they wished to be seen no longer as females.

Paul's reply to this situation is shot through with appeals to the Old Testament creation stories. The male is not required to cover his head during worship because "he is the image and glory of God," (my trans.). This reasoning uses the sentence in Gen. 1:27 about God's creation of the human being in God's image. The reference, however, is a loose one; the word "image" is expanded by the addition of "glory," which does not occur in the Old Testament verse but carries weight for Paul, since he uses it again in the immediately ensuing statement "but woman is the glory of man." This is followed by the sentence "for man is not out of woman, but woman is out of man: because indeed man was not created for the sake of woman, but woman for the sake of man" (11:8–9, my trans.). The echo of Genesis 2 is quite unmistakable. The Adam of this narrative is made by God from the dust of the ground; he is given the breath of life and becomes a living being (Gen. 2:7). The woman, on the other hand, is taken from Adam's side (Gen. 2:21–22). But this forming of woman out of Adam is done because Adam by himself is incomplete, in need of having a partner who is a part of his own being (Gen. 2:18, 23).

The allusions to the Genesis stories in 1 Cor. 11:2–16 are uncontested. But what purpose they serve is disputed. Paul is very frequently assumed to be defending a position that sets up the male as a superior creation of God in contradistinction to woman, who is by nature dependent on the male. Not only verses 8–9 are interpreted in this way. The opening sentence of the whole argument, "The head of every man is Christ, the head of the woman is the man, and the head of Christ is God" (11:3, my trans.), is understood to mean, in analogy to many Stoic and Jewish-hellenistic parallels,[9] an ontological hierarchy from God down to woman, who is at the lowest rung of the ladder; and the statement "the man is the image and glory of God, but the woman is the glory of man" (11:7) is interpreted to imply that the male alone is created in the image of God, as is indeed stated in certain rabbinical traditions.[10] But this interpretation runs into great difficulties, especially because it cannot do justice to Paul's continuation of his own argument in 11:11–12: "In the Lord woman is not without man, nor man without woman. For just as woman is out of man, so is man through woman. And all this is out of God" (my trans.).

The word "head" in its metaphorical meaning in 11:3 does not mean "authority" or "overlord" but "origin" or "source,"[11] and the subjects said to be "head" do not form a chain from the highest to the lowest or from the lowest to the highest. Rather, in the sentence "The head of every man is Christ, the head of the woman is the man, and the head of Christ is God," a sequence of ontological gradations is precisely not followed. Paul's interest lies in the establishment of relations in which the differences of male and female, Christ and God, are not nullified but understood as being essential components of a whole that is from God (11:12).

The intensive employment of the creation story in the context of a concrete situation in the gathering for worship in Corinth is intended to hold creation and redemption together. The new age, the life in faith, and the possession of God's Spirit do not cancel out what God has formed in his creation. What is true "in the Lord" that "woman is not without man and man is not without women" (11:12) is the reaffirmation of what is true in the act of creation, that "man is the image and glory of God and woman is the glory of man" (11:7).[12] Far from denying woman's participation in being, together with man, the image of God, the statement of 1 Cor. 11:7 attributes glory to both man and woman together: Man is created to bring honor and praise to God, and woman is created to be the person whose existence draws honor and praise from the man.

Romans 1:18–32 (esp. 23–27)

Because of the intense discussion about issues of homosexuality in recent years, this passage has received a great deal of fresh scrutiny that in some respects has helped the clarification of exegetical issues.[13] We are concerned solely with the use of the biblical creation accounts in Rom. 1:18–32 and with their possible impact on the interpretation of the passage as a whole. This section of Romans contains no direct quotations from Genesis 1–2, and reliance on an Adam typology as its background is not warranted.[14] There are, however, clear allusions to God's creative act and to some phrases in Genesis 1 that are an important part of Paul's reasoning.

Romans 1:18–32 is the beginning of an extended argument leading to the conclusion that, in the light of the revelation of God's power of salvation in the gospel (1:16–17), no human being will be justified in God's sight (3:20). Human life and history outside the rule of Moses' law are portrayed, as in an apocalyptic vision, like a mass of perdition that has rejected the knowledge of God, is caught in the primal sin of idolatry, and in consequence of that fatal error manifests all kinds of moral perversion, of which homosexual practices are isolated as the most telling example (1:18–32). Yet in a sharp turn of argument that soon becomes clearly directed at those who acknowledge their allegiance to the Mosaic Torah, Jewish reliance on the saving efficacy of God's law is also demolished (2:1–3:30). The entire opening section of Romans is intended to lead to the conclusion that "there is no distinction, since all have sinned and fall short of the glory of God"; they are, whether Jews or Greeks, recipients of God's gracious and unearned justification (3:23–24).

From the beginning of his argument against Gentile religion and morality in Rom. 1:18–32, Paul has in mind God as Creator, the cosmos as the creation of the invisible God, and Gentile religion as the fatally flawed attempt to seek in elements of nature the manifestation of the invisible God who defies all images. From the creation of the cosmos (1:20) God made the eternal divine power and godhead known. But in spite of that knowledge, the Gentiles did not glorify and praise the true God but enmeshed themselves in futility by transforming the glory due the creator into the glorification of creatures; they "worshiped and served the creature rather than the Creator" (1:25).

At this point in his argument Paul employs the rhetorical device of introducing a pair of interrelated concepts that are used three times in a row: the idea of "exchange" and the notion of "giving up." "Exchange" (*metallassō*) is of great importance in our context. Paul states, first of all, as a general principle, the Jewish conviction that Gentile religion is idolatrous because it substitutes the honor due only to the immortal God for the veneration of images of mortal beings. Gentile religion "exchanged the glory of the immortal God for images resembling a mortal human being or birds or four-footed animals or reptiles" (1:23). Already in this first use of the idea of exchange, an allusion to the creation story in Genesis 1 is involved. The sequence "human being (*anthrōpos*), birds (*peteina*), four-footed animals (*tetrapoda*), and reptiles (*herpeta*)" echoes Gen. 1:26, which says that the human being (*anthrōpos*) is to have dominion over the fish of the sea, over the birds (*peteina*) of the air, over the cattle (*ktēnē*, but cf. Gen. 1:24, *tetrapoda*), and over the reptiles (*herpeta*).[15] Paul's appeal to the Creator, and to creation, does not move in general abstracts, as in our word "nature," but it is informed very concretely by the biblical creation story. Paul had absorbed what "Creator" and "creation" signify by the creation narratives at the beginning of Genesis, and the store of these accounts provides him with the conceptuality of his argument.

The first exchange of legitimate for illegitimate worship is followed by a second one, in which for the first time in the passage the phrase "give up" also appears. The second exchange is not materially different from the first.

Again it is said to consist in a transference of allegiance from a worthy subject to an object not worthy of veneration. Gentiles "exchanged the truth about God for a lie and worshiped and served the creature rather than the Creator" (1:25). But in this second step, the initial and fundamental exchange of loyalties is accompanied by a general but observable degradation in the bodies of those who practice idolatry (1:24). The phrase "degrading of their bodies" allows no specificity. In the third step involving the exchange, however, the specificity is palpable. The substitution of the honor due the Creator with the religious reverence for mortal creatures leads, as a consequence, to a third exchange analogous to the first and second in that, again, a relationship established by the Creator is exchanged with another relationship, which has no foundation in God's creation. "Women exchanged natural intercourse for unnatural, and in the same way also the men, giving up natural intercourse with women, were consumed with passion for one another" (1:26–27). Paul chooses words for "men" and "women" in those verses that are otherwise not used in his letters, except in Gal. 3:28. The words "*thēleiai*" and "*arsenes*" derive from the storehouse of creation terminology in Gen. 1:27, in which the one human species (*anthrōpos*) is said to exist in the form of the union of two (*arsen kai thēly*). There is, for that reason, a strict analogy between the exchange of the Creator for creatures and the exchange of the Creator's act in ordaining the union of male and female for the union of members of the same sex.

On the basis of the foregoing observations, some conclusions may be warranted.

Several of the most important New Testament passages dealing with issues of sexuality appeal to the creation stories in Genesis 1 and 2. This affirms that in the new creation, in the life of faith, sexuality is neither inconsequential nor abolished.

It is striking that the same New Testament passages evoke the story of creation (Genesis 1 and 2) but never the account of the Fall (Genesis 3). Human sexuality is seen, in these texts, as a fundamental continuance of God's good creation. Actual sexual behavior, whether heterosexual or homosexual, is subject to all kinds of perversions, and therefore sadly connected with the Fall. But being born male or female is the undiminished actuality of God's good creation.

The New Testament passages discussed here deal with a wide variety of sexual questions: marriage and divorce, prostitution, gender differentiations in external appearance, and homosexuality. In all cases, the questions are decided by concentration on a single point: the creation of the one human form of life in the polarity of male and female. The distortion or abolition of this one crucial reality of being human is seen in the New Testament as outrage against the Creator.

All New Testament passages discussed above read the creation stories in Genesis 1 and 2 from a new vantage point. The Genesis narratives are now plunged into the light of the coming kingdom of God and of the justification of God in the work of Christ. This new understanding of the creation narratives intensifies the value of sexual life and heightens the demand expected in sexual behavior. The criticism of divorce and the rejection of prostitution go beyond Old Testament law, and the radicality of perceiving homosexual practices as an outcome of idolatry stretches Old Testament legislation into the arena of apocalyptic disaster.

The sections we studied contain without exception ethical mandates, or at least strong directives for sexual conduct. But they are also without exception mindful of a creational ontology that is given in the word form of the narratives of Genesis 1 and 2. Being male or female is a reality prior to law and morality. Actual sexual conduct may be conducive to honor this primal reality, but it will do so only in approximations. Human capacity to express the goodness of God's creation is limited, for heterosexual and happily married Christians as well as for anyone else. Therefore, human capacity or incapacity to live up to sexuality as God created it, or human experience or lack of experience of this gift of God, cannot be the measure by which we judge God's creation of human life in the polarity and partnership of male and female. The New Testament has resolutely chosen to make the revelation in Genesis 1 and 2 of human sexuality as God's good creation the measure and judge of our conduct, not the other way around.

Concerning the issue of homosexuality, which is demanding attention at the present time, it would follow from this study that it is a serious mistake to isolate the discussion of homosexuality from the wider scope of the New Testament's approach to human sexuality as the essential form of God's good creation. If the main thesis of this study is correct, it follows that homosexual practice cannot honor the creation of human life in the essential differentiation of male and female. Homosexual conduct is the practical, and today also the theoretical, denial that the human being is good as God's creature in the polarity of being male or female. In one form or the other, homosexual conduct fears or denies, despises or ridicules, the goodness of God's creation of male and female.

This consideration of the indebtedness of some New Testament teaching to the Old Testament creation stories can also leave no doubt that anybody in the Christian community may be allowed exemption from the searing criticism of sexual mores found in the New Testament. But we would be ill served, in discussions on homosexuality, divorce, obsession with sex, widespread promiscuity, or any other aspect of sexual behavior, to encapsulate ourselves in the dictates of contemporary cultural trends and the presumed necessities of our modern insights, to the neglect of the voice of the New Testament (and the Old Testament with it), which proclaims the ever-challenging, ever-liberating, distant glory of God's creation of the human as male and female.

NOTES

1. First Tim. 2:13–14 also refers specifically to the story of Adam and Eve in the discussion of the relationship between men and women. The emphasis in those verses is on the Fall and its consequences for the man–woman relation, not on the creation of man and woman. Since the latter aspect is the only topic of this chapter, 1 Tim. 2:13–14 has been omitted from consideration.
2. Contra A. E. Harvey, "Genesis versus Deuteronomy?: Jesus on Marriage and Divorce," *The Gospels and the Scriptures of Israel*, ed. C. A. Evans and W. R. Stegner, *JSNTSup* 104 (Sheffield: Academic, 1994), 55–65.
3. "The conditions of eschatological salvation are usually conceptualized as a restoration of primal conditions rather than an entirely new or utopian mode of existence with no links to the past," David E. Aune, "Early Christian Eschatology" *ABD* 2:595.
4. The need to understand the use of "body," *sōma*, in 1 Cor. 6:12–20 not as a confusing collection of unrelated meanings such as "person," "seat of sexual life," or "physical organism" has been cogently stressed by Ernst Käsemann, who seeks to define *sōma* in Paul's usage this way: "Corporeality is the nature of man (*sic*) in his need to participate in creatureliness and in his capacity for communication in the widest sense, that is to say, in his relationship to a world with which he is confronted on each several occasion" (*Perspectives on Paul* [Philadelphia: Fortress, 1971], 21).
5. Karl Barth, *Church Dogmatics* III/2 (Edinburgh: Clark, 1960), 307. I have corrected, at the end of the sentence, a glaring mistranslation that renders the German original "*personifizierte menschliche Untreue gegen den Menschen*" as "personifies human unfaithfulness against God."
6. O. Michel (*Paulus und seine Bibel*, BFCT 2:18 [Gütersloh: Bertelsmann, 1929], 166) assumes as background of the passage "*eine haggadistische Ausschmückung der Schöpfungsgeschichte*." James Moffatt (*The First Epistle of Paul to the Corinthians* [New York: Harper, n.d.], 152) speaks of *midrashim*.
7. Two good examples from the Greco-Roman background are supplied by Gordon D. Fee, *The First Epistle to the Corinthians*, NICNT (Grand Rapids: Eerdmans, 1987), 511, n. 81.
8. James Robinson, *The Nag Hammadi Library in English*, 3d ed. (San Francisco: Harper, 1990), 129, 138. Logion 22 is substantially cited in 2 Clement (ca. 140) but the interpretation given aims at Christian asceticism in sexual matters, not at the invalidation of the difference between male and female. See J. B. Lightfoot and J. R. Harmer, *The Apostolic Fathers: Revised Greek Texts with Introductions and English Translations* (Grand Rapids: Baker, 1973), 90.
9. Hans Conzelmann, *First Corinthians* (Philadelphia: Fortress, 1975), 187–88, provides a representative collection of evidence for chains of being that employ the word *eikōn*.
10. Particularly influential in promoting the idea that Adam alone is God's image is the book by Jacob Jervell, *Imago Dei: Gen 1,26f. im Spätjudentum, in der Gnosis und in den paulinischen Briefen*, FRLANT 76 (Göttingen: Vandenhoeck &

Ruprecht, 1960). This thesis is Jervell's starting point: *"Klar ist freilich, dass nur der Mann in unserem Zusammenhang gottebenbildlich geschaffen worden ist. Eben das ist auch für uns die Hauptsache"* (293).

11. See the thorough discussion in Fee, *First Epistle to the Corinthians*, 502–3.

12. Conzelmann (*First Corinthians*, 190) uses the phrase "in the Lord" in 11:11 to separate nature and creation from existence in faith. The verse "maintains the central idea that the cancellation of distinctions has its specific place, that they are canceled 'in the Lord,' not 'in us.' " But the sequence in v. 12, in which a definite allusion to Genesis 2 is introduced as the reason (*gar*) for v. 11, makes this understanding untenable.

13. Of the scholarly contributions, mention must be made of John Boswell, *Christianity, Social Tolerance, and Homosexuality* (Chicago: University Press, 1980); George R. Edwards, *Gay/Lesbian Liberation: A Biblical Perspective* (New York: Pilgrim, 1984); Victor P. Furnish, *The Moral Teaching of Paul: Selected Issues*, 2d ed. (Nashville: Abingdon, 1985, 52–82); R. B. Hays, "Relations Natural and Unnatural: A Response to John Boswell's Exegesis of Romans 1" (*JRE* 14 [1986]:184–215); and Robin Scroggs, *The New Testament and Homosexuality: Contextual Background for Contemporary Debate* (Philadelphia: Fortress, 1983). Not yet available to me was Marion L. Soards, *Scripture and Homosexuality: Biblical Authority and the Church Today* (Louisville, Ky.: Westminster John Knox, 1995).

14. The Adam typology as background for Rom. 1:18–32 is advocated especially by Jervell, *Imago Dei*, 312–31; Morna D. Hooker, "Adam in Romans I," *NTS* 6 (1959–60), 297–306; idem, "A Further Note on Romans I," *NTS* 13 (1966–67): 181–83; Alexander J.M. Wedderburn, "Adam in Paul's Letter to the Romans," Stud Bib 3, 1978 (*JSNT Sup*, 1980): 413–30; James D. G. Dunn, *Romans 1–8*, WBC 38A (Dallas: Word, 1988), 53–76; idem, *Christology in the Making*, 2d ed. (London: SCM, 1989), 101–2. It is, however, questionable whether a definite Adam typology lies behind Rom. 1:18–32. A recent commentator on Romans flatly rejects the use of Adam typology in this passage: "The alleged echoes of the Adam stories in Genesis are simply nonexistent" (Joseph Fitzmyer, *Romans*, AB 33 [New York: Doubleday, 1993], 274).

15. Many commentators see in Rom. 1:23 an allusion to Deut. 4:15–18, and it is entirely possible that this echo should be heard. But it needs to be observed that in Deut. 4:15–18 the list of idolized elements of nature is much longer, there is no mention of the human being, and the list of worshiped animals in Deut. 4:17–18 has less similarity to Paul's list in Rom. 1:23 than does the one in Gen. 1:26.

2

Textual Orientation

Choon-Leong Seow

Among Protestants the debate about homosexuality most often revolves around a few standard biblical texts. For some, exegesis of these scriptural passages provides the only legitimate basis for discussion. Other factors, such as the contribution of science and the testimony of experience, are "unscriptural" and hence subordinated to "what scriptures say."[1] The fact that the participants in this conference are primarily biblical scholars certainly suggests our general textual orientation. Yet the issue is not merely an exegetical one; it is not a question of what the biblical texts *mean*. Rather it is a hermeneutical issue, a theological issue, a question of how we understand the nature of God. Given the textual orientation of Protestants and the mandate of this book, this chapter will begin by examining the passages most commonly cited in the debate and then will consider the contribution of some marginalized voices from within the canon: namely, the wisdom literature of the Old Testament.

Typical Textual Orientation: The Standard Texts

There are four categories of texts usually cited by those who argue against homosexuality: (1) legal texts that explicitly forbid it, (2) narrative passages that are said to illustrate its wrongness, (3) New Testament lists of inappropriate and wrongful behaviors, and (4) the creation accounts in Genesis 1—2.

Explicit Prohibitions

In the first category are two texts, Lev. 18:22 and 20:13. These are the only texts in the Bible where homosexual intercourse is explicitly forbidden. Both of them are embedded in the portion of cultic-legal material known as the Holiness Code (Leviticus 17—26). Leviticus 18 begins with an injunction not to behave like the Egyptians and the Canaanites. There follows a series of explicit prohibitions addressed in the second-person masculine form (probably referring to the head of every household in the faith community) against sexual relations with women in one's immediate household and certain other female kin, sexual intercourse with a woman during her menstrual period, adultery, child sacrifice, homoerotic acts between men,[2] sexual acts between a person and an animal, and so forth. There can be little doubt about what the text says: "You shall not lie with a male as one lies with a woman; that is an abomination" (Lev. 18:22); "If a man lies with a male as with a woman, both of them have committed an abomination; they shall be put to death; their blood is upon them" (Lev. 20:13, my trans.). In the formulation of the laws in Leviticus 20, the death penalty is clearly stipulated for same-sex intercourse and other sexual violations. The texts are unambiguous on the prohibition. They are equally unambiguous about the penalty of death.

The Holiness Code is clear on many other issues as well. As one reads on, one finds that it is forbidden to crossbreed animals, sow two kinds of seeds in the same field, and wear clothing with two different kinds of fiber (Lev. 19:19; also Deut. 22:9–11). It is forbidden to eat meat with blood still in it (Lev. 19:26; cf. Lev. 3:17; 7:26–27; 17:11). It is forbidden to trim the hair at the side of the head or to clip the edges of one's beard (Lev. 19:27; cf. 3:17, 7:27; 17:10–14). The death penalty is prescribed for anyone consulting ghosts and familiar spirits (Lev. 20:6–8, 27). Children who slight their parents are also supposed to receive the death penalty (Lev. 20:9; see also Ex. 21:17).[3] A command is given to distinguish between clean and unclean animals; it is stipulated that people must not be contaminated by unclean creatures (Lev. 20:25).

Then in Leviticus 21, it is said, regarding priests: "They shall not shave any part of their heads or shave off the edges of their beards or cut their bodies" (Lev. 21:5, my trans.). A priest may not marry a prostitute, "a deflowered woman" (ḥălālâ),[4] a divorcee, or a widow; a priest may only marry a virgin "from his own people" (Lev. 21:7, 13–14, my trans.). No one who has any physical defects whatsoever is eligible to be ordained as priest; no one is acceptable who is blind or lame, has a limb too long or too short, has an impaired leg or an impaired hand, is hunchbacked, is thin or small (daq),[5] has defective eyesight,[6] has a festering rash or some other skin disease, or has damaged testicles (Lev. 21:17–20). Strictly speaking, of the entire Holiness Code, it is Leviticus 21 that most explicitly applies to the ordination to the ministry, for the chapter concerns the special qualifications of priesthood. Yet it is rarely discussed.

It hardly needs to be said that all the notions of purity and holiness as set forth in the Levitical code are culturally conditioned. The Holiness Code is unambiguous in its various stipulations and in the penalty for violation of the provisions. The more difficult and important question is the proper application of these provisions in our own context. Why are some laws pertinent to the question of the ordination of individuals to the ministry but not others? Why should the qualifications of priesthood in Leviticus 21 be secondary to the issue of homosexuality? Why do we decide that the laws apply but not the death penalty? The fact is we do not simply quote texts. We make decisions on theological and pragmatic grounds about what is applicable and what is not. Certainly the church has backed off on the penalty of death for the violation of some of these prohibitions, even as it insists on the validity of some prohibitions but not others. We also demur to the death penalty for children who do not honor their parents (Lev. 20:9), and when some modern nations practice the *lex talionis*, or law of retaliation ("an eye for an eye, a tooth for a tooth"), we judge their observance of antiquated laws to be incompatible with modern morality. Despite its avowed textual orientation, the church has historically made decisions about many ethical issues apart from the letter of the law. The church has changed its mind on many issues as it confronts new situations and learns new truths. Many have decided that the dietary laws no longer apply. We ordain people who have physical defects. We ordain people who cut their hair or shave their faces. We in the Presbyterian Church ordain women ministers and church officers today, even though many have argued against the ordination of women on the basis of scripture. Indeed, there are many practices that the Bible actually permits (like polygamy and concubinage) or even commands (like levirate marriage) that we, having heard the gospel, have rightly rejected. At the same time, there are things some biblical texts forbid (like divorce and remarriage after divorce) that we are compelled to reconsider on the basis of what we know today. We must not simply quote texts when we have to deal with difficult ethical issues. That is not the way the Bible is intended to be used. Rather, we must always interpret scriptures in the light of our understanding of the gospel.

There is a story told in 1 Samuel 21—22 of David and his entourage at the sanctuary at Nob. The men were hungry when they arrived at Nob, having fled from Saul. But the only food that was available at the sanctuary was the "holy bread" (see Lev. 24:5–9), which, by the established and commonly accepted code of holiness, could be received only by those who were consecrated as priests (see Lev. 24:9). Even though his troops had been on a secular mission and not a holy one, and they were not priests, David managed to define the men's holiness in an acceptable way and thus received the holy bread for his hungry men.[7] The story is cited in the New Testament in Jesus' defense of his disciples who had been picking grain in the field during Sabbath, in violation of the letter of the law (Matt. 12:1–8; Mark 2:23–27; Luke 6:1–5). Jesus referred to David's precedent, "How he entered the house of God when Abiathar was high priest, and ate the bread of the Presence, which was illegal for anyone but priests to eat" (Mark 2:26, my trans.). He then concluded with a daring theological interpretation of the Sabbath injunction: "The sabbath was made for humankind, not humankind for the sabbath; so the Son of Man is lord even of the sabbath" (Mark 2:27–28). We may observe in this connection that Jesus went beyond the letter of the law. He reoriented the text, as it were, and made a hermeneutical leap to interpret the Sabbath theologically. David's violation of the law had nothing to do with the Sabbath, yet Jesus appealed to David's action as a scriptural principle for pointing beyond the letter of the Sabbath prohibition. In each case—for David and for Jesus—human needs provided the hermeneutical key for understanding the legal tradition. In each case the theology is "from below," so to speak, beginning with the reality of human needs. Neither David nor Jesus began, as their interrogators did, with dogma—a theology "from above." To be sure, by defending the technical violation of the Sabbath injunction, Jesus did not render Sabbath observation invalid. The Sabbath principle of rest was still valid. But the radical hermeneutical move did relativize the Sabbath commandment, subsuming it under a theology of God's creation and human need.[8] The Sabbath was established for the good of humanity—as a sign of God's perpetual covenant (Ex. 31:15–17)—but the law was not meant to be absolutized. Hence, some Christian ethicists would apply Jesus' theological interpretation of the Sabbath injunction in the homosexuality debate as well: "Marriage is made for men and women, not they for marriage."[9]

As another illustration of how we might theologize on the basis of legal texts, we may cite the experience of Simon Peter mentioned in Acts 10. The apostle had a vision in which he saw all kinds of animals, reptiles, and birds. Being an observant Jew, Peter understandably demurred when he was asked to "kill and eat." But a voice—we are to understand here a celestial voice—said to him that the creatures which had been stipulated as unclean in the Torah are somehow declared "clean." The allusion in the text is clearly to the dietary laws—laws that were codified in the Torah and that to a large extent, identified the Jew. But here the laws are relativized. Moreover, it quickly becomes clear that the issue at hand is not obeying dietary laws themselves but the nature of God's grace and sovereignty. As the story unfolds, one realizes that a significant theological move is being made in the text. Despite the fact that for the Jew it was forbidden—illegal, *athemitos*—to be associated with Gentiles, the grace of God points one beyond the letter of the law. The conclusion that Peter draws from the vision is theologically significant: "God has shown me that I should not call any person common or unclean" (Acts 10:28, my trans.). Luke was concerned specifically with the inclusive grace of God that embraces Gentiles as well as Jews, but Luke's hermeneutical move from the explicit prohibition of the dietary laws to the inclusivity of God's grace for all people provides us with some insights for a theological reading of the Holiness Code.[10] On the literal level, the tradition is clear about the dietary laws. The Holiness

Code is emphatic about what constitutes purity. But Luke's application of the text pushes it beyond the literal concern with cultic purity on the part of humanity. Indeed, the gospel permits—nay, impels—us to come to the laws with new insights. Hence we as Christians do not and must not follow the laws without asking about the grace of God manifested in Jesus Christ.

The Torah is clear about many things, but we do not follow it without question. The law is clear about the practice of levirate marriage: When a man dies without leaving a son, the widow is not allowed to marry outside the family; her husband's brother or, failing that, some other next of kin is obligated to perform "the duty of a husband's brother [the *levir*]" (see Deut. 25:5–10).[11] The law is literally clear on that obligation, but we do not practice it today. So too we must admit what the Holiness Code says about male homoerotic acts: They are forbidden, and the penalty for violation of the law is death. But the church needs to make ethical decisions based not on the letter of the law but on larger theological issues.[12]

Narrative Examples

There are a couple of narrative passages in the Old Testament that are frequently used to illustrate the wrongness of same-sex intercourse: Genesis 19 and Judges 19. In the first passage, divine beings come down to earth to verify the reputation of Sodom and Gomorrah for wickedness. That reputation has been established and reiterated in the narrative up to this point in Genesis; the cities are said to be wicked and sinful, although nothing is said about the precise nature of their wickedness (Gen. 13:13; 18:20–21). Lot encounters the strangers and extends his hospitality to them in accordance with the expectations of his culture. That night "the men of the city . . . both young and old, all the people to the last man," surround Lot's house (Gen. 19:4). They demand that the two strangers be brought out so they may "know them." Lot implores the mob not to act wickedly, offering in place of the strangers his two daughters: "Let me bring them [the two daughters] out and you may do anything you want with them; only do not do anything to these men, *for they have come under the shelter of my roof*" (translation and emphasis mine). It is Lot's duty as a host to protect his guests.

The story is set in a culture quite distant from our own. The modern reader is horrified by Lot's offer of his two daughters.[13] Once again, it is the women who are sacrificed. Lot is prepared to victimize his own daughters in order to protect the strangers who have come under his roof. In accordance with the expectations of ancient Near Eastern hospitality,[14] protection of strangers in one's house took precedence over the love of one's children! This may seem odd to modern Western readers, but it is a notion of hospitality prevalent in many cultures, including ancient Israel's. So we interpret that ethical principle in light of its cultural context. Lot made an ethical decision in that cultural context, but it is not a decision we are expected to emulate wholesale. We live in a different world. And we are surely not required by the narrative example to practice an ethic of familial sacrifice.

In any case, the text raises several ethical issues, not just the issue of intended homoerotic acts. Indeed, the passage is not about homosexuality in general. It is certainly not about homosexual love. Rather, it is about rape, specifically same-sex rape. It is about gang rape. It is about violence. It is about the violation of a code of hospitality. It is about wickedness in general.

Beyond this passage, Sodom is mentioned several times in the Old Testament, but nowhere are homosexual acts raised as an issue. In Isa. 1:10 and 3:9, the problem is injustice. In Jer. 23:14, Sodom and Gomorrah are associated with general wickedness: adultery, lies, and injustice. In Ezek. 16:49, Sodom represents pride, excess of food, prosperous ease, and indifference to the poor and needy. That is what Sodom came to symbolize in the Old Testament: the sins of greed, injustice, inhospitality, insensitivity to the need and pain of others, and general wickedness. Repeatedly it is cited as an example of God's willingness to destroy an entire people because of all kinds of sins, but nowhere is homosexuality named as the particular wickedness that warrants destruction. Nowhere in the Bible is the sin of Sodom said to be homosexual acts. Only in Jude is the sin of Sodom and Gomorrah associated with sexuality, but there the wrong is not homosexual intercourse. Rather, the people of Sodom and Gomorrah are said to have "practiced immorality in the same way [as the angels] and pursued other flesh (*sarkos heteras*)."[15] In rabbinic exegesis as well, the sin of Sodom is rarely explained as homosexuality. According to one view, the affluent people of Sodom selfishly adopted a policy of maltreating strangers in order to discourage visitors to their city (Tosefta Sota 3:11–12). Inhospitality is usually identified as the problem (see also Wisd. Sol. 19:14–15; Matt. 10:12–15; Luke 10:10–12; Josephus, *Antiquities* 1 § 194). Thus, Sodom and Gomorrah became symbols of utter wickedness in general. Genesis 19 cannot be used as an illustration of homoeroticism as a sin. Homosexual gang rape does not define homosexuality any more than heterosexual gang rape defines heterosexuality.

The second passage in this category of illustrative narratives is Judges 19. A Levite from the hill country of Ephraim goes to Bethlehem to win back his concubine, who has left him and returned to her father's house. The narrative tells of the hospitality that the concubine's father extends to the Levite, and we are told of the conversation between the two men. (The woman is completely silent throughout the narrative.) The man, his concubine, and his servant begin their journey home. It is quite late in the day when they arrive at the city of Jebus, whose inhabitants are apparently non-Israelites. The Levite decides they should not dwell among outsiders, so

they move on to Gibeah, in the territory of Benjamin. No native of this Israelite town offers hospitality to these travelers, but an old Ephraimite
dwelling in Gibeah does. That night, some gangsters come to the house
and demand that the Levite be brought out so that they might "know him."
Like Lot, the old Ephraimite implores them not to act wickedly, "since this
man has come into my house; do not do this outrageous thing." Like Lot,
he offers them the alternative of women—his virgin daughter and the concubine of the Levite. One notes that there were other men in the house besides the host and the Levite (see Judg. 19:3, 9, 11, 13, 19). But the host offers the gangsters the women, saying: "Ravish them (Hebrew ʿannû,
literally, "humiliate them"!) and do with them what seems good to you; but
against this man do not do such an outrageous thing" (19:24). When the
gangsters persist, the Levite himself seizes his concubine and pushes her
out the door. According to the text, they rape her all night long. In the
morning, the woman came and fell at the door of the house "till it was
light." When the Levite finally opens the door and finds his concubine
sprawled on the floor, he says, "Get up, let's get going." But there is no answer. He puts her on the donkey and goes home. Then he takes a knife and
cuts her up—limb by limb—into twelve pieces and sends the pieces
throughout the territory of Israel.

This text has been used to indicate the wrongness of homosexuality. It
should be evident, however, that these gangsters who committed the outrage were not "homosexual," as we would use the term today. They were
out to humiliate the strangers, and when a woman was offered them, they
gang-raped her. It did not matter to them that a woman was offered to them
instead of a man. The issue, therefore, is not sexuality but violence, mistreatment of others, and wickedness in general. Judges 19 passes over other
ethical issues in silence, but we cannot. We, having heard the gospel, surely
cannot accept the sacrifice of women to the abuse of men.[16] Though the
passage seems to condone it, we condemn the invitation of the Ephraimite,
who told the ruffians to humiliate the women and do with them as they
please. Though the text is silent, we condemn the Levite who, upon finding his concubine on the floor, says simply, "Get up." It is peculiar that some
of us should see this passage as an implicit condemnation of homosexuality,
rather than of rape or violence. Why is it that we use this text to argue
against homosexual love when the violence actually committed is heterosexual? Why is it that people should focus on homosexuality in this story of
general violence but not condemn heterosexuality in the story of the rape
of Dinah by the Shechemites (Genesis 34) or the rape of Tamar by Amnon
(2 Samuel 13)? Do we, on the basis of those texts about heterosexual rape,
say that heterosexuality is wrong? Do we, on the basis of those texts, deprive
heterosexuals from holding office in the church? In those passages of heterosexual rape it is clear to us that the issue is rape, not heterosexuality. We

blame only the rapists, not others. So why is it that we think homosexuality is the problem in the accounts of homosexual rape? When we read the story of David's adultery with Bathsheba (2 Samuel 11), we identify the issue as injustice or the abuse of power, as the parable of Nathan makes clear (2 Sam. 12:1–15). We certainly do not question the legitimacy of heterosexuality. The narratives in Genesis 19 and Judges 19 are about wickedness in general and violence in the form of rape. They are not about same-sex love.

New Testament Lists

According to some modern translations of the Bible, homosexuality is either explicitly mentioned or alluded to in three New Testament passages where wrongful behaviors are listed (Rom. 1:26–27; 1 Cor. 6:9; 1 Tim. 1:10). Constraints of time and space and the limitations of my own professional expertise do not permit me to delve into the exegetical details of those passages.[17] Suffice it to say, homosexuality does not appear to be the central concern in any of those lists, although its mention has been highlighted in the debate about homosexuality. In none of these New Testament texts is there an explicit command or a prohibition regarding homosexuality.

The reference to homosexuality in 1 Corinthians 6 comes in the midst of an argument against lawsuits among Christians. The Corinthian Christians were taking their disputes to secular authorities for settlement. For Paul, it was bad enough that such disputes should even have arisen in the church, but it was worse that the Christians were expecting their disputes to be settled by outsiders—unbelievers. Paul would have preferred the matter to be resolved in private among Christians. Christians will judge the world and even angels, says Paul. So the world's judges cannot judge believers. Paul asks regarding those who are of the world, "Don't you know that unrighteous persons will not get into God's kingdom?" (6:9, my trans.). Why should Christians not be judged by outsiders? Look at them, says Paul. Look at all the things they do! The apostle gives a list of the kinds of things that unrighteous people do, and this is the context in which he mentions "the effeminate" (*malakoi*) and "the men who sleep with other men" (*arsenokoitai*).[18] The list is meant to be exemplary. It illustrates the kinds and ranges of vices committed by *unbelievers:* that is, the outsiders who are in no position to judge Christians. The homoerotic acts mentioned incidentally by Paul are peripheral to his main concern.

The point in 1 Corinthians 6 is the impropriety of lawsuits among Christians before unbelievers. It is peculiar, therefore, that we should overlook the impropriety of lawsuits before the world, which is the main point made by Paul in 1 Corinthians 6, and focus instead on an impropriety that Paul mentions only in passing. And so modern Christians continue to sue one another in secular courts or even sue the church without regard for Pauline authority on this matter. At the same time we call attention to homosexuality, as if that were what Paul intended for us to learn from his letter. This is not to say that Paul was not opposed to homosexual acts. He was—just as he was appalled by all acts of immorality, idolatry, thievery, drunkenness, moneygrubbing, slander, and so forth. The point of the passage, however, is lawsuits against other Christians before unbelieving judges, an admonition that many modern people seem to have decided on pragmatic grounds is no longer pertinent. How do we decide, then, that Paul's central point in the passage is no longer relevant but that a peripheral reference is?

In Romans 1 we have the most extensive biblical reference to homosexual practice, and the only one that refers to female homosexuality. In this passage Paul writes about the immorality of the pagan Gentiles: "Their females exchanged natural relations for unnatural, and their males likewise gave up natural relations with the female and were consumed with passion for one another, males committing shameless acts with males and receiving in their own persons the due penalty for their error" (Rom. 1:26–27, my trans.). It is apparent that Paul thinks homosexual acts are wrong.[19] For him, they typified pagan morality. His judgment on this matter, however, is not unique. It was a view shared by other thinkers of the Greco-Roman world, easily documented in the writings of Plato, Aristotle, the Stoics, Plutarch, Seneca, Dio Chrysostom, Philo, and others. As the Jewish historian Josephus put it:

> What of our marriage laws? The law recognizes no sexual intercourse, except the natural union of a man and a woman, and this only for the sake of having children. It abhors intercourse of men with men, and death is the punishment if anyone attempts it.
>
> (*Ag. Ap.*, 2 § 199)

Paul was not presenting a unique revelation he had received from on high but a perspective that was standard *in his culture*. For him, there was no question that homosexuality was a matter of choice, for he says, "They (the pagan women) *exchanged* natural relations for unnatural" and "they (the pagan men) *gave up* natural relations with the female." He associated the choice with insatiable lusts. He assumed heterosexuality was "natural" whereas homosexuality was "unnatural." Paul's opinion of what is "natural" was based on popular perception. It was a culturally conditioned point of view. Elsewhere, too, Paul uses the nature argument in insisting on the distinction between men and women: "Does not nature itself teach you that for a man to wear long hair is degrading . . . but if a woman has long hair, it is her pride?" (1 Cor. 11:14–15, my trans.). For Paul it is simply "unnatural" for men to have long hair (and so cutting the hair is assumed to be "natural") and for women to wear short hair. That view of what is "natural" and "unnatural" is also in accordance with his culture, the Greco-Roman world.[20] The fact that he opines what is natural or unnatural does not make that opinion binding for all generations. One is not constrained to agree with Paul that it is "unnatural" for a man to grow long hair or for a woman to cut her hair. Nor do we agree with the creation argument used by the writer of 1 Tim. 2:11–14 that since Adam was created before Eve, women must be subordinate to men. If one takes that line of argument to its logical conclusion, one may say that human beings are subordinate to vegetables and animals since vegetables and animals were created first, according to Genesis 1. We cannot disregard the historical and cultural context out of which the Bible comes.

Creation Theology

It must be admitted that the standard biblical texts—seven in all—that either mention or may allude to homosexual practice are uniformly negative about it. In this negativity they reflect a heterosexist bias prevalent in the ancient Near East. Christian ethical decisions cannot, however, rest on those seven texts, for the application of each text is fraught with difficulties. What we need is a different textual orientation. If a decision is to be made about homosexuality as a valid or invalid lifestyle, it has to be on theological grounds. It is for good reason, therefore, that many interpreters have turned to the Old Testament theology of creation. Some have argued on the basis of the creation account in Genesis 1 that heterosexual relations are normative: God created humanity as male and female, and the charge is given that people should "be fruitful and multiply" (Gen. 1:28). It has been noted, however, that Gen. 1:26–28 is not concerned with social relationships. The human creatures are not described as 'îš wĕ'iššâ, "man and woman" or "husband and wife," but zākār ûnĕqēbâ, "male and female."[21] It is in Genesis 2 that the human creatures are characterized by the sociological terms 'îš wĕ'iššâ. Exegetically it is evident that biology is the point in Gen. 1:26–28, not sociology. Nor is the text about sexual orientation; it is about the special status of humanity over against the other creatures of the earth. Unlike the other creatures of the earth, humanity is created in the image and likeness of God. Humanity is thus elevated above other creatures and portrayed as a reflection of the deity. To judge by what we know from other "creation texts" of the ancient Near East, we take this to mean that humanity is created as dignified and sovereign like the deity. Human beings are not, as Israel's neighbors had it, a servant class only for the use of the gods.[22] Rather, humanity was created in the divine image and likeness. At the same time, the text makes plain that human beings are different from God, inasmuch as they are biologically differentiated and therefore just like the other creatures of the earth. In their sexuality they are not at all like the God of Israel, they are like the animals.[23] The passage, then, concerns human beings as *biological* creatures capable of reproduction. So it is that when male and female were created, they were commanded to "be fruitful and multiply"—just like the animals (Gen. 1:22). The charge to procreate is a constant refrain in the so-called Priestly source (Gen. 1:22, 28; 8:17; 9:1, 7; Exod. 1:7). Of all the things said in the creation account, this command is reiterated in the Priestly account.

This presentation of reality is probably a deliberate response to Babylonian theology, as reflected in the Atraḥasis Epic (1700 B.C.E.). Whereas the gods in the Babylonian account have every intention of putting limits on the growth of human population—through drought, pestilence, famine, infertility, flood, and so on—the biblical perspective emphasizes the very opposite to be the intention of Israel's God: God intends for humanity to "be fruitful and multiply."[24] Viewed in this light, it seems clear that the intent of the author of Genesis 1 is to affirm the growth of human population.[25] Theologically, too, we must affirm with the Bible that procreation is good and that it is in God's creative intention. At the same time, we must admit that procreation is *not* an essential element of our being human.[26] People who are childless are no less human. Nor is heterosexual union an indispensable element of humanity. People who are celibate by choice or by circumstances beyond their control are no less human. Genesis does not in fact tell the full story of creation. Despite the clarity of the biblical text, we are aware that procreation is not a command that every human being can keep. There are some people who are biologically incapable of bearing children. Elsewhere in the Bible, too, the problem of human infertility is recognized. In the cultural environment of the biblical writers, such infertility or barrenness is regarded as a curse and often explained as a consequence of divine affliction. But for many of us, that is an antiquated and inadequate explanation of a human condition. Then, there are others who, for economic and pragmatic reasons, do not obey the imperative to have children. Indeed, some countries in modern times have found it necessary to legislate birth control, in effect mandating a disregard of the biblical command. Even apart from the law, modern social and economic realities may necessitate a reconsideration of the imperative to "be fruitful and multiply." Smaller families, it is commonly believed today in the West, provide better environments for raising children, so many couples choose to have smaller families. That decision is made today on pragmatic grounds, not on the basis of proof texts. We already make such decisions apart from our textual orientation. The accounts of creation in Genesis give what the biblical writers believed to be typical: Every creature is created according to its type. It does not, however, take into account the exceptions that are also created.

A Different Textual Orientation: The Wisdom Literature

The scriptures do not reveal all the realities of creation. There are many truths about creation that people may discern through observation of life and the world, and there are realities that may remain unexplained. This is the premise of the Old Testament's wisdom tradition, which is best represented in the Protestant canon in the books of Proverbs, Job, and Ecclesiastes and also the Wisdom of Solomon and Ecclesiasticus (Ben Sira) in the larger canon. As elsewhere in the ancient Near East, wisdom in the Old Testament may be defined as "a practical knowledge of the laws of life and of the world, based upon experience [and] the characteristic of practically all that it says about life is this starting point in basic experience."[27] The sages of Israel did not begin instruction with "thus saith the LORD." Rather, they observed the workings of the world, learned from human experiences, and dispensed instructions accordingly—without appealing to special revelation or to the experience of a particular people.[28] The result is not a systematic theology but a series of practical admonitions for living and how to cope with the vicissitudes of life.[29] Along with the "theology from above" that one discerns elsewhere in the Bible, wisdom sets forth a "theology from below," a theology that begins with humanity.[30] In contrast to the Torah and the Prophets, the tendency in the wisdom tradition is to avoid the language of divine causality in accounting for human experiences. So the doctrine of retribution as stated in normative wisdom is decidedly not theonomous; it does not attribute consequences of human actions to God.[31] For instance, one finds the following saying in Prov. 26:27:

> Whoever digs a pit will fall into it,
> and a stone will come back on the one who starts it rolling.
> A lying tongue hates its victims,
> and a flattering mouth works ruin.

One observes that there is no mention of the deity's involvement in the way things work out. The digger of the pit falls into it, the rolled stone rolls itself back, the flattering mouth itself works ruin. Evil brings evil, good brings good. The consequence follows the act as a matter of fact, as if by some law of nature.

The divergence in perspectives between the wisdom tradition and other parts of the Bible is also evident when one compares an injunction against vows stated in Ecclesiastes over against that stated in Deuteronomy. The version in Deuteronomy is dogmatic: "When you make a vow to YHWH your God, do not be slack in fulfilling it; for YHWH your God will certainly require it of you and it shall be an offense against you [if you do not fulfill it]" (Deut. 23:21 [Hebrew v. 22]). By contrast, Ecclesiastes states the matter in neutral terms: "When you make a vow to God, do not be slack to fulfill it, for there is no delight in fools" (Eccl. 5:4). Apart from the fact that the more generic name "God" is preferred over the more particularistic "YHWH your God," the admonition in Ecclesiastes resorts to circumlocution instead of the language of divine retribution: "There is no delight in fools."

Moreover, in the wisdom literature of the Bible, *tôrâ*, "instruction," and *miṣwâ*, "commandment," are used not so much of sacred laws but of human instructions, wisdom born of experience. The language of obedience to the *tôrâ* and *miṣwâ* in the wisdom literature is comparable to what we find in Deuteronomy, except that the "instruction" and "commandment" in the former come not as truths revealed by God but as teachings of mother and father and of sages (Prov. 1:8; 2:1; 3:1; 4:2; 6:20, 23; 7:1–2; 13:14). In other words, wisdom democratizes and desacralizes *tôrâ*, "instruction," and *miṣwâ*, "commandment." This is not to say that the perspective of the wisdom tradition is anti-Yahwistic or even nontheistic, but it is clear that the wisdom moves beyond the confines of purely theistic explanations and the idea of divine revelation. The unspoken assumption of the sages is that some things may be explained in nonreligious language. Not all events can or need be explained in terms of divine causes and effects. Wisdom is interested in what is natural, and it does not define what is natural or unnatural by what traditions say. Rather, the sages turned to the study of nature itself. So it is that Solomon, the consummate sage in the Old Testament, "would speak of trees, from the cedar that is in the Lebanon to the hyssop that grows in the wall; he would speak of animals, and birds, and reptiles, and fish" (1 Kings 4:32–33 [Heb. 5:12–13]). This interest is analogous to the "list science" of ancient Egypt and Mesopotamia.[32] In a late wisdom text, the sage's activity is said to have included astronomy, zoology, and botany (Wisd. Sol. 7:17–22). These are the things which "wisdom, the fashioner of all things, taught" (Wisd. Sol. 7:22). Wisdom is interested in the ancient equivalent of what we today call the natural sciences, and its assumption is that human beings can learn from such sciences some truths that are not specially revealed. Hence there is in the wisdom tradition the greatest regard for those who bring knowledge from the "natural sciences." In Ben Sira, for instance, physicians and pharmacists are extolled as experts whose skills are created by God for humanity's well-being (Sir. 38:1–15).[33] Wisdom recognizes that there is truth one can learn from natural sciences and human experiences. Thus, as W. Sibley Towner argues, the wisdom literature of the Bible provides us with a "biblically warranted, theologically validated affirmation of our 'secular' interpretation of experience comprehended within a theological framework built upon a doctrine of creation as the good handiwork of a creator who remains also sustainer and the ultimate redeemer of the world."[34] Here in the wisdom tradition of the Bible is *scriptural authority* for human beings to make ethical decisions by paying attention to science and human experiences.[35] We do learn from nature, and it is scriptural to reflect on human experience—even if human experience sometimes contradicts what we have always believed to be true. The wisdom texts of the Bible point us beyond a purely textual orientation in our ethics.

The book of Job makes this point well. At the outset we are told that Job is righteous; he is a fearer of God. From the standpoint of the orthodox tradition, however, there can be no question as to why Job suffers; he must have done something wrong to deserve his pain. And so his friends come along to confront him, appealing to the standard explanations for human suffering. Eliphaz even reports that he received a supernatural word and visions confirming the orthodox position. The friends of Job refuse to listen to his testimony and his insistence of innocence. For them, the standard explanations have priority over human testimony. So despite what they have observed and what they have known personally of their friend, they rely only on what they have always known to be true. But Job's innocence is a given, according to the prologue. And the epilogue asserts the same—indeed, attributing to God the judgment that Job was right and his friends wrong (Job 42:7). In the end the book does not account for the suffering of the innocent. It implicitly concedes that wisdom has no answer in this case. But the book does call into question the easy answers of orthodoxy. There are some things about creation that remain a mystery. Creation is not as orderly as one would like to believe. This point is emphasized in Israel's reactive wisdom tradition, as represented by Job and Ecclesiastes. To be sure, the wisdom tradition as a whole recognizes that God is the Creator of the universe, but wisdom also concedes that God's creation does include irregularities and unevenness—anomalies that no human being can explain or change. So one reads in Ecclesiastes (1:15; 7:13):

> What is crooked cannot be made straight,[36]
>   What is lacking cannot be counted. . . .
> See the work of God;
>   For who can make straight what He has made crooked?

Conclusion

Wisdom's perspective is admittedly unorthodox when judged by the viewpoints of the Torah and the Prophets. Noticeably absent from the wisdom texts of Proverbs, Job, and Ecclesiastes are the main themes that one finds elsewhere in the Bible. There is no interest in salvation history, no mention of the ancestors, the exodus, or the Sinai experience, no reference to the giving of the law, and no covenant theology. Indeed, the perspective of wisdom seems so different from the rest of the canon that the wisdom literature as a whole has proved to be a stumbling block for those who want to describe Old Testament theology in terms of a well-defined center. Wisdom simply does not fit the schemes laid out in the monumental Old Testament theologies of Gerhard von Rad and Walther Eichrodt. For some, the distinctiveness of wisdom's approach is such that questions must be raised about its legitimacy and authority.[37] Yet it is a fact that the wisdom literature is a part of the canon. It is a part of the Bible. One may suggest, therefore, that the perspective of wisdom is a needed corrective to the "theology from above" that one finds elsewhere. The presence of wisdom's perspective is a reminder that one cannot be too quick to speak for God and too ready to disregard the complexity of the world in which we live. We risk presenting an imbalanced theology when we reflect only from above, neglecting what is from below. In the wisdom literature we are instructed not to ignore nature, science, reason, and experience. The appeal for a place for reason and experience is, therefore, an appeal for a more wholesome *canonical* response to the problems that human beings face, a response that does not neglect the often marginalized voices of wisdom. And the way of wisdom, which gives credence to science and experience, is not at all unscriptural. It merely assumes a different textual orientation, one that ironically points us beyond the written texts.

NOTES

1. On the methodological difference between Protestants and Catholics in the use of scriptures and natural law in this debate, see Charles E. Curran, "Homosexuality and Moral Theology: Methodological and Substantive Considerations," *Homosexuality and Ethics*, ed. Edward Batchelor, Jr. (New York: Pilgrim, 1980), 90–91.
2. There is no reference to homoerotic practice among women anywhere in the Old Testament. The sole text in the New Testament that touches on the subject is Rom. 1:26.
3. The Hebrew verb *qillēl* does not just mean "to curse" (so NRSV; NIV) but literally "to make light, to slight." See Lev. 19:4; Judg. 9:27; 2 Sam. 16:5, 7, 10, 11, 13. Thus, NJPS translates the verb as "insult" while NEB has "revile." The Aphel of the verb in Aramaic means "to dishonor, disrespect." The Akkadian cognate is *qullulu*, "to reduce, diminish, discredit." The Hebrew verb is thus the opposite of *kibbēd*, "to honor" (literally, "make important, heavy").
4. Literally, "a pierced (woman)." See the comment of K. Elliger, *Leviticus*, HAT 4 (Tübingen: Mohr/Siebeck, 1966), 288–89.
5. The adjective is used of the gaunt cows in pharaoh's dream in the Joseph story (Gen. 41:3).
6. Hebrew *těballūl ʿênô*, literally, "obscurity of his eyes."
7. Walter Brueggemann concedes that perhaps "David plays loosely with the distinction of clean and unclean, but presumably he does not lie." The main argument is that they need bread. See his *First and Second Samuel*, Interpretation, (Louisville, Ky.: Westminster/John Knox, 1990), 154.
8. For this interpretation see Robert Guelich, *Mark 1-8:26*, WBC 34A (Dallas: Word, 1989), 123–25.
9. Tom F. Driver, "The Contemporary and Christian Contexts," *Homosexuality and Ethics*, ed. Edward Batchelor, Jr., 20.
10. See Jeffrey S. Siker, "How to Decide: Homosexual Christians, the Bible, and Gentile Inclusion," *Theology Today* 51 (1994): 219–34; reprinted as "Homo-

sexual Christians, the Bible, and Gentile Inclusion: Confessions of a Repenting Heterosexist," *Homosexuality in the Church: Both Sides of the Debate*, ed. Jeffrey S. Siker (Louisville, Ky.: Westminster John Knox, 1994), 178–94.

11. See Josephus, *Antiquities* 4.8, 23, and the comments in Patrick D. Miller, *Deuteronomy*, Interpretation (Louisville, Ky.: Westminster/John Knox, 1990), 165–66.

12. On law as a secondary genre to the values it enforces, see Waldemar Janzen, *Old Testament Ethics: A Paradigmatic Approach* (Louisville, Ky.: Westminster John Knox, 1994), 64–66.

13. For some interpreters the story shows that homosexuality in general was regarded as more abhorrent than heterosexual rape. So Robert Gordis ("Homosexuality and the Homosexual," *Homosexuality and Ethics*, ed. Edward Batchelor, Jr., 52): "The *practice* is clearly regarded as worse than rape" (emphasis mine). The passage is not concerned about a "practice," however. It tells of a horrible incident. The intention of the men of Sodom was rape, though a homosexual one. Today we know that rape is about violence and the use of power, not about sex. If it is true that the narrator of the story regarded homosexuality as worse than (heterosexual) rape, we must take that male and heterosexist bias into consideration in our hermeneutic. In any case, whether or not the author implicitly condemns it, homosexuality is not the ethical focus in the text.

14. See Simon B. Parker, "The Hebrew Bible and Homosexuality," *Quarterly Review* 11, no. 3 (1991): 6.

15. Jude 7. Homosexuality is not the issue, for the flesh that is pursued is called *heteras*, "other, different" (as in English "hetero-"). The point is that mortals transgressed the boundaries between human and celestial beings, even as celestial beings abandoned their positions to have sex with women—they of different flesh. See R. J. Bauckham, *Jude, 2 Peter*, WBC 50 (Dallas: Word, 1983), 14.

16. See also Janzen, *Old Testament Ethics*, 36–44.

17. See Victor P. Furnish, "The Bible and Homosexuality: Reading the Texts in Context," *Homosexuality in the Church: Both Sides of the Debate*, ed. Jeffrey S. Siker, (Louisville, Ky.: Westminster John Knox, 1994), 24–31; Abraham Smith, "The New Testament and Homosexuality," *Quarterly Review* 11, no. 4 (1991):18–32.

18. The precise meaning of these terms is debated. See the chapter by Dale B. Martin in this volume.

19. I am in agreement with Richard B. Hays that exegesis should not be confused with hermeneutics. As far as the plain sense of the text is concerned, I believe it is adequately clear that Paul, like others in his culture, was against homosexual acts by men and by women. See Hays, "Relations Natural and Unnatural: A Response to John Boswell's Exegesis of Romans 1," *Journal of Religion and Ethics* 14, no. 1 (1986):185.

20. See C. K. Barrett, *A Commentary on the First Epistle to the Corinthians*, Black's New Testament Commentaries (London: Black, 1968), 256–57.

21. See Phyllis A. Bird, " 'Male and Female He Created Them': Gen. 1:27b in the Context of the Priestly Account of Creation," *HTR* 74, no. 2 (1981): 129–59; idem, "Genesis I–III as a Source for a Contemporary Theology of Sexuality," *Ex Auditu* 3 (1987):31–44.

22. See *Enuma Elish*, Tablet VI, lines 34–35 (*ANET³*, 68), and *Atrahasis* 1:194–97 (W. G. Lambert and A. R. Millard, *Atrahasis* [Oxford: Clarendon, 1969], 56–57).

23. Note the command "Be fruitful and multiply" is first given to the animals (Gen. 1:22).

24. According to the Atraḫasis Epic, humanity had increased and become too noisy for the gods, hence the desire for limitations. See Anne Draffkorn Kilmer, "The Mesopotamian Concept of Overpopulation and Its Solution as Represented in Mythology," *Orientalia* 41 (1972):160–77, and W. J. Moran, "The Babylonian Story of the Flood," *Biblical* 40 (1971):51–61.

25. Contrary to the destructive intention of the gods in Atraḫasis, God promises the Israelites, "In your land women will neither miscarry nor be barren" (Ex. 23:26, my trans.). See Tivra Frymer-Kensky, "The Atraḫasis Epic and Its Significance for Our Understanding of Genesis 1–9," *Biblical Archaeologist* 40 (1977): 150.

26. See Gerald T. Sheppard, "The Use of Scripture Within the Christian Ethical Debate Concerning Same-Sex Oriented Persons," *USQR* 40 (1985): 23–25.

27. Gerhard von Rad, *Old Testament Theology* 1 (New York: Harper, 1962 [German edition 1957]), 418.

28. See John J. Collins, "The Biblical Precedent for Natural Theology," *JAAR* 41, no. 5, suppl. (March 1977): 35–67.

29. As Walter J. Harrelson puts it, "Wisdom operates without the necessity of a synthesis." See his "Wisdom and Pastoral Theology," *Andover-Newton Quarterly* 7, no. 1 (1966): 10.

30. See Walter Brueggemann, *In Man We Trust: The Neglected Side of Biblical Faith* (Atlanta: John Knox, 1972).

31. The classic exploration of this aspect of the wisdom tradition is Klaus Koch's "Is There a Doctrine of Retribution in the Old Testament?" *Theodicy in the Old Testament*, Issues in Religion and Theology 4, ed. James L. Crenshaw (Philadelphia: Fortress, 1983), 57–87. This influential article was originally published in German: "Gibt es ein Vergeltungsdogma im Alten Testament?" *ZTK* 52 (1955):1–42.

32. The ancient sages catalogued lists of things in nature in order to understand them. See Horst E. Richter, "Die Naturweisheit des Alten Testaments in Buche Hiob," *ZAW* 70 (1958):1–20; Gerhard von Rad, "Hiob XXXVIII und die altägytische Weisheit," *Wisdom in Israel and in the Ancient Near East*, VTSup 3, ed. M. Noth and D. Winton Thomas (Leiden: Brill, 1960), 293–301; A. Leo Oppenheim, "Man and Nature in Mesopotamian Civilization," *Dictionary of Scientific Biographies* 15 (New York: Scribner's, 1970–80), 634–66.

33. See R. E. Clements, *Wisdom in Theology* (Grand Rapids: Eerdmans, 1992), 65–93.

34. "The Renewed Authority of Old Testament Wisdom for Contemporary Faith," *Canon and Authority: Essays in Old Testament Religion and Theology*, George W. Coats and Burke O. Long (Philadelphia: Fortress, 1977), 146.

35. Indeed, James Barr has recently argued that "natural theology" is not found only in wisdom literature; it is in fact a biblical viewpoint, evident in both the Old Testament and the New. Barr concludes that "if the presence of natural theology within the Bible is recognized, it may mean that common ideas of the doctrine of scripture have to be revised" (*Biblical Faith and Natural Theology* [Oxford: Clarendon, 1993], 195).

36. The MT has the Qal infinitive *litqōn*, "is straight." The Qal of this verb is unattested elsewhere in Hebrew, however; the verb is always in Piel in the Bible

(see also 7:13; 12:9; Sir. 47:9), so the corresponding passive ought to be Pual. In Mishnaic Hebrew, too, the verb occurs only in Piel, Hiphil, and Niphal, never in Qal. Thus *lō' yûkal lĕtuqqan*, "cannot be straightened," may be compared with the rhetorical question *mî yûkal lĕtaqqēn*, "who can straighten?" (7:23). The passive ("be made straight") is supported in the ancient versions. The point is that some things in creation are contrary to what human beings may expect, but they are so by God's will and no amount of human effort will change their nature.

37. So, for instance, Hartmut Gese (*Lehre und Wirklichkeit in der alten Weisheit* [Tübingen: Mohr, 1958], 3) and Horst D. Preuss (*Der Segen in der Bibel und im Handeln der Kirche* [Munich: Kaiser, 1968], 40–42).

3

The Power of God at Work
in the Children of God

Robert L. Brawley

More than anything else, New Testament ethics is about the power of God. With startling irony, conspicuous portions of the New Testament push human behavior back to divine behavior and glean ethics as the fruit of living under God's rule. Some of us read the Bible as if it projects a way of life we then actualize. But for a forcefully reiterated line of thought in the New Testament, ethics does not depend on our ability to discern what is right and to do it. Rather, God's power is at work precisely in what we do *not* discern and do *not* do. We children of God do not even know how to pray as we ought (Rom. 8:26). Can we be counted on to act as we ought? Does the Holy Spirit help us in our limitations?

Truth to tell, much of our labor in ethics is futile. For one thing, the ground on which we base our efforts may be shifting sand. Paul's zeal for ancestral traditions led him to persecute the people of God (Gal. 1:13). So depending on ancestral traditions may mean stepping into quicksand. Whether tradition says, "You shall . . ." or "you shall not . . . ," it implies, "I am able." Unfortunately, evil wreaks havoc with the assumption that I am able (see Rom. 1:18–2:24). In the pyramid of devastating injustice I am not at the top, oppressing everyone below me. But I am not at the bottom either. So ethics as a human enterprise reveals our inadequacy. Indeed, we do *not* know how to pray as we ought, so we can hardly be counted on to *act* as we ought.

What is left, except for God's Spirit to lead us? But how are we to glean our conduct as the fruit of living under God's rule? There are at least two crucial aspects of being led by the Spirit of God. One is for us to experience God's power through direct relationships with God. The second is for us to know God and the nature of God's power. Therefore, this chapter has two corresponding tasks. One is to demonstrate biblical themes of direct relationships between God and human beings. The other is to reflect briefly on the literary characterization of God in the Bible. But a direct relationship with God and experiences of God's power are sticky wickets. For many modern people, power is an obstacle, and so is God.

God as a Problem

Experiencing God in a direct relationship may seem to be depressingly preposterous to many of us because God has no electronic mail address. We may not know whether there is a modem that will communicate with God, and even if we concede that such a modem might exist, how to get on-line bewilders us. Our inability to format ourselves for a relationship with God is reason enough for some of us to become agnostic about direct relationships.

This analogy may not appear accurate for today's Christian community, but many people have given up trying to know God. Although Wayne Meeks's *The Moral World of the First Christians* has validity in its focus on the social processes that formed the character of early Christian communities, it undercuts the New Testament's appeal to a profound relational dynamic of being led by the Spirit.[1] In the effort to pump vitality into human conduct, some strategies for biblical ethics are in fact prejudiced against God. Moreover, our uncertainties about direct relationships with God steer us away from experiences of the divine, so that we focus instead on principles, rationality, and the influence of peers. We may be adrift in understanding how God's Spirit might lead us and downright suspicious of anyone who claims a direct relationship with God. So we have settled for a rough equivalent of agnosticism. We are cut off from God.

To be enlightened, to taste the gift of heaven, to become companions of the Holy Spirit, to taste the good word of God and the powers of the age to come are pivotal but not extraordinary experiences in the New Testament. They may not fit our expectations, however. What is companionship with the Spirit? Characteristically, we sensationalize. If God's ways are not our ways, we may anticipate something spectacular. Our expectations tend to be spectacular experiences of the Spirit that animate our bodies and lips—leaping, prophesying, and speaking in tongues.

The New Testament offers its share of ecstatic spectacle (Acts 2:3–4; 3:8; 1 Cor. 14:1–40). But indeed God's ways are not our ways. So when Paul grounds the life of believers in a relationship with God, he gives quite a different reference point for experiencing the Spirit: the experience of being God's children. "When we cry, 'Abba! Father!' it is that very Spirit [of God] bearing witness with our spirit that we are children of God" (Rom. 8:15; cf. Gal. 4:6–7). In Romans 8 our cry to God from the heart as God's children is intimately related to our suffering and inadequacy. In our suffering and limitations we who have the Spirit groan inwardly as God's children—the voice of God's Spirit, who expresses our plea for us (Rom. 8:18–27).

In the spring of 1995 the Illinois Supreme Court directed that four-year-old Richard be taken from his adoptive family and placed in the care of his birth parents, whom he had never known. In the actual moment of transfer, Richard clung to his adoptive mother and cried, "Mama, don't let them take me. Mama, go with me." Richard's cry from the heart bore witness that he was her child. Likewise, when we suffer in a broken and fallen world and, like Richard, cry out to God, "Mama, don't let them—Mama, go with me," it is God's Spirit confirming that we are God's children. Our cry to God is on-line with God. We are formatted to experience that we are God's children (see Gal. 4:6–7; 1 John 3:1; Heb. 2:10, 14; 12:4–11).

Power as a Problem

Divine virility is justifiably on the wane. It is not merely that a masculine God needs a more suitable image, God's power to coerce is also appropriately diminishing. Power implies a relationship that is hierarchical and asymmetrical. Some of us may be quite satisfied with hierarchy and asymmetry in a relationship with a benevolent deity; after all, divine and human nature are inherently asymmetrical. In fact, all relationships are inherently asymmetrical, with the ironic exception of narcissism. But a coercive God in a coercive social order has the potential to take back all we have gained from the witness of the Spirit that we are God's children. Who wishes to be the child of a God who twists our arm?

Modern theology has criticized a coercive God as a perversion of biblical characterizations of God and a distortion of human experience.[2] The move away from coercive divine power leads toward the perspective that God's power persuades us but does not domineer.[3] In fact, Michel Foucault claims that Christianity spreads a new kind of power—pastoral power.[4] In pastoral power the shepherd suffers for the sake of the flock. Divine pastoral power means that God persuades and influences but does not coerce. Later I will return to the question: To what degree is such a God of persuasion compatible with New Testament ethics?

Living out of a Relationship with God

Bearing fruit under God's rule is not the only option for New Testament ethics. James tries direct exhortation, the conclusion of the good Samaritan makes the hero of the parable a role model (Luke 10:37), and 2 Thessalonians espouses imitation of Paul (3:7,9).[5] The options in the New Testament are multiple. To be led by God's Spirit, however, is prominent among options because (1) it is forcefully reiterated, (2) it lies at the heart of the good news, and (3) it derives from God's power. Actually, however, the reiteration is not monolithic but a combination of several distinct strains. I will discuss examples from the historical Jesus, Mark, Matthew, Luke-Acts, and Paul.

The Historical Jesus

Because the historical Jesus is available only through documents that represent developments of tradition, the methods for recovery are complex and debatable.[6] The points that follow are based on widely accepted criteria of early levels of the tradition, multiple independent attestation, and what is typical for the historical Jesus.

Jesus' own relationship with God and his conduct as the fruit of God's power at work in him are strongly attested. He defends himself in the Beelzebul controversy: "If it is by the finger of God that I cast out the demons, then the kingdom of God has come to you" (Luke 11:20).[7] Mark 14:36 preserves the Aramaic *Abba* for Jesus' direct address to God, an affectionate term implying a confidential relationship. The same intimate term probably lies behind other references to God as father (Luke 11:2), and Paul's use of it in Rom. 8:15 and Gal. 4:6 may stand in continuity with Jesus' language.[8] It is impossible to identify every single reference to Jesus' own relationship with God, but the multiple independent attestation of the imprint he left on the tradition leaves little doubt about that intimate relationship.[9]

These sketchy notices about the experience of the historical Jesus also fit his proclamation and enactment of God's rule. Swimming upstream against strong cultural and religious currents, Jesus issued a summons to an unrestricted and unbrokered kingdom of God. In a hierarchical society with stark inequalities in power patron–client relationships were rife, and brokers mediated transactions between one level and another.[10] Duplicating the social structure, religious leaders, practices, and institutions mediated the exchange between God and human beings. But in word and deed Jesus beckoned people to an unbrokered kingdom of God,[11] a direct relationship with God that bypassed temple, sacrifice, priest, synagogue, teachers of the law, and the law itself. In contrast to meals that reflected social inequalities and discrepancies in power, Jesus enacted the unrestricted rule of God in open table fellowship. His exorcisms were not mere healings but exhibitions of access to God's power outside established religion. Jesus himself, however, was not a broker of God's power but a concrete case of living out of a direct relationship with God.[12]

Mark

Mark preserves Jesus' emphasis on an unbrokered relationship with God and God's power at work in human lives. Within two verses of Jesus' appearance on the scene, Mark describes the descent of the Spirit upon him (Mark 1:9–10). The emphasis on the Spirit becomes a theme because (1) the descent of the Spirit recalls the prediction of John the Baptist that

Jesus would baptize with the Holy Spirit, and (2) the notice after the baptism that the Spirit drove Jesus into the wilderness underscores the significance of the Spirit (Mark 1:8–12). From his baptism on, Jesus lives out of a Spirit-endowed relationship with God as God's son.

Further, Mark 1:15 gives a summary of the mission of Jesus: "The time is fulfilled, and the kingdom of God has come near; repent, and believe in the good news." This statement of Jesus' mission and his Spirit-endowed relationship with God colors everything that follows. Thus, when Jesus' disciples harvest grain on the Sabbath and violate Sabbath laws, Jesus' vindication of them is not merely an assertion of their status over the Sabbath but also a concrete case of living under God's rule (2:23–28). Jesus' resolution of this controversy stands in an intertextual relationship with the making of the Sabbath in Gen. 2:1–3. The opponents imply that the disciples should keep the Sabbath for God's sake. Jesus implies that God has given the Sabbath for *their* sake. Living under God's rule enables Jesus' disciples to eat the food God provides for the welfare of humanity, and thus humanity has dominion over the Sabbath just as over the rest of creation (Gen. 1:26–29).[13] God's rule breaks the way of doing ethics by following laws and roots ethics in God's power at work directly in human beings.

On the other hand, Jesus defends a commandment from the decalogue in Mark 7:8–9 appearing to imply that the law brokers a relationship with God. Jesus overrides the traditions of the elders about washing hands and declaring corban by appealing to the Mosaic law (7:10–13). But there is a prior control on Jesus' appeal to the law—a heart close to God (7:6), an unbrokered relationship. Similarly, what is right about marriage and divorce depends on living under the rule of the God who provides for the well-being of humanity (Mark 10:2–9). That is, God joins husband and wife for their welfare so they will not be alone (Gen. 2:18).

The unbrokered kingdom is also reflected in a difficult passage about faith, in Mark 11:22–24. Many interpreters understand the text as a general principle that faith can move mountains. But Jesus actually speaks about removing "this mountain": namely, the Temple Mount. Jesus' call for faith in God juxtaposes living under God's rule to the Temple Mount. For those who live in a relationship of faith with God, the Temple Mount is removed and cast into the sea.[14] Faith is the unbrokered kingdom's alternative to the Temple. God's rule exists outside established religious channels.

In Mark this kingdom is relational in two senses. It is an unbrokered relationship with God and with others. The first and second commandments demonstrate the double nature of the relationship. Living under God's rule is loving God, and loving neighbor flows out of loving God (Mark 12:28–34).

Matthew

Matthew emphasizes the unbrokered kingdom as a relationship between God and God's children. The thematic endowment with the Spirit locates Jesus in a relationship with God, as does Mark; that is, the descent of the Spirit and the notice that the Spirit led Jesus into the wilderness recall the prediction of John the Baptist that Jesus would baptize with the Holy Spirit, and the descent of the Spirit empowers Jesus for his mission (Matt. 3:11–4:1). Similarly, Matthew summarizes Jesus' mission as does Mark: "From that time Jesus began to proclaim, 'Repent, for the kingdom of heaven has come near'" (Matt. 4:17), and this summary is a key to everything that follows.[15] Thus Jesus' endowment with the Spirit anticipates all he will do, and the canopy of God's rule covers everything in Matthew's story. Under that canopy God treats Jesus' disciples as God's own children, and they understand themselves to be God's children (Matt. 5:9; 7:9–11).

This relationship between God and God's children in which the children experience God's power for their conduct is particularly significant in the ethical teaching of Jesus in the Sermon on the Mount. In such a relationship Jesus' disciples experience the blessedness of being poor in spirit—recognizing the limitations of the human condition as "poverty" (Matt. 5:3)—as the point of departure for ethics.[16] Those who are poor in spirit do not presume to ground their conduct in human resources. Jesus' disciples derive their conduct from their relationship with God, out of which God's children act as God's children (Matt. 5:44–45).[17] The beatitudes are hardly ethical exhortations for disciples to become meek, or merciful, or peacemakers (as in *Did.* 3:7–8). Rather, the Spirit-endowed Jesus dramatizes the blessedness of what it means to live as God's children under God's rule.

But what about explicit discussions of the law (Matt. 5:17–48)? Do they fit the derivation of human behavior from God's rule? Like the beatitudes, Jesus' discussion of the law does not stand on its own but falls under the canopy of God's rule from Matt. 4:17. In the discussion itself, however, there is a curious dialectic between canonical law and Jesus' revision of it. On the one hand, the discussion values canonical law—"Not one letter, not one stroke of a letter, will pass from the law" (Matt. 5:18). On the other hand, the discussion violates canonical law with revisions that alter letters. What does it mean to do the least of these commandments in Matt. 5:19?

Though Matthew's Jesus values the letter of the law, doing the commandments is clearly not the letter of the law. Jesus revises the law on murder and adultery by going beyond the letter (Matt. 5:21–30). But he revises the letter of the law on divorce and oaths by annulling them and replacing them with his own opinions.[18]

Jesus' embodiment of God's will resolves some of the curious dialectic between valuing the law and revising it. The Spirit-endowed Jesus fulfills the law not in his radical interpretation of it (Matt. 5:21–48) but in enacting God's will in his life. Jesus' followers likewise are to enact the law and the prophets in loving God and neighbor (7:12; 22:40).[19] Living under God's rule (4:17) breaks the traditional understanding of law as the broker of God's will and makes ethics God's power at work in human lives.

When it comes to Jesus' own sayings in the Sermon on the Mount, readers of Matthew will find it extremely difficult to keep them as new prescriptions that broker God's will. Does turning the other cheek exhaust what Jesus means in Matt. 5:39? Rather than new laws, Jesus' sayings are open-ended focal instances of what it means to live under God's rule.[20] The charge to be perfect as God is perfect is not an isolated injunction but grounds love—even love of enemies—in a relationship with God as *"your heavenly Father"* (Matt. 5:43–48). To be perfect as God is perfect means that nothing less than the God who is God of God's children is the norm for love.[21]

Luke–Acts

Luke–Acts is another witness to an unbrokered relationship between God and God's children. Jesus' special relationship with God surfaces early and often in Luke. When Jesus first appears on the scene as an angel's promise, he is already identified as God's son (Luke 1:32,35). Luke reiterates Jesus' relationship to the Spirit around his baptism even more than do Mark and Matthew. Luke 4:1 explicitly characterizes Jesus as full of the Spirit, and Jesus reinforces the coming of the Spirit upon him in 4:18: "The Spirit of the Lord is upon me, because he has anointed me." Luke-Acts makes this a potent theme in that Peter reiterates the anointing of Jesus with the Spirit in his summary of Jesus' mission (Acts 10:38). So Jesus' own ethical concern for the poor, the captives, the blind, and the oppressed is the fruit of his thematic endowment with the Spirit (Luke 4:18; 7:22).

After his emphatic endowment with the Spirit, the Lucan Jesus gives his own programmatic statement about his purpose: "I must proclaim the good news of the kingdom of God to the other cities also, because I was sent for this" (Luke 4:43). Thus, God's rule as Jesus' purpose is a key to everything in Luke-Acts. Further, God's rule has formidable connections with two additional Lucan themes. One theme is God's covenant with Abraham. God's rule in and through Jesus is the particular way God's promise to bless all the families of the earth comes to completion (Luke 1:55, 72–73; Acts 3:25). The other theme is bearing fruit. In his sermon on the plain, Jesus reiterates John the Baptist's antithesis of bad fruit/good fruit (Luke 3:8–9; 6:43). If readers take 6:45 out of context, it appears that good fruit flows from the inner motivation of good people. But in its context, good fruit flows first from God's rule and a relationship with Jesus as Lord (6:46).[22]

Loving enemies in Luke 6:35 is a particular case of bearing fruit to God under the umbrella of God's promise to bless all families of the earth. If readers take 6:32–36 out of context, it appears that loving enemies confers the status of God's children on disciples, and they are to love enemies in imitation of God: "Be merciful, just as your Father is merciful" (6:36). But in the context of God's rule, loving enemies derives from the status of being God's child. "You will be children of the Most High" (6:35) is a manifestation of this status. Moreover, imitation of God is deficient because disciples can hardly imitate God's kindness. God shows mercy in giving the blessings of creation to the ungrateful and wicked. God's children can only act analogously and derivatively in that they have experienced the mercy of *their* father (6:36). Lucan ethics is a matter of God's children bearing fruit to the God who promises to bless all families of the earth.

Paul and the Problem of the Law

What is the relationship between the Spirit of God and the law? Do Old Testament prescriptions and prohibitions remain valid for Christians? Does Paul excommunicate the law? James Dunn has argued that the tension in Paul between Christ and the law has been widely misunderstood.[23] Noting that Paul broaches the antithesis between Christ and the law only in the context of defining the people of God, Dunn concludes that the negative aspect of the law is its distortion as an exclusivistic ethnic marker. So the "works of the law" that Paul places in antithesis to Christ are ethnic practices such as circumcision, Sabbath observance, and keeping kosher.[24]

Dunn's understanding of the law implies that (1) the problem of the law has to do with the inclusion of Gentiles in God's people corporately rather than as individuals and (2) the law has a positive function for believers once it is liberated from ethnicity.

(1) Is the problem of the law corporate or individual? In a context of social conflict in Galatia, where opponents insisted that Gentiles become Jewish proselytes, Paul made faith God's one way of salvation for Israelites and for Gentiles. So justification by faith has to do with corporate rather than individual relationships with God (see Gal. 4:10; 5:2–6).

But with due respect to Dunn, the problem of the law does not end with ethnic exclusivism. When Paul deals with ethical behavior—as distinct from becoming a part of the people of God—justification by faith takes on decidedly individual relevance. This is clear in Romans 6. Paul claims that all who believe are justified by God's grace (Rom. 3:24; 5:20–21). This claim, however, can be distorted as a free pass for sinning. Paul's response to this distortion of his gospel sets justification by grace against the law (Rom. 6:14). In this specific context of human conduct, Paul's notion of justification has to do with *individual* behavior.[25]

(2) Does the law continue to have a positive function for believers?

Dunn contends that when the law is liberated from Jewish nationalism, it has an abiding constructive role for people of faith.[26] The law does not motivate or enable Christian conduct, but it does inform it.

Clearly, Paul affirms that the law is holy, just, and good (Rom. 7:12). The problem with the law is that the power of evil uses the law to deceive human beings. For Dunn, construing the law as an ethnic distinction constitutes the deception. So when ethnic distinctions fall away, the law lights the pathway of obedience to God. But is that what is at stake? If in fact Paul wishes to reclaim the law, why does he speak so often about freedom from it (Rom. 6:14; 7:4,6; Gal. 3:25; 4:26,30; 5:1,18)?

One reason Paul speaks about freedom from the law is the nature of the deceptive power of evil. For Paul, human beings are under the power either of evil or of God—a compulsory alternative.[27] Not only does the power of evil use the law to imply ethnic distinction, it also uses the law to persuade us that we are serving God when in fact we are not. And that leaves but one other alternative. We may think that if we keep the law we will be offering life to God as it should be lived. For Paul it is the reverse. Life is what God offers us (Rom. 3:24). Our infatuation with what we do obscures what God does and so deceives us into thinking we serve God when we serve the power of evil.

Moreover, we may construe the law as God's will and still misconstrue the will of God. Is it possible to understand the law as God's will and precisely because of that understanding to persecute the people of God (Gal. 1:13–14)? Dunn attempts to do two commendable things: to show the sociological dimension of misconstruing the law as an ethnic boundary and to maintain the validity of human efforts to obey God's will. But beyond the sociological factor, Paul points to a problem with our efforts to obey God's will. Our efforts throw us into reliance on ourselves, hinder us from deriving our behavior from God, and leave us but one other alternative—to serve the power of evil.[28] We can construe the law as God's will and still misconstrue the will of God.

Does the summation of the law as love of neighbor establish the continuing role of the law? I will return to love as a criterion for ethics, but for the moment two other issues are at hand. First, other than living in the Spirit, Paul defines love of neighbor only negatively: "Love does no wrong to a neighbor" (Rom. 13:10; cf. Gal. 5:14). Thus, love of neighbor can hardly be construed as a law that decrees what one can or cannot do. Rather, love of neighbor implies a pivotal shift from law to the things against which there is no law (Gal. 5:23). Second, this love is nothing other than life in the Spirit—God's power at work in God's children.[29]

When Paul contrasts justification by faith with justification by works of the law in Gal. 2:16, more is at stake than ethnic markers. So Paul claims to have died to the law *as a way of life*, with the result that his way of life now is to live out of a relationship with God in and through Christ (Gal. 2:19–20).[30] Consequently, the law of Christ in 6:2 cannot be a reclamation of the Mosaic law as a guide for believers. Rather, the law of Christ is Christ himself as the one through whom God rules.

A particularly pertinent case is 1 Cor. 6:12–20. In exhorting the Corinthians to adjudicate their own grievances, Paul claims astoundingly that the saints will judge the world (6:2). A parallel in Rom. 4:13 speaks of God's promise to Abraham and his descendants that they will inherit the world. The parallel shows that Paul's claim that the saints will judge the world presupposes the Abrahamic covenant. So the eschatological fulfillment of the Abrahamic covenant is also what is at stake in 1 Cor. 6:9–11. Paul is not ousting the unjust here and now but disqualifying them as heirs of the future when the saints join God in ruling the world. The unjust in 6:9 who will be excluded stand in contrast to the saints in 6:2 who will be included.

The Corinthians, however, do not qualify as unjust. They are consecrated to God, and as such they claim the slogan, "All things are lawful for me" (1 Cor. 6:11–12). Paul is probably dealing with sexual promiscuity— males engaging in sex with prostitutes. On the one hand, Paul gives a direct exhortation: "Shun fornication" (6:18). On the other, he persuades his readers by reminding them of their relationships with God. "The body is not in a relationship with sexual immorality but with the Lord, and the Lord is in a relationship with the body" (6:13, my trans.).

Paul develops his reminder of their relationships with God in a triadic pattern. (1) "Do you not know that your bodies are members of Christ?" (1 Cor. 6:15). (2) "Do you not know that your body is a temple of the Holy Spirit within you?" (6:19). (3) "[Do you not know] that you are not your own? For you were bought with a price" (6:19–20). The passive verb in the last sentence conceals God as the one who buys the "slave." So Paul reminds the Corinthians of their relationship with Christ, with the Holy Spirit, and with the God who pays the price for them. Further, he makes it clear that the power of God that raised Jesus is available to them through the relationship by which believers are united with the Lord in one spirit (6:14, 17).

Paul resorts to no law here. But is it not possible to be misled when we think we are being led by God's Spirit? Indeed Paul scores that very point in discussing spiritual gifts in 1 Cor. 12:1. Even people who worship idols can, so to speak, get the spirit. So Paul develops criteria for determining whether behavior derives from God's power or not. (1) The criterion in 1 Cor. 6:12 is what is beneficial. The same criterion surfaces in 10:23; 12:7,12–26; and 14:1–33. (2) Love is closely related.[31] The hymn to love appears in 1 Corinthians 13 precisely to establish love as a criterion for congregational relationships.[32] Love appears with similar force in Gal. 5:13–14, 1 Cor. 8:1, and Rom. 13:9–10, where in all three cases it coincides with benefiting others (see also 1 Cor. 8:1; 1 Thess. 4:9; Rom. 14:15). (3) Additionally, 1 Cor. 12:3 establishes the confession that Jesus is Lord as a criterion for what it means to be led by God's Spirit. The basis for the criteria of love and edification in Rom. 14:15 is God's love for those for whom Christ died (cf. Rom. 15:2–3), and the outcome of the criteria of love and edification is a manifestation of the relationship with God—"God is really among [the Corinthians]" (1 Cor. 14:25).

Biblical Characterizations of God

Earlier I suggested that biblical characterizations of God are crucial, if one is to be led by God's Spirit, and that such characterizations occur through reiteration and emphasis. To touch superficially on the character of God, a God of persuasion resonates strongly with a great deal of the characterization of God in the Bible. "The LORD, the LORD, a God merciful and gracious, slow to anger, and abounding in steadfast love" (Ex. 34:6; see Ps. 103:8; Jer. 32:18; Jon. 4:2). Hosea's God entreats Israel with warm and tender compassion (Hos. 11:8). The Lucan God rejoices over repentant sinners like a woman rejoicing over finding a lost coin or a father rejoicing over finding a lost son (Luke 15:8–32). For Paul, God's kindness is a persuasive power to lead to repentance (Rom. 2:4).

In two particular ways, however, a God who is persuasive but not coercive is deficient for much of the New Testament. First, the power of God that raised Jesus from the dead entails more than persuasion and influence. God's power to raise Jesus is probably what the Gospel of Mark anticipates when Jesus promises that his contemporaries will see God's rule come with power (Mark 9:1); in Acts, God raises Jesus in mastery over the power of death (Acts 2:24). Second, the power of God apparent in the resurrection of Jesus foreshadows a final divine triumph over the power of evil. In 1 Corinthians 15, God's power triumphs ultimately over every opposing power (15:24–28), and Hebrews and Revelation have their own versions of the ultimate divine victory (Heb. 1:13; 10:13; Rev. 21:2–4). So on the one hand, God's power surpasses persuasion and influence. On the other, the power of God that bears fruit in human conduct is heavily weighted on the side of persuasion and influence.

If reiteration and emphasis are criteria for characterization, certainly the law qualifies as a forceful part of the characterization of God. God's covenant at Sinai consistently characterizes God in the New Testament as well as the Old. Readers of the New Testament can hardly fail to characterize God as the giver of the law at Sinai. So God is the kind of God who does not want human beings to kill one another, to wound one another in sexual betrayals, or to deprive one another of the basis for sustaining life by theft. In an ethic that derives from our relationship with God, the law comes in not to light our pathway but to characterize the God whose children we are. But in a question about divorce, Jesus drives the characterization of God back to a situation before the Mosaic law (Mark 10:6–9). Jesus appeals to the character of God as the one who joins male and female so they will not be alone (Gen. 2:24). Thus, the law is *part* of the characterization of God.

But analytical methods in biblical studies have caused us to fragment covenant traditions into separate trajectories, when in fact much of the Bible collapses them into one. The one covenant that dominates is God's promise to Abraham: land, descendants, and blessing of all families of the earth. The Mosaic and Davidic covenants are particular ways God is bringing the promises to Abraham to fulfillment.[33] This also is what God's messiah is about—God's covenant fidelity.

Toward a Synthesis

This sampler of notions of deriving ethics from a direct relationship with God provides the basis for underscoring four additional points.

By and large, first, grace, faith, redemption, salvation, sanctification, and justification are relational. Grace and faith are not qualities that believers receive and possess. Rather, they are relationships in which believers stand.[34] Grace is God's power in relation to believers, and faith is the believers' dependence on the God of power.

Second, over against modern individualism, living out of a relationship with God is repeatedly communal in the New Testament. It is communal in two senses. Ethics is not merely individual fidelity but a relationship with God that embraces communal relationships: "We do not live to ourselves" (Rom. 14:7). Ethics is also communal as we make decisions about what being led by God's Spirit means. In this sense Paul's exhortations are his effort not to establish new laws but to contribute to the community's determination of how the Spirit leads. Even though the sin in Matt. 18:15–20 initially offends on a one-to-one basis, the purpose of reproof is restoration to community; and, further, the community adjudicates controversy as nothing less than God's judgment when they are gathered in Jesus' name.[35] Paul's charge to the Thessalonians to test everything is addressed to the congregation in the second person plural (1 Thess. 5:21, cf. 4:18; 5:11; similarly 1 Cor. 14:24; 1 John 4:1).[36] The congregation tests, holds fast to what is good, and keeps away from every form of evil. In Acts, although Paul alone has a vision that calls him to Macedonia, his entourage comes to a corporate agreement on God's call (Acts 16:9–10). Notably, both Paul's conversion and Peter's mission to Cornelius involve the confirmation of double visions; that is, the vision of one person contains and authenticates the vision of another (Acts 9:10–16; 10:5–6, 19–22).[37] Making and implementing ethical decisions is communal.

Third, some interpreters warn that theocentric ethics detracts from human efforts to obey God. But because actual human beings live out of their relationship with God, theocentric ethics does not drain away human activity but safeguards it as an indispensable component of the relationship. Believers are not passive but embody God's power.

Last, the option of deriving ethics from a relationship with God banks on a high assessment of God's power. The power that rules over believers is the power that raised Jesus from the dead and will ultimately triumph over every form of evil. Nevertheless, inasmuch as it depends on faith, it is conspicuously characterized as the power of persuasion.

A Word on a Current Debate

What does an ethic deriving out of a relationship with God mean in the present debate in the Presbyterian Church (U.S.A.) on human sexuality? Some answers, I think, are marked by dialectic. (1) Such an ethic is not an easy permissiveness. It depends on God's power. (2) God's power produces conduct that is loving and beneficial. (3) The focus on the relationship of believers to God calls us to attend to our own relationship with God and restrains us from being judgmental about others. But (4) behavior is not a matter of idiosyncratic judgment. Rather, the Christian community, as two or three gathered together in the name of Jesus, as session, congregation, presbytery, synod, and General Assembly, tests the spirits to see if they are from God. (5) In testing everything, it is appropriate for the church as community to give guidance. (6) For an ethic that depends on our relationship with God, however, it is inappropriate for the church to give "definitive" guidance. As a global decision, definitive guidance constitutes a new law and curiously is like a Marxist class analysis. The leading of God's Spirit has to do with complexity and particularity, rather than Marxist generality. (7) Finally, in order for us to be led by God's Spirit, both in human sexuality and in the debate about human sexuality, the church might call us all to our relationship with God. For of such is the ethic of God's power at work in the children of God.

NOTES

1. Wayne A. Meeks, *The Moral World of the First Christians*, Library of Early Christianity (Philadelphia: Westminster, 1986). For a reference to being led by the spirit of Jesus, see p. 140.
2. See Dorothee Soelle, *The Strength of the Weak: Toward a Christian Feminist Identity* (Philadelphia: Westminster, 1984), 97–105. For the notion that power is not a unilateral effect of one party on another but a reciprocal relationship see Bernard Loomer, "Two Kinds of Power," *Criterion* 15, no.7 (1976): 12–29.

3. See Anna Case-Winters, *God's Power: Traditional Understandings and Contemporary Challenges* (Louisville, Ky.: Westminster/John Knox, 1990), 129–31.

4. Michel Foucault, "The Subject and Power," *Michel Foucault: Beyond Structuralism and Hermeneutics*, ed. Hubert L. Dreyfus and Paul Rabinow (Chicago: University Press, 1983), 214. See Loomer, "Two Kinds of Power," 28.

5. Franz Laub shows that elsewhere in the Pauline epistles imitation of Paul has to do with the Spirit's power to sustain us in tribulation. Also, imitation of Christ is not an ethical appeal but an expression of a common destiny with Christ (*Eschatologische Verkündigung und Lebensgestaltung nach Paulus: Eine Untersuchung zum Wirken des Apostels beim Aufbau der Gemeinde in Thessalonike*, Münchener Universitäts-Schriften [Regensburg: Pustet, 1973], 80–84).

6. For a discussion of methods see Robert L. Brawley, "Table Fellowship: Bane and Blessing for the Historical Jesus," *Perspectives in Religious Studies* 22 (1995): 13–31.

7. John D. Crossan, *The Historical Jesus: The Life of a Mediterranean Jewish Peasant* (San Francisco: Harper, 1991), xix.

8. Gerhard Kittel, "*abba*," *TDNT* 1.5–6; Hans Conzelmann, "Jesus Christus," *RGG* 3, no. 3:633. Joachim Jeremias overstated the singularity of Jesus' usage (*The Prayers of Jesus* [Naperville, Ill.: Allenson, 1967]). Geza Vermes gives evidence that *abba* was used by other Jewish charismatics in Jesus' time to express their intimacy with God (*Jesus the Jew* [New York: Macmillan, 1973], 210–11). Mary D'Angelo relates Jesus' use to Roman imperial order rather than to intimacy ("*Abba* and 'Father': Imperial Theology and the Jesus Traditions," *JBL* 111 [1992]: 611–30). Questions of the historical Jesus aside, the Abba of Mark 14:36 is the God of the relationship described by "not what I want, but what you want." Cf. John Ashton, "Abba," *ABD* 1:7–8.

9. So Marcus J. Borg, *Jesus: A New Vision: Spirit, Culture, and the Life of Discipleship* (San Francisco: Harper, 1987), 15.

10. Halvor Moxnes, *The Economy of the Kingdom: Social Conflict and Economic Relations in Luke's Gospel*, OBT (Philadelphia: Fortress, 1988), 36–47; idem, "Patron-Client Relations and the New Community in Luke-Acts," *The Social World of Luke-Acts: Models for Interpretation*, ed. Jerome Neyrey (Peabody, Mass.: Hendrickson, 1991), 241–50.

11. Beyond doubt the historical Jesus proclaimed the kingdom of God. Leander E. Keck, *A Future for the Historical Jesus: The Place of Jesus in Preaching and Theology* (Philadelphia: Fortress, 1981) 32; Crossan, *Historical Jesus*, 284—Crossan sets the brokerless kingdom of God over against a brokered empire by major divisions; Conzelmann, "Jesus Christus," 633–35.

12. On meals, healings, and Jesus' refusal to be a broker see Crossan, *Historical Jesus*, 261–353; Brawley, "Table Fellowship."

13. See Robert L. Brawley, *Text to Text Pours Forth Speech: Voices of Scripture in Luke-Acts*, Indiana Studies in Biblical Literature (Bloomington, Ind.: Indiana University Press, 1995), 1–2.

14. Werner H. Kelber, *Mark's Story of Jesus* (Philadelphia: Fortress, 1979), 61–62.

15. Jack D. Kingsbury, *Matthew as Story* (Philadelphia: Fortress, 1986), 4–5, 38–77.

16. So Hans D. Betz, *The Sermon on the Mount: A Commentary on the Sermon on the Mount Including the Sermon on the Plain (Matthew 5:3–7:27 and Luke 6:20–49)*,

Hermeneia (Minneapolis: Fortress, 1995), 114–15. I take awareness of the human condition as primarily experiential rather than cognitive, as does Betz.

17. Hans D. Betz, *Nachfolge und Nachahmung Jesu Christi im Neuen Testament*, BHT 37 (Tübingen: Mohr/Siebeck, 1967), 122–23; idem, *The Sermon on the Mount*, 97.

18. Betz takes Matt. 5:27–37 as Jesus' interpretation of God's intent in the law rather than as a revision of the law (*Sermon on the Mount*, 209–10).

19. Ulrich Luz, *Matthew 1–7: A Commentary* (Minneapolis: Augsburg, 1989), 260–65. W. D. Davies envisions the Sermon on the Mount, though not detached from the life of Jesus, as "Messianic Torah" surpassing Mosaic Torah in interpretation (*The Setting of the Sermon on the Mount* [Cambridge: University Press, 1964], 93, 96, 431, 435).

20. Robert Tannehill, *The Sword of His Mouth* (Philadelphia: Fortress, 1975), 67–77.

21. Daniel Patte, *The Gospel According to Matthew: A Structural Commentary on Matthew's Faith* (Philadelphia: Fortress, 1987), 82–84.

22. See Robert L. Brawley, *Centering on God: Method and Message in Luke-Acts*, Literary Currents (Louisville, Ky.: Westminster/John Knox, 1990), 185–211.

23. James D. Dunn, *Jesus, Paul, and the Law: Studies in Mark and Galatians* (Louisville, Ky.: Westminster/John Knox, 1990).

24. Dunn, *Jesus, Paul, and the Law*, 99–101, 131, 159, 184–88, 191–200, 219–24. See also James D. Dunn, *Romans 1–8*, WBC 38a (Dallas: Word, 1988), lxiv–lxxii; E. P. Sanders, *Paul and Palestinian Judaism: A Comparison of Patterns of Religion* (Philadelphia: Fortress, 1977), 75, 180–82.

25. "Universalism and the most radical individuation are here two sides of the same coin" (Ernst Käsemann, *Commentary on Romans* [Grand Rapids: Eerdmans, 1980], 22).

26. Dunn, *Jesus, Paul, and the Law*, 200, 231; idem, *Romans 1–8*, lxxi–lxxii. In contrast to Dunn, Käsemann contends that "the third use of the law is still inconceivable to the apostle" (*Commentary on Romans*, 215).

27. Rudolf Bultmann, *Theology of the New Testament*, 1 (New York: Scribner's, 1951), 197–203; Otto Merk, *Handeln aus Glauben: Die Motivierungen der paulinischen Ethik*, Marburger theologische Studien 5 (Marburg: Elwert, 1968), 30–32. For a parallel in the Jewish environment see 1 QS 3:13–4:26.

28. See Käsemann, *Commentary on Romans*, 194, 202–12.

29. Herbert Braun, *Gerichtsgedanke und Rechfertigungslehre bei Paulus*, UNT 19 (Leipzig: Hinrichs, 1930), 65; Wolfgang Schrage, *Die konkreten Einzelgeboten in der paulinischen Paränese: Ein Beitrag zur neutestamentlichen Ethik* (Gütersloh: Mohn, 1961), 72.

30. Hans D. Betz, *Galatians: A Commentary on Paul's Letter to the Churches in Galatia*, Hermeneia (Philadelphia: Fortress, 1979), 147.

31. On edification as a criterion see Laub, *Eschatologische Verkündigung*, 69, 89–91; Merk, *Handeln aus Glauben*, 145–48 and passim.

32. Merk, *Handeln aus Glauben*, 145, 228; cf. 170–73.

33. Ronald E. Clements, *Abraham and David: Genesis XV and Its Meaning for Israelite Tradition* (Naperville, Ill.: Allenson, 1967), 47–60, 81–82.

34. Käsemann, *Commentary on Romans*, 24, 174, 310. Modern theology also emphasizes the relational nature of God. See Case-Winters, *God's Power*, 225–27.

Grace and faith express something of the reciprocity Loomer emphasizes in relational power ("Two Kinds of Power," 23–24).

35. Patte, *The Gospel According to Matthew*, 252–55.
36. Laub, *Eschatologische Verkündigung*, 93–94.
37. Robert L. Brawley, *Luke-Acts and the Jews: Conflict, Apology, and Conciliation*, SBLMS 33 (Atlanta: Scholars, 1987), 59–60.

Part 2

The Bible and Human Sexuality

4

Marriage in the Old Testament

J. Andrew Dearman

Marriage is a primary social institution in any culture. In ancient Israel it was the basis of kinship relationships; these were the building blocks of the broader society in the ancient Near East, of which Israel was a part, and the most important means by which social relations were ordered.[1] Ancient Israelite culture was also part of a preindustrial society whose kinship structure was patrilineal and patriarchal. For a proper understanding of marriage in the Old Testament, it is necessary to evaluate the institution from within its host culture(s); otherwise, one risks anachronism and misunderstanding by way of explanation. The same principle applies in theological interpretation. Some cultural assumptions applicable to marriage in ancient Israel may be obsolete in modern societies. Nevertheless, the Old Testament also places marriage in such transcultural contexts as God's intention for the nurture of humankind in community and as a model for the divine–human relationship. In doing so, the Old Testament is a major source for the New in its treatment of the subject and, together with it, calls into question modern attempts to define marriage from the perspectives of personal rights and freedom.

In what follows, Israelite marriage is examined in three categories. The first considers the topic in light of the creation accounts in Genesis. Typically, creation stories provide part of a culture's worldview and help to define its theological self-understanding. In the Genesis accounts one finds the theological basis of marriage rooted in the complementary nature of humankind as male and female created in God's image, where the one-flesh union of husband and wife is the foundation of human community. The second category considers marriage in the context of Israelite custom and Pentateuchal instruction. Customs and legal codes preserve ordering processes for societies, and law provides for the application of justice when order fails. Israelite marriage combined patrilineal and patriarchal structure with the functions of providing familial security and community order. The third category considers the marriage metaphor in the prophetic corpus. Marriage may be useful as an analogy in many spheres, but the prophetic corpus employs it to portray the relationship between the Lord and his people, thereby defining Israelite religion as a unique reflection of the marriage bond itself.

The Creation Accounts as a Paradigm for Marriage

The two accounts of creation (Gen. 1:1–2:3 and 2:4–3:24) are foundational to the understanding of marriage in the Old Testament. Both devote major attention to the relationship between man and woman. They are etiological narratives that convey the significance of their topics through the description of origins. God's design is paradigmatic for the respective roles of men and women in society. Even the account of disobedience and expulsion from the garden (Genesis 3) portrays Adam and Eve in representative roles. Virtually all aspects of Israelite marriage reflected elsewhere in the Old Testament find their etiological counterpart in the creation accounts.

In the first account, the creation of man and woman in the image of God comes at the conclusion of God's design of the cosmos. The six-day scheme of creation is set out with correspondences between days 1 and 4, 2 and 5, 3 and 6. Days one and four concern the relationship between light (1) and the heavenly bodies (4). Days two and five concern the relationship between the firmament dividing the waters (2) and the birds and fish that move in the sky and the water respectively (5). Days three and six concern the relationship between land and vegetation (3) and animals and humankind (6). Creation of humankind is the climactic act on the sixth day, accompanied by a unique conferring of privileges and responsibilities through divine blessing (Gen. 1:26–31). Nevertheless, humankind as male and female is also joined to all living things who exist "according to their kind" (days 3, 5–6) and who can be fruitful, or reproduce (also days 3, 5–6). Marriage is an outworking of these two traits: The relationship between man and woman is a result of divine blessing, and the relationship affirms what is humanly "according to kind" and capable of reproduction.

The exalted place for humankind is affirmed by the narration that humanity as *male* and *female* is made in the image of God (Gen. 1:26–27). The majority of biblical scholars have concluded that whatever else is communicated by the phrase "created in the image of God," the terms "image" and "likeness" refer to material form and correspondence in appearance, a functional representation where the image points to the source of its identity.[2] Nothing else in the Old Testament bears this privilege of image and likeness because nothing else represents God's own relationship to creation as does humanity in its kind as male and female. Biological complement is also rooted in the blessing God confers on humanity (1:28). Man and woman are given the privileges to subdue the earth and to have dominion over animals. These privileges most likely underscore the function of being created in the image of God. Man and woman (as *male* and *female*) exercise their dominion as stewards of the creator in a representative theomorphic sense. Marriage and family are the institutional setting for male and female in God's creation.

The second account (Gen. 2:4–25) elaborates on the place of man and woman together in God's creation. The terms *male* and *female* are not used in this account, but they are presupposed by the climactic affirmation that man and woman form a one-flesh union (2:24). The first "man" is a creature formed from the earth (2:7), reflecting in a literal way the correspondence suggested in the previous account between the land (= day 3; Gen. 1:9–13) and the creatures who inhabit the land (= day 6; Gen. 1:24–31). Even the designation "the man" (*ha'adam*) is an etiological acknowledgment of the organic relationship to the earth (*'adamâ*).[3] According to divine assessment, it is not good that the man be alone (2:18). None of the animals, however, can provide satisfactory companionship: literally, a "helper suitable for him."[4] In this dilemma the second account provides illumination of Gen. 1:26–27. "The man" is related to the animals as steward, but they do not provide the companionship reflective of the divine image. Only man and woman together share that privilege. Indeed, no other creature except the woman, not a human male, not even one of the semi-divine "sons of God" (see Gen. 6:1–4) is able to bond fully with the first Adam.[5]

The second account provides two affirmations of the "suitable companion": the woman is literally of the same flesh and blood as the man (Gen. 2:23), organically related[6] and made for him; and, as paradigm for the unique bond between the two, a man (husband) shall separate from his parents and cleave to "his woman" (wife),[7] and the two shall become one flesh (*basar 'ehad*). In the process of leaving parents and cleaving to each other, man and woman complete the symbolic circle of their one-flesh origins (2:21–22) in a literal act of embodiment. Becoming one flesh assumes both sexual union and a resulting bond; however, the significance of "one flesh" is not completed through these actions. Flesh (*basar*) indicates kinship as well,[8] for in leaving his parents and cleaving to his wife, a man forms a family unit as a result of the marriage bond. Here is the etiology of both marriage and family in a nutshell. Children are a result and extension of man and woman in the uniqueness of their one-flesh union.

Disobeying God's instruction leads to brokenness in the relationship between man and woman (Gen. 3:1–24). Nevertheless, nothing negates the uniqueness or the appropriateness of their union; its paradigmatic significance for society is assumed.[9] To support the one-flesh union, the desire of the woman shall be for her husband, even though the combination of her manual labor for the family's subsistence and the birth of children is painful (Gen. 3:16).[10] The comment that her husband "shall rule over her" is patriarchal and probably reflects the cultural primacy of the man in subsistence efforts (farming, gathering, and herding). Children were a key to family survival. The intensive process of birth and nurture kept the mother closer to the domicile as manager of the household, although her duties were not limited to child rearing (see Prov. 31:10–31). The manual labor of the man is likewise difficult; eventually he will succumb to the struggle with the soil and become dust (3:19). These circumstances of labor and "hierarchical" gender roles result from the disobedience of the man and the woman; they are not "creation mandates" but prospective explanations of physical existence outside the garden. Nevertheless, Adam "knew" (*yada'*, "engage in sexual intercourse") his wife Eve, they produced children, and thus their labor began a pattern for their descendants (Gen. 4:1–2).

Marriage in Israelite Culture and Customary Law

As part of the kinship system in ancient Israel, marriage not only regulated family structure and identity but also was closely linked to the central institutions of property ownership and inheritance. Marriages were typically negotiated between families of a larger kinship group (clan or tribe), allowing the kinship group to maintain possession of its property and form a protective association. This form of kinship marriage is endogamous, as opposed to marriage between members of different tribes (exogamous). The primary social unit was the *bet-ab*; literally, the Hebrew phrase means "house of the father," and it included a man (the patriarch or *pater familias*), his wife or wives, and sons and unmarried daughters. Legal status for all in his house was determined through him, although every member of the house possessed certain rights and responsibilities. "House," therefore, meant more than domicile; it was actually the term for the family itself, including its property. If his sons were married, they (and their houses) remained linked to his house through the common possession of family property and other familial duties. In groups with a pastoral lifestyle (so-called semi-nomads), the sons would remain a part of the tent family. Married daughters were members of their husbands' house, yet they themselves provided a kinship link between the two families now joined through marriage. Slaves, servants, and concubines, where applicable, were included.

When the patriarchal head of the family died, his sons inherited the bulk of the house. Family descent (name and legal status) and property, and the responsibility to maintain them, were passed from father to son. A house had membership in a clan (*mišpaḥah*), which was a kinship association comprised of houses headed by uncles, brothers, and male cousins, all linked to an eponymous ancestor. These related houses played direct roles in the institution of marriage, particularly when one of the families was threatened with the loss of property. First, the cousins of these houses were likely prospects for intermarriage (endogamous marriage within a tribe or clan).[11] As noted, this provided for the maintenance of the family's possessions within the clan. Second, should a man die without an heir, one of his brothers or another male clan member could be expected to cohabit with his widow in the hope that an heir would be born (levirate marriage).[12] Third, family honor and maintenance of property required the protection of the larger clan. In dire circumstances, a man might mortgage (sell) his property, his family members, and even himself to creditors. It was the expectation that, if possible, another male of the clan (gō'el, a kinsman redeemer)[13] would redeem the family property and family members from their respective bonds.

The intertwining of families through patrilineal descent and patriarchal authority can be seen in other marriage terminology. A husband can be called ba'al or 'adôn (Ex. 21:3, 22; Deut. 21:13; 24:1; Isa. 54:5; Mal. 2:11; Gen. 18:12). Although they are not synonyms, both terms are closely related and mean "lord" in a broad sense. Ba'al includes particularly the concept of ownership or possession, while 'adôn is particularly associated with preeminent status. One who possesses is ba'al; one in authority is 'adôn. In Hebrew a woman betrothed or publically declared as engaged is 'ōrasâ/ me'ōrasâ. As a wife she is ba'ulâ. These are grammatically passive terms, reflecting her status as someone first dedicated to her husband and then possessed by her husband. The term ba'al can be used as a verb with a man as subject, meaning to marry a woman or to take her as a wife. The more frequent term for marriage is the common verb "to take." A man takes (laqah)[14] a woman and she becomes (hayah le) for him a wife. These verbs signify the legal transfer of the woman from her father's house to that of her husband.

Not much is known about the social mechanisms ("rites of passage") used by two families in contracting and entering a marriage in ancient Israel.[15] Nor is there much in the Old Testament about the marriage ceremony itself, although a variety of customs probably existed. One can draw out elements of the process, but the description is composite and subject to the variations of time, place, and local custom.

The process was initiated by the man's family. The father of the woman had to give his approval. She too may have had some choice in the matter (see Gen. 24:8, 57–58), but typically neither the man nor the woman had autonomy in the manner of the marriage proposal. Upon receipt of a gift (mōhar, "bridewealth," Gen. 34:12),[16] the father declared that his daughter was engaged or betrothed. Apparently the engagement was made public knowledge and considered binding. Since a gift had been given, honor and customary law required the completion of the marriage, with the eventual transfer of the woman to the house of the man. Justifiable cause must be shown to negate the engagement. A feast or celebration may have taken place (see Gen. 29:22) to honor the consummation of the marriage. Sexual intercourse took place in the domicile of the man. A symbolic phrase "to spread the garment over" signified the consummation of the marriage (Ruth 3:9; Ezek. 16:8). The man and his family expected the woman to be a virgin at the time the marriage was consummated. Apparently a symbol of her virginity was preserved, in case there was a dispute over this issue (Deut. 22:13–21). Patrilineal descent, patriarchal custom, and the honor of both families were at stake. Her virginity and her dowry[17] were brought to the man's family. In summary form "she became to him a wife" (Gen. 24:67).

Divorce could be initiated and carried out by the man, but the details and the extent of its practice remain obscure. The one legal passage concerned with the mechanism of divorce (Deut. 24:1–4) presupposes a particular set of circumstances and does not preserve a general mandate regarding the institution.[18] Polygyny was permissible, but its frequency in Israel is unknown.[19] Both Judaism and Christianity understood the thrust of the Old Testament to be toward monogamy, and it is likely that the predominantly monogamous practices of Jews and Christians corresponded to earlier Israelite practice.[20] Explicit references to polygyny are infrequent; they exist primarily in the ancestral accounts in Genesis (29—30) and the politically arranged marriages of the kings. Concubines and female slaves had an acknowledged status in ancient Israel, but the extent of their legal status over against that of "wives" is also obscure.[21] They maintained certain rights with regard to sexual activity (Ex. 21:7–11; Deut. 21:10–14) and their place in the house.

Adultery was considered a crime against the husband; fornication, incest taboos, seduction, and rape were considered crimes against the father or the husband.[22] The prescribed penalties could be harsh (Ex. 22:15–16 [16–17E]; Lev. 18:6–18; 20:10; Deut. 22:22–29), including death for both man and woman engaged in adultery. Adultery was also a sin against God (Ex. 20:14, 17; Deut. 5:18, 21), as were homosexual acts and bestiality (Lev. 18:21–22). Each was a source of pollution to the community. All required purging, atonement, and purification (Lev. 18:24–29; cf. Hos. 4:1–3). Homosexual acts and bestiality are attributed to the Canaanites (Lev. 18:24), but this does not explain the full force of their rejection. The issue is a concern for the integrity of the family; this is the context in which the practices are mentioned (Lev. 18:6–23). Their rejection is probably based on the same presuppositions proposed in our analysis of the creation accounts. Homosexuality and bestiality do not conform to the description of existence "according to their kind," and the sexual unions they represent are incapable of "reproducing." This is only consistent with humankind as male and female. Adultery, incest, fornication, and rape, likewise, are a violation of the one-flesh bond of husband and wife. All the forbidden sexual relations in Lev. 18:6–23 threaten the proper function of the family. Both the creation accounts and the legal codes base their understanding of legitimate sexual activity on the order, commitment, and obligation established in marriage rather than on the need for sexual gratification. The enjoyment of sexual relations is understood as something wonderful, but marriage is its proper context.[23]

Several aspects of Israelite marriage are made more comprehensible by comparing the prescriptions in the Old Testament with legal codes and judicial decisions from the ancient Near East. The best sources for the latter come from Mesopotamia, and there are now a number of studies that attempt to compare the biblical and cuneiform materials.[24] Two complicated elements in the discussion concern the degree to which there was a common legal tradition in the ancient Near East (of which Israel was a part), and whether the legal codes (e.g., the code of Hammurabi: Ex. 21:1–23:19; Deut. 12—26) represent state law enforced by a central administrative and judicial system. Since the biblical marriage "laws" have several correspondences with the cuneiform tradition, the question of commonality is simply one of degree and not of kind. The question of the legal codes as state law is probably to be answered in the negative. Cuneiform records of judicial decisions do not cite the legal codes in handing down a ruling, and the rulings may differ from those preserved in the codes. The legal codes are therefore better understood as treatises on law as the foundation of society, with summaries of actual cases compiled to illustrate the application of justice.[25]

Three interpretive principles follow from such a conclusion, each of which influences the understanding of the "marriage laws."

First, the legal prescriptions of the Old Testament regarding marriage are summary in form and incomplete. One may see this illustrated in the "law" of levirate marriage in Deut. 25:5–10. The Deuteronomic prescription concerns the responses of a widow and her brother-in-law to the circumstance that her dead husband had previously fathered no heir to preserve his name and inheritance. From two different narratives (Genesis 38 and Ruth) it appears that marital "options" to produce an heir were not limited to a brother-in-law. This is what one might expect if Deut. 25:5–10 is not a comprehensive prescription of the institution of levirate marriage.[26]

Second, careful attention to comparative material from the ancient Near East may also suggest a more complex legal setting for a marriage law than the summary form indicates. Stated differently, the biblical prescription may assume a prior legal status or the operation of customary law that is not stated explicitly. For example, the prohibition of divorce and remarriage in Deut. 24:1–4 probably served to prohibit a type of fraud whereby a first husband divorces his wife because of "indecency" he found in her, keeping either her dowry or the compensation due her, and then remarries her after she receives support money or compensation from a second husband. The circumstances behind this kind of fraud are attested elsewhere[27] but the Old Testament is silent about types of compensation and where they are applicable when a man and woman divorce. It is also possible that the divorce and remarriage is understood by the Deuteronomic compiler as a violation of purity boundaries or as an example of adultery.[28] It is likely that matters of compensation are also at issue in the question of a bride's virginity in Deut. 22:13–21; the dispute concerns more than the honor of the bride and the two families joined through the marriage.[29]

Third, the remedies or penalties given in the prescription texts may be understood as guidelines or illustrations of a just response rather than an unalterable requirement. For example, the penalty prescribed for adultery is death (Lev. 20:10–12; Deut. 22:22, 23–24). The observations of Prov. 6:30–35, however, imply that the husband of the adulterous wife had several legal options regarding his wife's paramour, since the adulterous relationship is understood as a crime against his rights. Compensation for damages in cases of adultery was an option commonly chosen in the ancient Near East.[30] Moreover, the prophetic model of YHWH's "divorce" of Israel and Judah on the grounds of adultery also represents punitive measures taken against them (e.g., legal separation, stripping, exposure) short of execution (Hos. 2:3–15 [1–13E]; Ezek. 16:37–39; 23:26).

Marriage as Theological Metaphor in the Prophets

The prophetic tradition preserved in the Old Testament adopted the metaphor of marriage as a means of depicting the relationship between the Lord and his people.[31] One can only speculate how far back this insight goes in Israelite thinking, but the origin of a concept is often less important than its actual employment. The metaphor is widespread in the prophetic corpus, but it has been understood frequently as a synonym for the covenant concept, a major interest of scholars in preceding decades.[32] Marriage and covenant are not synonyms in the prophetic corpus, but there is some overlap in meaning (see Prov. 2:17); both are concepts used to describe the relationship between Israel/Judah and the Lord.[33]

To summarize by way of introduction: Various aspects of the marriage metaphor are employed in the prophetic corpus. The Lord plays the roles of husband and father (parent). These roles also allow the Lord to prosecute his spouse or children. Israel and Judah can be either spouse or children. Jerusalem and Samaria also play the roles of wife and daughter. Sexual infidelity in various forms is a common metaphor for Israelite or Judean failure. Divorce is one measure used to describe divine judgment. Marital reconciliation, even when going beyond the options of the legal codes, is employed as the means to overcome the alienation provoked by infidelity.

A primary theme of the prophetic books is that the Lord has chosen Israel (Judah) as his own. The marriage metaphor is employed in a variety of ways to underscore this theme. Amos states that YHWH had known (*yada'*) Israel in ways different from other clans (*mišpaḥot*) of the earth (Amos 3:1–2). The use of the verb "to know" in the context of a chosen clan evokes the image of intimate knowledge that leads to conception (see Gen. 4:1). Hosea uses the marriage of the prophet to Gomer as a central metaphor to depict the relationship between Israel and the Lord (Hosea 1—3), including the role of children, adultery, and divorce. Both Jeremiah (2:2; 31:32) and Ezekiel (16, 23) employ variations on the theme of divine election as the institution of a marriage bond. In Jer. 31:32 the covenant (*berît*) established with Israel at the exodus is described as the Lord taking Israel in marriage (the verb is *ba'al*). Isaiah 5:1–7 contains a love song for a "beloved" and his vineyard. Vineyard can be a symbol of the female beloved (S. of Sol. 8:12).[34] Owner and vineyard play a role like that of Hosea and Gomer; in both instances the primary relationship at issue is that between the Lord and his people (5:7).

The same theme of divine election can be portrayed by reference to the personified capital cities of Jerusalem and Samaria, typically as "daughter" (*bat*) or "virgin" (*bethulâ*). The city personified as a female is part of a recognized metaphor in the ancient Near East.[35] "Daughter" is more explicitly a familial term, but "virgin" connotes a woman whose lack of sexual experience is due to her preservation for her future husband. Amos describes Israel as a virgin (5:1–2), even though Israel is a masculine name (see Jer. 3:6). Ezekiel develops an allegory in which Jerusalem and Samaria are sisters raised by the Lord and married to him (16; 23).[36] Personified Jerusalem plays an assortment of marital roles in Isaiah 40—66, a section of scripture originating in the exilic and early postexilic periods. She is a restored daughter (52:1–2; 62:10–12; cf. 40:1–2), a barren woman who bears children (54:1–3), a forsaken wife now reconciled to her husband (54:4–8), a queen and bride (62:3, 5). In these roles she represents the people. As married land and nursing mother, she also provides sustenance for the people (62:4; 66:10–11). The Lord is husband (54:5), bridegroom (62:5), and like a nursing mother (49:15–16); in these roles of restoring Jerusalem and people, the Lord is faithful to a family bond that has been temporarily destroyed.[37]

Gender-specific images are necessary to play a metaphorical role, but they apply inclusively to Israel or Judah. The capital city as female represents her people as a whole just as Israel in the role of son represents all the people in their identity as an heir to the inheritance (*naḥalâ*) of the Lord. It is even permissible to mix roles for the purpose of proclamation. In Hos. 1:2–9 (cf. 11:1–9) the people of Israel are represented by Gomer (wife), Loruhamah (daughter), and Jezreel (son).

If divine election is portrayed in marital terms, the failures of Israel and

Judah are depicted as sexual infidelity. In Hosea, Gomer's adultery and harlotry represent the infidelity of Israel against the Lord; even her children are termed children of harlotry (1:2–3). According to the most probable interpretation of chapter 2:3–25 [2:1–23E], Hosea's divorce proceedings against Gomer symbolize the Lord's rejection of Israel (2:3–15 [1–13E]); this is the necessary background to the language of courtship, betrothal (*'aras*), and "bridewealth" in 2:16–25 [14–23E], where the Lord pursues and reacquires the people in marriage. This moves beyond the options preserved in the legal codes. In 2:16 [18E], Israel will no longer call YHWH "my ba'al" but "my husband" (*'îš*). Here the term *ba'al* is understood in its significance as the title for another deity who has seduced Israel from its devotion to the Lord. As an obedient sign (3:1–5), Hosea acquires another adulteress (probably Gomer) to illustrate the Lord's action on behalf of wayward Israel. In chapter 11 the Lord is depicted as the parent (father) of rebellious children (Israel). This familial imagery is part of the root metaphor of marriage. The decision of the Lord to break with tradition (that is, not to prosecute the rebellious son; cf. Deut. 21:18–21) is only possible because the Lord is God and not "man" (*'îš*; 11:9). Again, the customary legal prescription—that an adulterer and an incorrigible son receive the death sentence—is overridden by the love of the husband/father, who declares that he will not be bound by the legal options of an *'îš* (man).

In the initial chapter of Isaiah, Jerusalem is personified as a prostitute (1:23; *zônâ*).[38] This is a betrayal of her identity as daughter and virgin. Fornication is tantamount to adultery. Like adultery, charges of prostitution or harlotry can be employed as a metaphor for idolatry (see Hos. 4:12–14). The vineyard of the beloved (5:1–7) that produced putrid grapes is like the children of harlotry born to Gomer in Hos. 1:2–9. The relationship between owner/vineyard and husband/wife is analogical but recognizable in Israelite culture.[39]

Jeremiah and Ezekiel are graphic in their employment of the sexual infidelity motif (Jer. 2:20–25, 33–37; 3:1–10; Ezekiel 16; 23), using the language of fornication, promiscuity, and adultery. In both books, the breach between the Lord and the people is compared to divorce. Jeremiah indicates that a return to the Lord raises the issue of defilement (Jer. 3:1–5; see also Deut. 24:1–4). The issue is resolved in chapter 3 as a decision of the Lord to do what the Deuteronomic law forbade: In mercy the Lord would take back the defiled people whose adultery was considered a marriage to their lovers. Jeremiah himself is forbidden to marry as a sign that the Lord is estranged from the people (16:1–4). In the language of restoration, Israel is once again a virgin, and the wonder of this turning is described as a female who encompasses a man (Jer. 31:21–22). The latter image formulates the miracle of restoration in a reversal of the patriarchal family structure.

In Ezekiel the graphic imagery of sexual infidelity exceeds even that of

Hosea. Jerusalem is depicted as a female foundling whom God adopted and married (16:1–8), who subsequently committed adultery (16:15–34), and who was divorced and judged (16:35–43). Chapter 23 portrays Jerusalem and Samaria in allegorical fashion as promiscuous sisters whom the Lord married and later judged. Because of their adultery, the two suffer the maximum penalty (23:36–49). The description of the sexual infidelity leaves little to the imagination; as with similar passages, the infidelity is code language for cultic and ethical failures and idolatry. Similarly, the language of judgment for adultery stands for the defeat and exile of Israel and Judah.

In summary, the marriage metaphor provides a rich vocabulary of divine commitment to Israel and terminology to describe Israel's failures. In his patriarchal role the Lord acquires a spouse, becoming the husband of his people. The commitment of the Lord to the intent of the marriage bond extends beyond the legal options preserved in the Old Testament for dealing with infidelity. Judgment or divorce are the expected actions, but they are temporary. The bond of matrimony and family is renewed. The language of adultery identifies defection from the Lord by analogy to the breaking of the most intimate bond known in human community. Defection as adultery is misdirected passion and misplaced loyalty. It is also finally a form of self-love. This is what unites the critique of idolatry and that of social injustice in the prophets: both are defective attempts to secure well-being apart from the familial bond established by the Lord. Thus it is no coincidence that the marriage metaphor and the exclusive worship of the Lord are bound closely in the prophetic corpus. The two are predicated on a unique bond at the center of social life and religious devotion.

Addendum: Old Testament Marriage in the New Testament and the Nature of Biblical Interpretation

It is not satisfactory for a Christian interpretation of the Old Testament and its teachings about marriage to ignore the New Testament and its own contributions to the subject. To borrow a marriage motif, it is not good that the Old Testament be alone; it needs a corresponding helpmate. This does not make it obsolete. The Old Testament is preparatory for God's supreme revelation in Jesus Christ; this is both a historical and a theological perspective. Together the Old and New Testaments preserve the historical character of God's self-revelation.

In what follows, one can only point briefly to the kinds of appropriation and supplementation that the New Testament offers the Old.

1. There is affirmation that the creation accounts are foundational for the understanding of marriage and sexuality (e.g., Mark 10:1–10/Matt. 19:3–9; Rom. 1:18–27).
2. There is adoption and adaptation of the marriage metaphor to

portray the relationship between Christ and the church (e.g., 2 Cor. 11:2–3; Eph. 5:22–33; cf. Rev. 21:2). Salvation as adoption and inheritance are also rooted in the Old Testament conception of the family (e.g., Rom. 8:14–17; Eph. 2:19).

3. There is acceptance of the view that the marriage bond is the proper context for sexual relations between man and woman (e.g., 1 Cor. 7:1–7).

4. There is acknowledgment that divorce (and thus the laws that regulate it) results not from God's intention for marriage but from human fallibility (Mark 10:5/Matt. 19:8; cf. 1 Cor. 7:12–16).

5. There is recognition that the eschatological horizon revealed in Christ shows marriage to be limited to a role in "this age." The "age to come" does not contain marriage (Mark 12:18–27/ Matt. 22:23–33). Celibacy is a viable option for Christians in the church, the new family of faith (1 Cor. 7:8–9, 25–40).

The New Testament is not a simple affirmation of all the Old contains about the institution of marriage. Thus, from the New Testament one may discern faithful ways of reading the Old Testament material that are "scriptural" and instructive for the life of the church but which do not originate from the Old Testament itself. On a fundamental level, however, the Old and the New Testaments have a common assumption about marriage and society. Both operate on the assumption that persons draw their fundamental societal identity as members of a family (and by extension they draw their theological identity from a community of faith).[40] "Rights" are first privileges of membership rather than the means of self-fulfillment or keys to personal autonomy. If this is, broadly speaking, the biblical perspective on social institutions, it differs markedly from a dominant perspective of modernity. The option to return to preindustrial, patriarchal societal norms is neither viable nor desirable for modern communities of faith; what is required in the task of faithful biblical interpretation is recognition that modern cultural assumptions may hinder as well as help with theological understanding.

NOTES

1. Two full-length studies on marriage in Israel are David R. Mace, *Hebrew Marriage: A Sociological Study* (New York: Philosophical Library, 1953); Raphael Patai, *Sex and Family in the Bible and the Middle East* (Garden City, N.Y.: Doubleday, 1959). On the link between kinship and marriage see Jack Goody, *The Oriental, the Ancient, and the Primitive: Systems of Marriage and the Family in the Pre-industrial Societies of Eurasia* (Cambridge: University Press, 1990), and K. C. Hanson, "BTB Readers Guide: Kinship," *BTB* 24 (1994): 183–94. It can be ar-

gued that a systemic analysis of a family is the most important element in cultural interpretation; see Emmanuel Todd, *The Explanation of Ideology: Family Structures and Social Systems* (Oxford: Blackwell, 1988).

2. Gunnlaugur Jónsson, *"The Image of God": Gen. 1:26–28 in a Century of Old Testament Research*, ConBot 26 (Stockholm: Almqvist & Wiksell, 1988).

3. Some interpreters propose that "the man" of 2:7f. should be understood as androgynous before the removal of the rib and creation of the woman. See the discussions in Phyllis Trible, *God and the Rhetoric of Human Sexuality* (Philadelphia: Fortress, 1978), 72–143, and William E. Phipps, *Genesis and Gender: Biblical Myths of Sexuality and Their Cultural Impact* (New York: Praeger, 1989), 1–35. Both refer to the creature as "sexually undifferentiated." The use of the definite article with "adam" in Genesis 2 also seems to preclude taking the term "adam" as a personal name, although the chapter is inconsistent in this matter (cf. 2:20). Whatever may be said about the gender of "the man" before the creation of the woman, the goal of the narrative in chapter 2 is to support the role of man and woman in one-flesh union as the paradigm for marriage and family. Perhaps it would be more faithful to the narrative to say that the purpose of "the man" cannot be fully realized without the woman who corresponds to him completely in creaturely humanity. It is not just that the woman was created for the man; he is not fully a man without her. In their companionship the two reflect the image of God.

4. The Hebrew phrase in 2:18, 20, '*ezer kănegdō*, is perhaps best rendered as "a helper corresponding to him." The term "helper" ('*ezer*) does not imply inferior status but one who supplies what is lacking. The Lord is the "help/helper" of Israel (see Ps. 121:1–2).

5. The priestly rejection of homosexual acts and bestiality (Lev. 18:22–23) is consistent with this interpretation of the one-flesh union as the legitimate setting for sexual relations.

6. Genesis 2:23 affirms this in an etiological pun; she is "woman" ('*iššâ*) because she was taken from the "man" ('*îš*). The terms '*îš* and '*iššâ* are also the common designation for husband and wife respectively (e.g., Ruth 1:2–3).

7. This language of forming an intimate bond is also used in Deut. 10:20; 11:22; 13:4. Israel should "cleave" to the Lord and reject other deities.

8. For the term "flesh" (*bašar*) as a term for sexual organs see Lev. 15:2–3, 19. For the term "flesh" as indicating kinship see Gen. 29:14; 37:27; Lev. 18:6; 2 Sam. 5:1; Isa. 58:7.

9. The naming of the woman as Eve, "the mother of all living," confirms this (Gen. 3:20).

10. Carol L. Meyers, "Gender Roles and Genesis 3:16b Revisited," *A Feminist Companion to Genesis*, ed. Athlya Brenner (Sheffield: Academic, 1993), 118–41, has shown that Gen. 3:16 refers to an increase in (physical) labor to sustain the family *and also* to the pain associated with childbearing. A traditional interpretation has understood the labor as that associated with birth.

11. Incest taboos forbade marriage or sexual relations between primary members of the husband's and wife's families (see Lev. 18:6–18; 20:10–21). Levirate marriage (Deut. 25:5–10) is an exception.

12. Raymond Westbrook, *Property and the Family in Biblical Law*, JSOTSup 113 (Sheffield: JSOT, 1991), 69–89.

13. Westbrook, *Property and Family*, 58–68. The verb "to redeem" (*ga'al*) has its

sociological setting in family custom. It is the basis for the noun "redeemer" used to describe the activity of the Lord in redeeming his people. See note 37.

14. Occasionally the verb is *qanah*, meaning "acquire" (see Ruth 4:10).

15. Werner Plautz, "Die Form der Eheschliessung im Alten Testament," *ZAW* 76 (1964):298–318.

16. Édward Lipiński, *mōhar*, *TWAT* 4:717–24.

17. Anthropologists use the term "indirect dowry" to refer to gifts from the man's family that are given to the bride. These may function as indications of status and honor for the man's family as well as the woman's.

18. Raymond Westbrook, "The Prohibition on Restoration of Marriage in Deuteronomy 24:1–4," *Studies in Bible*, ed. Sara Japhet, ScrHier 31 (Jerusalem: Magnes), 387–405; Carolyn Pressler, *The View of Women Found in the Deuteronomic Family Laws*, BZAW 216 (Berlin: De Gruyter, 1993), 45–62.

19. W. Plautz, "Monogamie und Polygynie im Alten Testament," *ZAW* 75 (1963):3–27; Gordon P. Hugenberger, *Marriage as a Covenant: A Study of Biblical Law and Ethics Governing Marriage Developed from the Perspective of Malachi*, VTSup 52 (Leiden: Brill), 84–123.

20. Polygamy is a good example of a social institution practiced in antiquity but outlawed in many modern states. It is still an issue, however, for churches in some places; see S. Dwane, "Polygamy," *Church and Marriage in Modern Africa*, ed. T.D. Verryn (Johannesburg: Ecumenical Research Institute, 1975), 221–27, and W. G. Blum, *Forms of Marriage: Monogamy Reconsidered* (Nairobi: AMECEA Gaba, 1989). The laws restricting marriage to heterosexual monogamy in modern states are likely to face increasing scrutiny as other forms of cohabitation (e.g., homosexual couples, bisexual groups) seek societal legitimacy and legal protection. It will be interesting to see how the tolerance of polygamy in the Old Testament plays a role in arguments for extending the rights of marriage to other forms of cohabitation.

21. Karen Engelken, "*pileges̆,*" *TWAT* 6:587–89; idem, *Frauen im Alten Israel: Eine begriffsgeschichtliche und sozialrechtliche Studie zur Stellung der Frau im Alten Testament*, BWANT 130 (Stuttgart: Kohlhammer, 1990).

22. Raymond Westbrook, "Adultery in Ancient Near Eastern Law," *RB* 97 (1990): 542–80.

23. The goodness of sexual attraction is given expression by the bride and groom in the Song of Songs. Love is as strong as death (8:6), but it should not be stirred up before its time (2:7; 3:5; 5:8; 8:4).

24. Clemens Locher, *Die Ehre einer Frau in Israel: Exegetische und rechts-vergleichende Studien zu Deuteronomium 22: 13–21*, OBO 70 (Göttingen: Vandenhoeck, 1986); Raymond Westbrook, *Studies in Biblical and Cuneiform Law* (Paris: Gabalda, 1988); Meir Malul, *The Comparative Method in Ancient Near Eastern and Biblical Legal Studies*, AOAT 227 (Neukirchen-Vluyn: Neukirchener, 1990); Bernard M. Levinson, *Theory and Method in Biblical and Cuneiform Law: Revision, Interpolation, and Development*, JSOTSS 181 (Sheffield: JSOT, 1994).

25. The Pentateuch also has a high percentage of cultic and ritual texts (e.g., Leviticus) which have application in a worshiping community but not as state law in the modern sense.

26. Variety in custom may have meant a limited application of specific laws. For example, the ancestral accounts record the marriage of Jacob to two sisters

(Genesis 29—30), something later forbidden, according to Lev. 18:18. Similarly, a man is not to marry his half-sister (Lev. 18:9), but 2 Sam. 13:13 assumes that Amnon could marry Tamar, his half-sister, if the king permitted it. It is possible that the "laws" of Leviticus 18 were formulated after the account of Amnon and Tamar to constrict earlier practices, but it is also possible that the customs for the marriage of royal offspring were different. See Susan Rattray, "Marriage Rules, Kinship Terms, and Family Structure in the Bible," *SBLSP*, ed. Kent H. Richards (Atlanta: Scholars, 1987), 537–38.

The Old Testament does not contain an explicit reference to a woman initiating divorce. Does this mean she was unable to divorce her husband under any circumstances? This is a complicated issue, but there is some evidence that a woman could secure a divorce in ancient Near Eastern societies. During the Persian period (fifth to fourth centuries B.C.E.), Jewish women at Elephantine in Upper Egypt could secure a divorce. For references and discussion see E. Lipiński, "The Wife's Right to Divorce in Light of an Ancient Near Eastern Tradition," *Jewish Law Annual* 4 (1981):9–27.

27. Westbrook, "The Prohibition on Restoration of Marriage."
28. The woman is described as defiled (the verb is *ṭamaʾ*) and the action is described as an abomination (*tōʿebâ*) to the Lord in 24:4. See the discussions in Pressler, *View of Women*, 45–62, and Hugenberger, *Marriage as a Covenant*, 76–81.
29. Pressler, *View of Women*, 28–29.
30. Westbrook, "Adultery."
31. Andre Neher, "Le symbolisme conjugale: Expression de l'histoire de l'AT" *RHPR* 34 (1954):30–49; Nelly Stienstra, *YHWH Is the Husband of His People: Analysis of a Biblical Metaphor with Special Reference to Translation* (Kampen: Kok Pharos, 1993).
32. E. W. Nicholson, *God and His People: Covenant and Theology in the Old Testament* (Oxford: Clarendon, 1986).
33. The connection between covenant and marriage is given thorough examination by Hugenberger, *Marriage as a Covenant.*
34. Helmer Ringgren, "The Marriage Motif in Israelite Religion," *Ancient Israelite Religion*, ed. Patrick D. Miller et al. (Philadelphia: Fortress, 1987), 421–28.
35. Marcia M. Biddle, "The Figure of Lady Jerusalem: Identification, Deification and Personification of Cities in the Ancient Near East," *The Biblical Canon in Comparative Perspective*, ed. K. L. Younger et al. (Lewiston, N.Y.: Mellen, 1991), 173–94.
36. Julie Galambush, *Jerusalem in the Book of Ezekiel: The City as Yahweh's Wife*, SBLDS 130 (Atlanta: Scholars, 1992).
37. Isaiah 40–66 has sixteen references to the activity of the Lord in "redeeming" (the verb is *gaʾal*) Israel or Jerusalem. The verb has its institutional origin in family law, where a kinsman acts to redeem a family member in distress (see note 13).
38. Jerusalem's "prostitution" (1:21–23) is actually described as acts of injustice and unrighteousness (see note 39).
39. The bad grapes are also described as injustice and unrighteousness in 5:7 (see note 38).
40. It is no coincidence that the primary audience of the Old Testament is Israel and the primary audience of the New Testament writings is the church.

5

Exploring the Implications of Paul's Use of *Sarx* (Flesh)

Elizabeth Gordon Edwards

This chapter represents an extraordinary discrepancy between the conception of an idea and its birth. My consciousness contains no awareness as to the "whence" of the idea's seed, but somehow the desire to *redeem* Paul's use of *sarx* germinated. The intention was to demonstrate that Paul's use of *sarx* was not as negative as usually thought and thus to repair in some small way the damage presumably caused by misunderstanding Paul in this manner, especially in relation to the area of sexuality.[1] The original design was quite innocent and, if I may say so, quite "virtuous" as well! For whatever reason, I longed to uncover a more authentic view of Paul's understanding of *sarx* and thereby to salvage part of his reputation *and* to mend to some degree the distorted impressions surrounding *sarx*, which impressions in turn had their ill effects both directly and indirectly on people's view of "Christian" sexuality. After extensive study, however, I found the original intent to be faulty. Redeeming Paul's use of *sarx* is a futile task; an abortion is required. The original conception of Paul's use of *sarx* was found wanting, its development into a birth was aborted, and a new birth for this chapter has taken place. The truth appears to be that not only is Paul's view of *sarx* indeed negative but also, when one apparent source of this negativity is explored, it is clear that this source has had decidedly ill and lasting effects on other parts of Paul's writings as well. The purpose here is thus to expose the source and effects of Paul's use of *sarx* rather than to redeem that view. This exposure does not claim to be new on the biblical studies scene; for many, the observations are probably quite readily apparent. Nonetheless the imperative is to spell out some of these observations in order either to open the door for those who do not give adequate attention to the particularities of New Testament writers or, for those for whom the door is already open, to push it even wider ajar. This writer finds it fascinating that what had been intended as a corrective word study has evolved into an exercise in awareness as we ever seek to understand, interpret, and incorporate into our own views New Testament views on various issues and realities, especially that of sexuality, one replete with sensitivity and explosive potential.

Three presuppositions that were involved in this chapter's initial conception need to be expressly stated. First, people in general believe Paul to have a negative view of *sarx*. Second, this belief in turn contributes to the opinion that the New Testament views sexuality quite negatively. Third, Paul's view of *sarx* is in fact *not* all that negative. The first and second presuppositions remain: It is the third that has been surprisingly overturned. In regard to the first presupposition, quite frequently in recent months I have inquired of laypeople and clergy as to their view of *Paul's* understanding of *sarx* (flesh). Invariably the response has been: "Negative, of course!"—or words to that effect. In regard to the second presupposition, it must be admitted that no explicit proof can be offered that this is the actual chain of events or train of thought in people's minds, but I believe it to be accurate, whether or not people make a conscious or an unconscious connection between "flesh" and "sexuality"—*sarx* and "sex," to put it more crudely but more clearly.

In regard to the third presupposition, I assume that Paul used *sarx* at times in a pejorative sense, blaming it for certain sins committed out of human weakness; at other times it was used in a purely neutral sense, referring simply to the "stuff" of human beings and other animals; and still other times it was used in a sense that has no relation whatsoever to either human weakness per se or human "stuff," but to a realm of existence, to an "age," to an orientation.[2] It was thought that this last sense easily predominated and that its meaning could be seen to override the other senses too easily assumed as dominant by most readers of Paul. Initial study bore out this impression; the following are six categories I discovered in Paul's uses of *sarx*:[3]

1. "All flesh" and "flesh and blood": This easiest of all expressions to grasp, with its Septuagint background, simply refers to human beings.

2. Relatives/kinspeople: This infrequent use (e.g., Rom. 11:14) simply points out the physical relatedness of an ethnic group of people.

3. *kata sarka* ("according to flesh"): This phrase basically means "from a merely human point of view," whether as a neutral term (e.g., Jesus' human descent, Rom. 1:3) or with negative connotations of self-directed activity and attitude, with closedness to others and to God's ongoing self-revelation and creation (e.g., Rom. 8:4).

4. *en (tē) sarki* ("in [the] flesh"): This phrase, with or without the article, demands some subtle subdividing, but enough consistency exists to see it as referring either to the actual "substance" or "material" of flesh itself (Rom. 2:29) or to the physical existence of human

beings in this life (Gal. 2:20) or to such existence without apparent awareness of another realm of existence that transcends this visible one (Rom. 7:5).

5. Joined with ideas such as "weakness" or "desire": This group is the most difficult to acquit from pejorative associations, especially since Paul makes statements about the law as weak through the flesh (Rom. 8:3); and exhorts his readers not to use freedom as an opportunity for the flesh (Gal. 5:13) or not to complete the desires of the flesh (Gal. 5:16).[4]

6. In contrast to/in tension with an opposing or contrasting force or reality such as *pneuma*/spirit or *nous*/mind: In these references one can comprehend the meaning of *sarx* only in the context and only from the perspective of the contrasting reality (e.g., Rom. 7:25; 8:6–12; Gal. 3:3).

Before discussing my own categories, it will be of interest to consider Schweizer's categorization of Paul's uses of *sarx* in the *Theological Dictionary of the New Testament* (TDNT) and to note his apparent desire to downplay any pejorative connotations. He lists seven categories:[5]

1. Body ("whole of [one]'s physical existence");
2. Earthly sphere ("not as sinful and hostile to God, but simply as limited and provisional");
3. "Flesh and blood, all flesh" (without reference to any sinfulness);
4. As object of trust ("What is sinful is not the *sarx*, but confidence in it");
5. *kata sarx* with a verb (which concerns an orientation of one's life to *sarx* versus Lord);
6. As subject of sin (but *sarx* itself is not a power, over against the power of Spirit; rather *sarx* as a norm "becomes a power which shapes" one);
7. The vanquished *sarx* (*sarx* has been crucified; "this message is new and typical of Paul").

It is perplexing that Schweizer felt a need to separate out items 4 and 7 rather than simply combining these two. Would not *sarx* as an object of trust be exactly what has been crucified in identification with Jesus in the crucifixion of his literal *sarx?*

Another basic work to consider is that found in the standard reference work on New Testament Greek, *Greek-English Lexicon of the New Testament* (BAGD). Its entry for *sarx* contains eight different sections:

1. material covering bones;
2. body itself, as substance;

3. person of flesh and blood;
4. corporeality, physical limitations, life on earth;
5. human/mortal nature, earthly descent;
6. external/outward side of life, as seen by unregenerate person;
7. in Paul especially: the willing instrument of sin, so subject to sin that wherever flesh is, all forms of sin are also, and no good thing can live in flesh;
8. source of sexual urge, without suggestion of sinfulness.

Each of the foregoing sections includes a citation from Paul, with the very significant exception of the final section (8) (unless the bibliographical references given under [8] imply the inclusion of certain of Paul's verses under that particular meaning). It is obvious that according to these categories, several meanings are perceived as neutral, whereas one (7) is seen quite negatively, three (4, 5, 6) somewhat negatively, and none in any explicitly or even implicitly positive manner.

In studying the six categories I previously presented,[6] I sought to posit the final category as Paul's major one, overshadowing others (especially 5) with the hypothesis that he simply used the word *sarx* to describe that other reality/orientation/realm without specifically associating it with our human "material" and thus without condemning it as such. In retrospect this view is naïve at best. Paul *did* in fact choose the term *sarx* for this contrasting reality *because of the negative associations with which he imbued it.*

Before proceeding further, let us examine the adequacy of these six categories. Can each instance of *sarx* in Paul's writings be subsumed under one of these six? Some instances seem to defy categorization, e.g., Rom. 9:8 contrasts children of the *sarx* with children of God. We understand that the former refers to people who have come into being through the expected natural, sexual manner and that the latter relates to people who have come into new being—the work of God versus the work of nature; the fulfillment of God's promise versus the initiative of human beings. But does this verse become grouped under a sort of sexual or natural section or is it more logically placed under a section concerning the human being's will to control against allowing God to rule?

Another problematic verse, not only in terms of categorization but in general terms as well, is 2 Cor. 12:7, with its famous and tantalizing reference to Paul's *skolops tē sarki* ("thorn in the flesh"): Should this be subsumed under "flesh as actual substance," or is its meaning far more elusive than that? That is, was Paul even necessarily speaking about a physical ailment or handicap, as people may too quickly assume, or was he simply using this image to depict a difficulty or a hindrance he had or experienced—one that had no setting in his flesh or physical being at all?

Of course, even when one can quite confidently categorize a particular reference, this does not mean that the significance of the reference is at all self-evident. Consider the significant and problematic passage in Rom. 8:3. In what way did Jesus appear in "sinful flesh"? Was he in *real* flesh, or was his incarnation somehow different? Does the "likeness" qualification refer to the sinlessness of Jesus' flesh, or was his flesh different, lacking susceptibility to the working of sin's power?[7] Aside from this question so central to both Christology and soteriology, one must interpret the use of *harmartias* ("of sin") in this text, i.e., What sort of genitive does it represent? Is it simply descriptive in the place of an adjective ("sinful")? Does it refer to a necessary attribute of flesh, or is it describing a particular type of flesh? Is Paul stating something other than that Christ became incarnate, or is his point that the effectiveness of the redemption God brought about through Jesus depended upon Jesus' total identification with humanity and involvement in the realm and activity of sin as then construed? These are some of the verses that resist or confuse categorization, but the process of categorization, nonetheless, serves a purpose.[8]

Looking at the six categories above from a different angle, we can conclude that *sarx* in Paul could refer to (1) the human being her/himself or the "stuff" of which we humans are made; (2) descendants, relatives, or kinspeople; (3) the human's earthly existence; (4) our "pre-Christian" life; (5) an orientation of a person toward her/himself; or (6) that aspect of our humanity that allows sin to take over in us and desires to be active. Amalgamating some of these groups, it may be helpful to observe four divisions: (1) the material, tangible "stuff" itself, whether part of or all of a human being, and being in it (or as it); (2) the fact of physical relationship (via the male); (3) the symbol of an orientation of being that is contrary to God; and (4) the symbol of being controlled, involuntarily, not by it, but somehow because of it or through it. Thus, one can say that *sarx* refers in Paul either (1) to that visible aspect of a person (more accurately that which enables a person to be in and relate in the world), that existence as flesh in the world, or to a person her/himself (possibly a kinsperson) or (2) to a particular quality of existence—namely, to one oriented contrary to God (or to that through which an alien power can take control of a person and turn that person from God).[9] The second possibility is most nebulous and elusive (What is the "that"?—a tangible something? or something other?), and the first one demands explanation. What is the connection between that visible substance of which a person is comprised and that orientation directed away from God? Further, is the connection direct and necessary?

These questions lead us back to the statement above—namely, that for Paul the use of *sarx* for a realm of existence contrary to God was a meaningful, intentional choice. It was not an arbitrary choice of a neutral-laden term; rather, for Paul *sarx* in the literal ("material") sense does have a pejorative connotation, and there is a direct relation between the negativity of the literal use and the negativity of the symbolic use; that is, between its meaning as "material" and its connotation of a "realm of existence." This may be obvious, but I need to express it because of my original sense that *sarx* as Spiritless realm did not mean that *sarx* as flesh itself was inherently negative or "evil." I was, however, wrong.

If Paul speaks of all human flesh in a pejorative way, this would push toward a dualistic anthropology that few want to claim for the New Testament. If Paul were influenced by a Greek philosophy that viewed the soul as trapped in the (evil) body of flesh,[10] this would distort a Christian understanding of the human being as an integrated whole—body/flesh, soul/spirit, and any other components a person is thought to have or consist of (e.g., personality or mind/intellect). In our desire to counter any unnecessary negative references to *sarx* in Paul, it would be highly desirable if we could point to passages in which Paul specifically declared the goodness of flesh as the matter of which human beings created in God's image are comprised. No such explicit references actually exist, however.[11] The current interest in creation theology and feminist affirmation of the body, focusing on God's creation of humanity as good rather than on humanity's need for salvation, finds no support in Paul's theology. Had Paul written more about our goodness and less about our sinfulness, the rediscovery of this basic theological truth experienced in recent years would not have been so welcome as filling a void and responding to a silence too long tolerated.

In speaking of the *soma* ("body"), Paul is far more positive than he is in his use of *sarx*. Despite some opinion that both can be interchangeable and despite both Greek words being used in the Septuagint to translate the same Hebrew word (*basar*), it is quite evident that Paul perceived of the body in a much more whole, extensive, all-encompassing manner.[12] The *soma* refers not only to the human being in her/his visibleness but to the human being in all her/his way of being, relating, and acting in the world, in an individual manner; that is, expressing her/his individuality. For Paul there is no *sarx* other than what we know in this life, but there is the reality of another new, transformed *soma*. (Note the careful change from *sarx* to *soma* in 1 Cor. 15:39–40.) Thus *soma* is totally necessary for any existence whatsoever of the individual, but *sarx* is temporary, and necessary only for life as we know it. This somewhat idealistic, even fantasizing manner in which Paul can conceive of a different kind of *soma* is not matched by any such view of *sarx*. This means that for Paul there *sarx* has a decidedly negative connotation—one that affects any real effort to see our bodily existence in all its facets, including sexuality, as positive and good and holy.

I now repeat the conclusion to which my study has unavoidably but lamentably led: It is not possible to redeem Paul's view of *sarx*; too much negativity is imbedded in it, and even the meanings/aspects that do not appear exceptionally pejorative lend themselves to negative connotations and contribute to the ultimate outcome that—as much as Paul may have intended otherwise—his use of *sarx* has been a decided disservice to the authentically Christian view of sexuality as a positive, essential aspect of personhood, as a gift and a blessing.

Perhaps we should be grateful that Paul did not make hostile statements against the flesh and against sexuality to any greater extent than he did. Those who followed him, however, those influenced by him, *did* make such hostile comments, to the detriment of us all.[13] Although Paul cannot be totally blamed for such comments that came upon his heels, he did open himself up to them and did nothing to protect his thoughts from those who might misconstrue his reluctance to speak very positively about *sarx*.

Since it appears impossible to "redeem" Paul's view of *sarx*, the question now becomes, Can we understand it any more deeply in Paul's own context so that its harmful effects can be neutralized by an awareness of the context of his own thought?

Paul's Context and Particularity

Paul's Maleness

It has been only in recent years that serious consideration has been paid to the particulars of a New Testament writer's situation so as to provide a more accurate lens through which to grasp God's Word. Only too recently has the relativity of the words of the Bible been appreciated in such a way as not to lessen the authority held toward God's written Word, but on the contrary, to come even closer to the meaning of it available to us these many centuries later. The patriarchialism in which and through which—and to which—the Bible was written has been unmasked, thanks to the work of many feminist and womanist exegetes and theologians. The thought forms and the assumed structures are male and oriented toward males. This truth is highly evident in Paul, and his words need to be understood for what they are: the words of a particular male in a particular time in history and in a particular culture and place. What area would be any more affected by his maleness than the area of sexuality itself? Furthermore, I am convinced that any references to *sarx* or to *soma* made by Paul not only come out of his maleness but are also dependent upon—and to some degree determine—his views on the reality of sexuality and his own sexuality as well.

By now it is well recognized that not only do women and men learn differently, know differently, experience differently, feel differently,[14] but they also perceive themselves, including their own bodies differently. The very phenomenon of having (or *being*) a body is different for males than for females. Consequently, it follows that one's view of one's flesh (*sarx*) differs according to one's gender. Thus Paul's view of *sarx* is without doubt determined by his gender as male; Paul was not writing a sort of inspired, "objective" account of theology, revealed to him apart from his own sexuality. He spoke not only out of his patriarchical context, but out of his own personhood, his maleness included. This means that in general he would have possessed a more alien view of "the body," of his body than would a female in general.[15] His view of (his) sexuality would have been outside of himself, rather than within, and he would have envied the ability to create and possessed a definite fear of visible, obvious failure (thus the need to compete and strive and succeed). This means also that he would have thought more in terms of opposites—of "this or that"—than in terms of "both/and."[16] In addition, his view of his own sexuality would have been more threatening to him as an instrument or a power to subdue or control, because of the more aggressive aspect of male sexuality (versus the receiving nature of female sexuality). Surely for one who can create other flesh to which she is connected by flesh itself and which she can nourish through or by her own flesh, the reality of *sarx* is utterly different than it is for one who has a part (or *the* [as then believed] part) in the creation of another human being, but who is not himself connected to that human being and is not the carrier or bearer of that other human being. Surely, that is, the reality of flesh is more positive and wondrous and benign for the female than for the male, given a certain context and framework of belief.

In Susan Bordo's careful and exciting study about the body, out of concern for those suffering from eating disorders, she discusses Western views of the body as found in Plato, Augustine, and Descartes. (And Paul is certainly connected with one if not two of these thinkers.) She speaks about the "dualist axis" in terms of the body experienced as "the not-self, the not-me"; the body experienced as "confinement and limitation"; the body experienced as "the enemy"; and finally the body experienced as "all that threatens our attempts at control."[17] Bordo explains that these factors represent an "imagery of dualism,"[18] and we have already mentioned that Paul struggled to maintain the unity of the body, the integrity of the total person, as a core belief of Christian faith. But there is an inherent human tendency especially evidenced among males to see the body as other than oneself, and a seed of this belief or tendency is surely in Paul's thought, no matter the work to dissolve it.

Most significantly for this study, it is particularly striking that one of the meanings of *sarx* in the Septuagint is "penis" (e.g., Gen. 17:13; Lev. 15:2, 3) and that for Paul himself this is the referent in at least one or two places (Rom. 2:28; Gal. 6:13). (When meanings of *sarx* are categorized, this reference comes under actual "substance," e.g., BAGD.) If one accepts Dunn's idea (see note 8), then the concept of penis is somehow present, even if subtly, in each one of Paul's uses of *sarx*. This is startling! That is, even if Paul were not conscious of the association with the male genitalia for each usage of *sarx*, he somehow made the connection unconsciously. It therefore follows that whatever views males hold in common about their genitals and whatever view Paul may have held in particular about his genital organ is somehow involved in Paul's total concept of *sarx*. This revolutionary thought points to the source of some pejorative nuances in Paul's view, whether or not they derived from earlier literature and thought, as colored by whatever view he held of the penis and of his own penis. One need only attempt to imagine what it would be like to learn that a woman who had greatly influenced our view of *sarx* actually had connected, in her conscious and/or unconscious mind, *sarx* with "womb" or "vagina." Would anyone doubt that this association had influenced the way she used *sarx* or the meaning she gave it?

It is incumbent on us, therefore, to attempt to understand to some degree Paul's view of the male sexual organ. If we look for some totally explicit reference, we will find none. The two references mentioned above need first to be considered: Both relate to circumcision. Romans 2:28 refers to the visible sign of a man's Jewishness and Gal. 6:13 refers to the visible source of boasting for his opponents. Thus, first of all, the penis for Paul is the location of the Jewish male's identity; for a man "under the law," it is a necessary mark of identification. Other than these two verses, the clearest reference in Paul to the penis is found in 1 Thess. 4:4: *skeuos*—literally "vessel." (Interestingly only 1 Thessalonians among Paul's letters contains no use of *sarx*.) The debate has been lengthy as to whether this word does indeed refer to the penis (as the vessel that holds the semen), or whether it instead refers to "wife" or "body."[19] To a great extent one's decision turns on Paul's use of the verb *ktasthai*, which can mean "to get for oneself, gain, be in the course of acquiring/procuring"[20] or "to gain control,"[21] at least in this instance. Rarely noted is the verb's present tense, which lends a continual sense to whatever translation is given. This precludes the translation "procure a wife." Because Paul is so enigmatic here, I believe that the reference is to the male sexual organ and to having control over it and thus using it (so to speak) "in honor and holiness," as the text reads.[22] Such an interpretation lends credence to the body's being experienced as something to control, something alien that functions contrary to one's own will. This issue of control of one's sexual instincts and desires is far more relevant and urgent for men than for women because of the aggressive nature of the male role.

At this point, in considering 1 Thess. 4:1–8, an extremely important question arises: the issue of holiness for Paul. What constitues "holiness" and of what it is comprised? In 4:3 Paul reintroduces the term *hagiasmos* ("holiness, sanctification"), having spoken in 3:13 about his prayer for the Thessalonians (that their hearts be "blameless in holiness" in the parousia), and here in 4:3 he states that their holiness is God's will. He proceeds then to talk about *porneia* ("fornication," with ambiguity as to specific meaning) as if sexual conduct is not only the initial and primary aspect of holiness but perhaps the only aspect.

It is extremely difficult to discern where a "break" should be made in this chapter and whether 1 Thess. 4:9ff continue the topic of "holiness." If they do, then there is no reason not to see 1 Thess. 4:13–5:11 as also speaking about "holiness," since there is no great difference between the way he introduces his comments on *philadelphia* and those on the dead. The entire structure is extremely problematic. In favor of seeing the discussion of "holiness" concluding at 4:8 is the smooth yet forceful manner in which Paul brings in the Holy Spirit to grant authority to his words and also to give hope for the fulfillment of them. If so, then "holiness" consists of one's sexual conduct, which in turn is basically not letting one's sexual desires take control. It can, of course, be argued that this was the sole topic covered only because Paul knew either from experience with the Thessalonians or from word about them that this was a definite trouble spot for them. This is conceded. Nonetheless, it would have been possible for Paul to indicate that the topic he was about to cover was but one aspect of the demand of holiness upon them. A disconcerting point is Paul's reference yet again to God's will in 5:18, but without any reference to holiness. It is unclear what God's will refers to in this verse, for the "this" could go back to rejoicing, praying, and giving thanks or ahead to not extinguishing the Spirit (v. 19) (an implicit allusion to holiness), on through abstaining from every form of evil (v. 22). The fact that "abstaining from fornication" in 4:3 so nicely parallels "abstaining from every form of evil" in 5:22 gives support to the last option. The conjunction "for" (*gar*), however, in 5:18b lends greater credence to God's will as a reference back to the preceding. Either way, there is no explicit mention of "holiness" in this reference to God's will.

The concluding benediction, however, very beautifully refers to holiness when Paul prays that God will "sanctify them (to be) whole" (v. 23) in the parousia. It is not easy to draw implications about the concept of holiness in 4:1–8, but it does seem to demonstrate the *intimate relation in Paul's thought* between *holiness and wholeness*. It thus presses home the imperative for a person not to "be at odds" with a particular part of him/herself, for somehow that very "fragmentation" is a sign of an absence of the holiness that is God's will. This verse of Paul's prayer for the Thessalonians also reminds us of Paul's deep concern for the need to see as a whole all aspects that comprise an individual person. When Paul mentions "your spirit and soul *(psyche)* and body," he surely includes either within the *psyche* or the *soma* the reality of *sarx*. It is strange that he may localize the issue of "holiness" in sexuality, as 4:1–8 seems to indicate, but if so, he may well have known holiness to relate integrally to each aspect of a human being, and for him to single out one aspect of an individual's reality—sexuality—may reveal that Paul had an over-concentration on (if not an obsession with) this particular area of concern.

On the basis of 1 Thessalonians 4 we can say that the male genital organ for Paul is something to be controlled. Men can surely identify quite readily with such an idea, since contrary to women's experience, the penis does seem to have "a life of its own." If it can stand for *sarx* as a whole, then *sarx* becomes something that needs to be controlled, especially in light of God's demand for holiness, an aspect of which is obedience to God's will, a doing that requires a control of that doing. It is refreshing that male writers are willing to discuss this aspect of their lives, this part of their bodies, with an openness and vulnerability unknown before; in part, the feminist thought and focus on spirituality can be credited for this change.[23]

Other Aspects of Paul's Sexuality

It is common to debate the marital status of Paul. It *should* be common to recognize that whatever that status was affected Paul's viewpoint on marriage, divorce, homosexuality—sexuality in general. One point is certain: It is not definite according to his letters whether he was then married, had been married, or was never married. One writer who respects our ignorance in this matter and uncovers our assumptions as such is Brendan Byrne, who performs a superbly openminded exegesis of the key passages (1 Cor. 7:7–8 and 9:4–5), showing how we cannot know whether Paul was speaking of his own celibacy or continence.[24] The point is that we do not know Paul's situation. We do know that he had certain interesting "parenting" instincts: for example, his comparing himself to a nurse or mother with her children and to a father with his (1 Thess. 2:7, 11); his longing for Christ to be formed in the Galatians (who in turn are in Paul's womb, unless Paul's birth pangs are sympathetic ones, as is possible) (Gal. 4:19); and his speaking of Onesimus as someone he begat (or birthed) (Philem. 10). These are interesting images and expressions for Paul to use. They are endearing, to be sure, but also surely reveal some of his innate desires and needs, which he saw fulfilled in some of his missionary activities and associations.

Another point bearing consideration is Paul's concern for the *sperma* ("seed") in whom God promised a fulfillment of God's blessings (Gal. 3:8, 16, with reference to Genesis 12; and Rom. 4:13, 16, 18, with particular reference to Genesis 15). Of course, this line of thinking was quite prevalent and is even seen elsewhere in the New Testament (e.g., 1 John 3:9, plus the numerous references therein to begetting ["*gennao*"]). Holy Spirit is for Paul, surely, the bearer of this *sperma* (!) since it is by Holy Spirit that we are enabled to call God "Abba Father" (Gal. 4:6), thereby being assured that we are God's children (the Spirit giving proof as circumcision had previously done). It is hard to know what to make of Paul's sexually charged terms and images, but it is worthwhile to give them thought as we attempt to comprehend the sexuality of the person on whom so much of our own thinking about sexuality has been based.

Paul's Jewishness

The foregoing comparison between Spirit and circumcision leads us into another aspect of Paul's context and his sexual self-understanding. Not only was he one of the specific people who belonged in a special way to God, but his identity was also greatly caught up in the outward sign of his belonging to this people—namely the rite of circumcision. Whether Paul's views on sexuality and the equal inclusion of women into the new reality of God's realm affected his outreach to the (non- and not-to-be-circumcised) Gentiles or whether his sense of mission to the uncircumcised affected his view of sexuality and women is impossible to know. (Though fascinating to ponder, it probably has not an "either-or" but a "both-and" solution.) Far too little work, I believe, has been done on the integral relation between Paul's focus on circumcision (i.e., rejecting the need for it) and his views on women and sexuality generally. It is certainly questionable whether any reticence towards living out aspects of his sexuality contributed to his vehemence about the gospel's universality and his seeing faith and baptism (with the coming of the Holy Spirit on the whole body and person) as the new locus and guarantee of covenant membership. It is fascinating that in some sense he was aware of the violent action characterizing circumcision when he speaks about the circumcised "dogs" as "the mutilation" (Phil. 3:2) and when he alludes in apparent pun fashion to his opponents "castrating" or "excommunicating" themselves (Gal. 5:12). Somehow circumcision operated for Paul in a most significant fashion, both personally and theologically . . . fascinatingly!

Paul's Eschatology

Among the many areas of Paul's life and thought that could be studied in light of his sexuality, one that deserves attention is Paul's eschatology, specifically his varying understandings of it and the relation between *chronos* (chronological time) versus *kairos* (time constituted by moments filled with significance).[25] Also worth studying with a different key in mind is his concept of the reign of God and the parousia of Christ, which receives less emphasis in his later writings and gives way to the tension of living in two ages at the same time. Moreover, it has been demonstrated that men and women view the future differently. Whereas men see it as a task to be analyzed and conquered, women see it as belonging to them.[26] These differing viewpoints deserve special attention in studying Paul.

Paul's Soteriology

Additional areas that require extensive study in Paul are concepts of sin and redemption, in light of issues related to sexuality. Men and women perceive and experience "sin" differently. It is now somewhat commonly recognized that guilt and shame are distinct. The New Testament, of course, sees the Christ event as dealing with guilt, in terms of forgiveness, reconciliation, etc., rather than with shame. Shame is viewed more as the woman's counterpart to the man's guilt.[27] Dwyer makes an insightful and potentially significant comment when he says that for women sexuality is something one is, whereas for men it is what one does.[28] This distinction would seem to relate integrally to the theory that men experience guilt for what they have done, whereas women experience shame for who they are. Such an observation has tremendous implications for understanding Paul. It points out, not surprisingly, the intimate relation between perspectives on sin and views towards sexuality.

Other Areas in Paul

These few topics have been sketchily discussed in order to hint at the immense possibility, if not necessity, to re-vision Paul and his theology in light of aspects of his sexuality. Other areas also require careful analysis. This chapter has served only to explore the central issue of the effect of Paul's own sexuality on matters related to sexuality, as well as its effect on other topics.

Many other related questions need to be addressed. For example, was Paul, despite his conditioned maleness, actually right about *sarx* being the place or vehicle of entry for sin, that is, for alienation from God, other, and self? Despite his negative view of flesh, influenced both by his maleness and a male's view of the body (amidst the Jews for whom "body" was most important), is it possible that his opinions in certain areas related to *sarx* are nonetheless accurate? That is, does the sexuality of a person provide symbolically, if not actually, the central place wherein all the manifestations of alienation from God/other/self occur? Is it possible that certain "works of the flesh" (Galatians 5) are indeed such, ultimately, because of their source and that to which they can be likened, even though they are not ostensibly sexual in nature? Did Paul choose the command "you shall not desire" (Rom. 7:7) in a very accurate manner, because he knew both that desire so often expressed in sexual ways is also at the root of other acts of alienation and that this particular command epitomizes the human tendency to live in the Spiritless realm of existence?

These questions, and similar others, are most tantalizing ones. They prompt one to wonder whether Paul's writings and thought would have been different had he been a Paula, and if so, in what ways they would have differed. Would a common core have existed between two such writers? Or is it impossible to imagine any expression of ideas apart from the particular sexuality of a particular person? Granted, God happened to call a man ("from his mother's womb"); this is no basis for complaint, only a call for deeper understanding. The Christian view on sexuality cannot be considered apart from the writer as a person in his or her specific circumstances, sexuality included, even if our New Testament writings all derive from persons sharing the same male gender. It is thus our responsibility to recognize the male source of all the New Testament writings as we seek to uncover and understand anew its words, its good news, and its demands, not by stripping it of its male-associated perspectives, but by recognizing them and acknowledging their effects on the product we have. If we sense a negative perspective on what we know God "called good," it is our task to unmask that negativity, rather than to accept it as infallible, unquestionable truth. It is incumbent upon us to sift through the New Testament words that derive from particular circumstances and to proclaim the blessing of our sexuality as a God-given gift, to be lived out in responsibility, to be experienced with thanksgiving, to be respected in others, and to be trusted and embraced in all its ambiguity and wonder, in all its mystery and awesomeness.

NOTES

1. Elizabeth Grosz helpfully offers four meanings to the term sexuality: a "drive" or "impulse"; an "act" or "series of . . . behaviors"; "an identity" (gender); or "a set of orientations, positions, and desires." She then astutely comments that sexuality is "incapable of ready containment . . . ; it infects all the activities of the sexes, underlying our understandings of the world well beyond the domain of sexual relations. . . . Our conceptions of reality, knowledge, truth, politics, ethics, and aesthetics are all effects of sexually specific—and thus far in our history, usually male—bodies, and are all thus implicated in the power structures which feminists have described as patriarchal . . ." (*Volatile Bodies* [Bloomington: Indiana University Press, 1994], vii–ix).
2. This writer has surely been influenced over the years by ideas such as Bultmann's " . . . all that is 'outward' and 'visible,' all that has its nature in external 'appearance' belongs to the sphere of 'flesh' . . . the sphere of sinning . . . it . . . opposes God as His enemy" (*Theology of the New Testament*, Vol. 1 [New York: Charles Scribner's Sons, 1951], 235–36) and by others also affected by Bultmann.
3. The letters assumed to be authentically by Paul himself are Romans, 1 and 2 Corinthians, Galatians, Philippians, 1 Thessalonians, and Philemon.
4. In statements such as these, it is almost as if Paul is restraining himself from declaring flesh to be evil (much as he refrains from stating that the law is anything but "holy and good" [Rom. 7:12]—but one feels him on the verge, "between the lines," as it were—since the law was created/given by God, as also was flesh created/given by God).
5. Edward Schweizer, *TDNT* 7:125–35, "*sarx.*"

6. The tendency to categorize uses, especially of *sarx*, is a puzzling one. What promotes it, other than the obvious need not to have seventy-two different "meanings" of *sarx* in Paul? (Paul also uses an adjective [either *sarkinos* or *sarkikos*], meaning "fleshly," nine times.) One point is the immediate recognition that one use echos LXX usage, and one wonders whether the LXX is the source of the other apparent meanings as well; one also wonders whether Paul is formulating an entirely new range of meaning when he seems to refer to a manner of existence or realm or orientation or age. Also, there exists an urge not to have the negative meaning present in some instances present in all.

7. Vincent P. Branick (*CBQ* 47 [1985]: 246–62). He concludes, rightfully, to my mind, that "by choosing the word 'flesh,' Paul evokes Christ's solidarity with sinful humanity. He was one of us, even in our sinfulness. He was our very flesh" (261). (Branick's willingness to break away from the traditional view of Jesus as "sinless" is appreciated; it is a view that I have long upheld, especially in regard to Gal. 3:13, and one that is increasingly recognized in feminist interpretations of who Jesus was.) Another valuable and thought-provoking comment on this verse is made by Gerd Theissen when he observes that Christ "takes the place of flesh [and] of the law . . . the id and the superego [becoming] the symbol of an integration of originally antagonistic tribunals. Christ becomes a 'coincidence of opposites'" (*Psychological Aspects of Pauline Theology* [Philadelphia: Fortress Press, 1987], 249).

8. A discussion that completely disavows this process of categorization is presented by James Dunn in his article concerning Rom. 1:3–4 ("Jesus—Flesh and Spirit: An Exposition of Romans I.3–4," *JTS* 24 [1973]: 40–68). He asserts that such classification into "separate . . . pigeon-holes" is impossible; rather there is a " 'spectrum' of meaning, and individual uses are often less like a point in the spectrum and more like a range of meaning within the spectrum" (44). His point is well taken, but he himself succumbs to the temptation and manages to list four usages: neutral, physical body; weakness, mortal; in contrast to a superior realm; and *kata sarka* as negative (44–46). Nonetheless, what is valid in his argument is that there is a fluidity in each use, not a stable or stagnant meaning. What is more, his point will be capitalized on below.

9. In this attempt to "get down to the core essential different meanings," i.e., in combining 1–4 into only two groups, two dangers appear: One is of overlooking the determination of relationship via the male as a separate category, thus blurring the clear relation perceived between *sarx* and the male genitals or seed, and the other is that 3 and 4 actually describe result (3) and instrument or vehicle (4), so that to combine the two into one is admittedly misleading.

10. A discussion of this dualism and the insistence that Paul did not indulge in such thought can be found in numerous places; e.g., Frank Bottomley, *Attitudes to the Body in Western Christendom* (London: Lepus Books, 1979), 37ff. Even Bottomley, however, acknowledges inconsistency on Paul's part: "Sometimes, however, Paul does seem to slip into a kind of dualistic anthropology in which 'body' is opposed to 'spirit'" (184 n.6). (It is as if we all have so much at stake in maintaining Paul's non-dualistic way of thinking! What is the source of so great a sense of threat? Why so much investment? Is it still the fear of some sort of docetism, some denial of the reality of the Incarnation, some dread of no real Resurrection or resurrection of us all?!) The debate has a long history, as it seems to continue on; for example, several decades ago W. D. Davies

wrote: "It is our contention . . . that the Pauline distinction between the *sarx* and *pneuma* is not a replica of Hellenistic dualism, nor again simply to be explained from the OT. It is rather the complex product of Paul's OT background and his Rabbinic training." He then proceeds to argue why it is wrong to think that "in his use of *sarx* Paul reveals that he had virtually departed from his Jewish faith and accepted the typical Hellenistic dualism, which opposed matter to mind, and that he regarded sin as innate in the empirical nature of man [*sic*]" (*Paul and Rabbinic Judaism* [Philadelphia: Fortress Press, 1948], 17–18). This writer cannot comprehend why it has to be an "either-or" question. Why cannot Paul be seen to be in tension with these views?

11. Unfortunately when Paul alludes to our having been created in God's image, the context is quite negative, e.g., Rom. 3:23, where human beings fall short of the glory of God; and 1 Cor. 11:7ff., where man but not woman is granted the identity as "image of God." Naturally these sparse references are understandable since Paul's focus dwelt not on the past creation, for the most part, but on the future, the new creation, and the final consummation of the initial creation. His passion is for what we now are as compared to who we were before Christ, not really for any regaining of our original image.

12. Such a comment is contrary to the work of John A. T. Robinson in his well-known study *The Body* (London: SCM Press, 1952). On p. 12 he writes: "Our contention will be that the Pauline use of *sarx* and *soma* is to be understood only in the light of these [Hebraic] assumptions, and, consequently, that the Greek presuppositions . . . are simply misleading if made the starting point in interpreting Paul's meaning," asserting that we are to maintain the integration of flesh and "body" that the single Hebrew word denotes.

13. See Peter Brown, *The Body and Society* (New York: Columbia University Press, 1988), 122–38.

14. The literature is fortunately vast on this important issue; see M. F. Bleneky et al., *Women's Ways of Knowing; Development of Self, Voice, and Mind* (New York: Basic Books, 1986) (e.g., 15ff., on five epistemological categories); Carol Gilligan, *In a Different Voice* (Cambridge, Mass.: Harvard University Press, 1982); and Donna Wilshire, "The Uses of Myth, Image, and the Female Body in Re-Visioning Knowledge" (*Gender/Body/Knowledge: Feminist Reconstructions of Being and Knowing* [New Brunswick, N.J.: Rutgers University Press, 1989]), where she presents a fascinating set of columns of knowledge vs. ignorance and spirit vs. flesh and male vs. female (95ff.).

15. "Alien" is one of the terms that Susan Bordo uses in her discussion of views of the body (*Unbearable Weight: Feminism, Western Culture, and the Body* [Berkeley: University of California Press, 1993], 144).

16. Ann Belford Ulanov mentions this point in *The Feminine in Jungian Psychology and in Christian Theology* (Evanston: Northwestern University Press, 1971), 191, as does also Wilshire ("The Use of Myth," 96). This significant point in and of itself has undesirable effects on the theology of Paul if not the whole New Testament; it relates, for example, to a male tendency towards dualism.

17. Bordo, *Unbearable Weight*, 144–45; my use of the word "threaten" happens to coincide with hers. The body in recent decades has become an important object of study, with extremely fascinating results. See Alison Jaggar and Susan Bordo, ed. *Gender/Body/Knowledge: Feminist Reconstructions of Being and Knowing* (New Brunswick, N.J.: Rutgers University Press, 1989); *Theology and Body*

(Philadelphia: Westminster Press, 1974). The essays therein pertinent to this paper are Sam Keen, "Toward an Erotic Theology," Bernard Aaronson, "The Experience of the Body and Transcendence," and Gwen Kennedy Neville, "Women's Bodies and Theology." Neville speaks about the "source of embarrassment" women's bodies have been "to theologians since the beginning of theology itself" (75). All this work offers new insight into the Incarnation and as well "This is my body . . . ."

18. Bordo, *Unbearable Weight*, 144.

19. BAGD lists three options: wife, body, and *membrum virile*. Each option has ample support. Unfortunately, using Paul as a resource to solve the problem is not exceedingly helpful; his only other uses of *skeuos* occur in Romans 9 (three times), each using the imagery of a potter and a pot/vessel to stand for people of God's creation (vv. 21–23), and in 2 Cor. 4:7 where he speaks about having "this treasure in earthen vessels," referring presumably to the fragility and mortality of our bodies. This last reference is not conclusive for determining Paul's meaning in 1 Thess. 4 as "body," since the context is so different.

20. LSJ. The perfect tense is given the meaning "possess" or "hold," and the perfect participle is translated "master" or "mistress"; otherwise the meaning "control" is absent.

21. BAGD offer two possibilities for translating *ktasthai* here: "take a wife for himself" or "gain control over his own body." Interestingly enough, the option of "gain control over his own genital organ" is not listed, despite the option included under *skeuos*.

22. I also believe that the same subject is in view in the ensuing verse (v. 7) rather than a change of subject to that of a "business matter" having taken place. That is, the warning is not to become involved with another man's wife, thereby exercising control over one's sexual urge. The very fact that Paul's manner of expression and argument is so elusive and convoluted speaks in favor of his touching on the sensitive subject of sexuality.

23. A commendable example of this new trend is James B. Nelson, "Embracing Masculinity" (*Sexuality and the Sacred*, ed. James B. Nelson and Sandra P. Longfellow [Louisville, Ky.: Westminster John Knox Press, 1994], 195–215). He writes about the underevaluation of the penis and the overevaluation of the phallus—flaccid vs. erect—and how the "price is paid by all who suffer because of patriarchy" (200).

24. Brendan Byrne, *Paul and the Christian Woman* (Collegeville, Minn.: Liturgical Press, 1988), 75–79. He mentions Yarbrough as an exception to the usual attitude when she says that it is "impossible to know if Paul was never married, widowed, or divorced" (79).

25. Ulanov describes "the feminine sense of time" as "individual," as "a series of unique occurrences," as "*kairos* rather than *chronos*" (*The Feminine*, 177). Luise Schottroff made reference to this sort of male-vs.-female way of seeing time in her paper "Feminist Observations on the Eschatology of Q," presented at SBL Annual Meeting of 1992.

26. John Dwyer, *Human Sexuality: A Christian View* (Kansas City, Mo.: Sheed & Ward, 1987), 145–48. (This relates, to this writer's mind, to the act of bearing children.) Dwyer writes that "a woman has a distinctive relationship to the future . . . not something which she has to conquer . . . not a problem 'out there' [but] as part of her (147).

27. Ulanov discusses a similar distinction between men and women by reference
    to Valerie Goldstein's work: "For a woman sin is not pride, an exaltation of
    self, but a refusal to claim the self God has given. Women refuse this self by
    hiding behind self-doubt and feelings of inadequacy (*Receiving Woman* [Phila-
    delphia: Westminster Press, 1981], 134), citing Goldstein's work.
28. Dwyer, *Human Sexuality*, 14–17.

6

The Holiness Code and Human Sexuality

Sarah J. Melcher

In his writings, Claude Lévi-Strauss recognizes the "inevitability of biological heredity." Nature has determined the structure and characteristics of biological descent, muses Lévi-Strauss in *The Elementary Structures of Kinship;* culture is "powerless before descent." Culture, however, has the means to impose further constraints. Incest prohibitions or, more broadly construed, the cultural rules for the exchange of women, when effectively enforced, more narrowly define the acceptable limits for descent within the particular culture. The fundamental function of incest rules is "to ensure the group's existence as a group."

A Corporate Explanation

If one wishes to discover a rationale for the distinctive shape of sexual prohibitions in a particular culture, Lévi-Strauss directs us to look for a corporate explanation. In other words, rules for sexual intercourse can perform a protective function. According to Lévi-Strauss, the group not only decides who are appropriate sexual partners for individual members, it also controls the distribution of scarce resources. These two forces can be interdependent in complex ways. In his words, "The group controls the distribution not only of women but of a whole collection of valuables.[1]

Lévi-Strauss's descriptions seem particularly apt for the sexual prohibitions of the Holiness Code, Leviticus 17—26. The text we now have before us may provide a corporate or communal motivation for the distinctive shape of these sexual prohibitions. Perhaps Lévi-Strauss's anthropological theory can inform our interpretation or serve as an explanatory model, if our analysis is rooted in the text and uses an appropriate literary method.

The Approach to the Text

Despite general agreement that a lengthy process of oral tradition, composition, editing, compiling, and shaping stands behind the present form of the Pentateuch, scholars of Hebrew scriptures have diverse theories concerning the nature of this process. How were the various pieces assimilated within the Pentateuch? In what social setting did they originate? In what relative temporal order were they incorporated? The questions concerning the pieces are many. Within the published works of Pentateuchal scholars, abundant attention and effort have converged on reconstructing the literary history of the pieces through source criticism, form criticism, and historical criticism.

More recently, scholarship has begun to follow an additional direction in the study of the Pentateuchal literature. James Muilenburg's Presidential Address to the Society of Biblical Literature marks a turning point. Speaking in 1968, he urged the biblical scholar to

> supplement his [*sic*] form-critical analysis with a careful inspection of the literary unit in its precise and unique formulation. He will not be completely bound by the traditional elements and motifs of the literary genre; his task will not be completed until he has taken full account of the features which lie beyond the spectrum of the genre. . . . For the more deeply one penetrates the formulations as they have been transmitted to us, the more he concentrates on the ways in which thought has been woven into linguistic patterns, the better able he is to think the thoughts of the biblical writer after him.[2]

Throughout his speech Muilenburg stresses the uniqueness of the literary unit and the importance of the manner in which its final form has been constructed. When he speaks of "formulations as they have been transmitted to us," he reminds us that we have received those formulations woven into the very fabric of the literary unit. What has been transmitted to us is what we have before us: the *final form* of the text.

James A. Sanders and Brevard S. Childs refine our apprehension of the final form through their "canonical" approaches, which perceive the biblical text as a product of communal decision and process. This process produced a sacred canon.[3] In a canonical reading, the literary analysis takes into account both the process involved in producing sacred literature and the distinctive character of the literary product. Childs advocates an exegesis that takes its perspective from the final canonical form.

> A study of the biblical text reveals that this concern to pass on the authoritative tradition did not consist in merely passively channeling material from one generation to another, but reflects an involvement which actively shaped both the oral and written traditions. A major hermeneutical move was effected in the process of forming an original law, prophetic oracles, or ancient narrative into a collection of scripture through which every subsequent generation was to be addressed.[4]

Literary analysis of the final form has gained adherents and has enjoyed increased credibility since Muilenburg's call and the refinements by Sanders and Childs. J. Cheryl Exum and David J. A. Clines, in their introduction to *The New Literary Criticism and the Hebrew Bible*, describe the essays in that volume as eclectic. Those interpretations explore diverse kinds of approaches or combinations of methods. What the essays have in common, in part, is an "outlook . . . about the primacy of the text in itself" and a concern with the texts' own "internal articulation."[5]

Robert Polzin presents a very fine argument for attempting a comprehensive literary analysis of a passage before attending to historical problems. After assessing historical issues, the interpreter can then refine the literary analysis. His carefully reasoned chapter in *Moses and the Deuteronomist*, "Criticism and Crisis within Biblical Studies," negotiates a meeting place between the proponents of historical criticism and the practitioners of final-form literary analysis.[6] Polzin makes two important points that are especially relevant in this context. First, he assumes that the present text does make sense. Though the present biblical text came into being through a "long and complicated editorial process," the resulting text we have before us has been deliberately arranged by competent hands. Second, a thorough and comprehensive literary study of the text with attention to its particular construction is an important preliminary to drawing historical conclusions. Then, as Polzin suggests, historical criticism can deepen an understanding of that literary analysis.

Gerhard von Rad acknowledges that the Holiness Code had undergone a deliberate compiling/editing/composing that has greatly affected its final form. As a result of this process, the predominant impression created in Leviticus 17—26 is that of divine address.[7] Whatever the literary history of its pieces or their original social setting, the editing process on the Holiness Code has created a document of sufficient conceptual and literary coherence to justify its consideration as a literary unit.[8]

This chapter arises from a larger study, which attempts a comprehensive literary analysis of the laws of sexual practice in the Holiness Code. That study employs a multifaceted approach—rhetorical/conceptual/semiotic. In this chapter, some conceptual characteristics will be examined in a broad way to suggest a possible interpretation for these laws of sexual practice. Certain key terms and phrases as they are used specifically in the Holiness Code will be examined, with particular focus on their employment in the sexual prohibitions. This analysis is informed by the terminological studies of Jacob Milgrom and the conceptual commentaries of Max Kadushin.[9] Without doubt, this is not the comprehensive literary analysis for which Polzin argues. That is attempted elsewhere. Rather, the present chapter lifts out some features of the conceptual portion of the more comprehensive analysis.

The Distinctiveness and Coherence of the Holiness Code

Within the Holiness Code, our analysis focuses on the texts about sexual practice: Lev. 18; 19:20–22, 29; 20; 21:7, 9, 13–15.

Many of the same interpretive issues that have characterized Pentateuchal studies generally hold true specifically for the Holiness Code. One difficulty in interpreting the document is to account for its growth by accretions over an extended period, while acknowledging its remarkable conceptual coherence. Frequently scholarship occupies itself in deciding the relative order and social setting of the various layers of material. Since the evidence is limited to that which can be gleaned from the final edited form of the document, much of this work is rather speculative. This concentration on the layers of the Holiness Code has resulted in relative neglect of the perspective of the final form. The Holiness Code shows a sophisticated use of rhetoric, and neglect of this aspect is a significant oversight. Someone, either a final editor or several representatives of the community, made a decision about how the final form of the document should look and what it should contain.

The debate has occupied scholarship since 1866, when Karl Heinrich Graf first hypothesized, on the basis of characteristic literary traits and general literary structure, that chapters 18—26 formed a piece having compositional integrity.[10] It was August Klostermann who first coined the term *Heiligkeitsgesetze*, or Holiness Code, to characterize this part of Leviticus, because of the frequent appearance of holiness terminology and formulas.[11] Some have questioned the compositional integrity of the Holiness Code, but the scholarly consensus sees it as an integral whole— literarily and conceptually distinct from the Priestly material contained in Leviticus 1—16.[12]

The most satisfactory resolution of these interpretive issues is the theory of the Holiness School. This theory has developed through the work of two scholars, Jacob Milgrom and Israel Knohl, who have worked both separately and in concert to advance this theory. What is especially satisfying about the theory is the idea of two "schools," the Priestly School and the Holiness School, which collected, composed, and edited the legal material of Leviticus over an extended time. This theory accounts for both the gradual accretion of the material, the homogeneity of the pieces of the Holiness Code in their underlying concerns and conceptual focus, and their distinctiveness from the passages of the Priestly School. Israel Knohl's most cogent statement for his theory of the Holiness School, which meticulously distinguishes between these two schools based on literary characteristics and conceptual concerns, is set out in *The Sanctuary of Silence*.[13] Milgrom's delineation of these two sources is found in his important commentary *Leviticus 1—16*.[14]

If we accept Knohl's careful source-critical work and treat the material in Leviticus 17—26 as part of the distinctive work of the Holiness School, evidence for interpreting the laws of sexual practice can be gleaned from the laws themselves and from other material of the Holiness School distributed throughout the Pentateuch.[15]

Conceptual Aspects: "The Sons of Israel"

Of special importance for this study of human sexuality in the Holiness Code is the address of the *bĕnê yiśrā'ēl*, the "sons of Israel." Words spoken by YHWH to Moses are to be conveyed to a corporate body, the *bĕnê yiśrā'ēl*.[16] In that way the narrative framework provides a conceptual vantage point from which to view the regulations on sexual practice. Since that narrative framework provides for the corporate address of the *bĕnê yiśrā'ēl* and since the legal and paranetic material it frames is intended for them (see 17:1–2, [8], [12]; 18:1–2; 19:1–2; 20:1–2; 21:24; 22:17–18; 23:1–2, 23–24, 33–34, 44; 24:1–2, 13–15, 23; 25:1–2; 26:46), we look for a rationale for these sexual regulations at a corporate level. Leviticus 17:2; 21:1, 17, 24; and 22:2, 18 imply an address directed to Aaron or to his sons, but the Holiness Code's material is predominantly directed to the *bĕnê yiśrā'ēl*. Most of the Holiness Code's laws about sexual practice are found in Leviticus 18 and 20. In both chapters introductory verses depict YHWH instructing Moses to speak to the sons of Israel. The idiom *bĕnê yiśrā'ēl*, is the Holiness Code's favorite designation for the community. Thus the community is most often perceived, in terms of descent from a common ancestor, as the "sons of Israel."

This chapter renders *bĕnê yiśrā'ēl*, as the "sons of Israel" rather than a more inclusive translation such as that of the RSV and NRSV (the "people of Israel.")[17] A possible rationale for the final redaction of the sexual laws of the Holiness Code is clearer if translation does not obscure grammatical gender, so unless otherwise indicated, all translations herein are my own. Grammatically, the *bĕnê* portion of the phrase is a masculine plural noun. The primary meaning of the singular form, *bēn*, is "son." One encounters the same problems for a generic use of this phrase as those encountered when using English terms like "man" or "mankind."[18]

Grammatical structure and literary context suggest that the adult male members of the community are the persons addressed by these texts of sexual practice. The laws in their final form in the Hebrew text employ second-person masculine or third-person masculine verb forms. The exhortatory framework uses a second-person *plural* form of address: for example, "You (pl.) shall not do," or "You (pl.) shall keep my statutes."[19] Within the laws of chapter 18, the second-person masculine *singular* form is preferred: for example, "You (sing.) shall not uncover your sister's sexual organs." Chapter 20, in contrast, prefers to express its laws in the third-person masculine *singular* verb form.

Nowhere in these laws is a woman or group of women addressed directly. Generally speaking, the woman is represented as the passive recipient of the man's "seed." She is most often specified as the inappropriate partner for sexual intercourse. The Holiness Code only rarely portrays a woman as the initiator of prohibited sexual intercourse. Leviticus 19:20–22, 29 follows the general tendency. Leviticus 21:9 discusses the possibility of the priest's daughter indulging in promiscuous behavior, but the verse is concerned with how this behavior reflects on her father. In 18:23b, the woman is pictured as the initiator of inappropriate sexual intercourse, as she is prohibited from having intercourse with an animal. Leviticus 20:16 treats the same topic and in a similar manner shows the woman as initiator of intercourse. Verses 17 and 18 of chapter 20 are notable exceptions to the rule as well, where the woman is shown as a full participant in prohibited sexual behavior.

The exceptions prove the rule—in general the woman is portrayed passively as an unsuitable sexual partner for the adult male. It is the adult males of the community, the "sons of Israel," who are addressed here, to indicate inappropriate sexual partners for them. Since women are discussed in the third person rather than addressed directly in the second person, one gains the impression that the "sons of Israel" have jurisdiction over proper sexual conduct for females.

The idea that these passages are written for the men of the community is not new. The Damascus Document (A) 5,8–10 paraphrases Lev. 18:13 and touches upon this concern for address.

> 8/ Moses said, "to your mother's sister you shall not draw near, she is the flesh of your mother." 9/ The law of forbidden sexual relationships; for men 10/ it is written, but like them are the women.

This medieval copy of the document (earlier fragments were found near the Dead Sea, one manuscript dating from 75–50 B.C.E.) sees the laws as written on behalf of the men in the community, supporting a crucial point for this interpretation. The composer of these lines must explicitly apply these laws to women as well, a point that is not evident in the original laws of forbidden relationships from Leviticus.

In the introductory verses of Leviticus 18 and 20, *běnē yiśrā'ēl*, identifies the addressees as a group defined in terms of descent. The group becomes a continuous line of descendants, stretching indefinitely through the generations, all descendants of the common ancestor Israel, an ancestor from a foundational time in the community's history. It is a powerful designation for the community, evoking images of perpetual existence but grammatically evoking an image of male descent. Its appearance in this literary context of exclusive forms of masculine address enhances the impression of patrilineal descent.

Idioms of Sexual Intercourse

Scholars have often referred to the Holiness Code's laws of sexual practice as "marriage laws," but the Hebrew uses idioms of sexual intercourse. Only the special laws for the priests use the idiom of marriage. *Yiqqaḥ 'iššâ* is the common biblical expression for a man "taking a woman in marriage." Leviticus 21:7, 13, 14 employs this same expression but stresses the inappropriateness of certain women by putting the nouns before the verb. Elsewhere, especially in chapters 18 and 20, the idioms are those of sexual intercourse: for example, "the sexual organs of [a designated woman] you shall not uncover" or "a man who lies with . . ." or other proximate expressions.[20] Joanne Dupont characterizes 18:17, 18 as marriage laws because of the idiom *lō' tiqqaḥ* in both verses, but she disregards the purpose clause, "to uncover sexual organs."[21] The verses may indicate marriage, but the addition of the purpose clause modifies the concern, bringing these verses into line with the other expressions. The latter half of 20:17 clearly pertains to intercourse, as it begins, "He sees her sexual organs and she sees his sexual organs." The subject of these laws overall is with inappropriate sexual intercourse. If we grant that the laws about the priests are a special case because of the idiom of marriage, all the other laws of sexual prohibition concern sexual intercourse.

But are the marriage laws for the priests really a special case? Though Lev. 21:7, 13, 14 clearly refers to marriage, 21:15 states explicitly the concern: "So, he will not profane his seed among his people, I am YHWH, who sanctifies him." Because of the great priest's heightened state of holiness, he must follow stricter restrictions for marriage partners. Only a premenstrual female is appropriate for marriage, because that "he must not profane his seed among his people." "Seed" here can mean both "progeny" and "semen" simultaneously.[22] In spite of the use of the marriage idiom, the concern is with the act of intercourse *and with its results.* Purity of descent is the stated object of these laws for priests (21:7, 13, 14).

All the laws of sexual practice are not strictly "incest laws," since they include the situation of the female slave in 19:20, the situation of the menstruant in 18:19 and 20:18, and intercourse with animals in 18:15, 16 and 20:15, 16. At most, we can say that these are laws prohibiting intercourse with certain designated partners.[23]

Though a "son of Israel" does not possess the same holy status as a priest, the need for progeny with pure lines of descent may be the primary motivating element behind this compilation of laws about sexual intercourse. The priestly concern to avoid profaning seed may find its equivalent in the "defilement" of the son of Israel's seed in 18:20, 23. It is likely that this arrangement of laws is concerned throughout with the *results of intercourse*. The laws for the priests are based on the same principles as the others, but because of the priest's heightened holy status, sexual intercourse outside the boundaries of marriage is not even contemplated.

"Sexual Organs" or "Sexual Function"

Most frequently the concept *'erwâ* appears in the form *'erwat* of a [woman designated as inappropriate]. This basic usage denotes "sexual organs" of a woman. In chapter 18, *'erwâ* has another related connotation as well. When it is used in construct with a noun referring to a man, it connotes the man's jurisdiction over the woman's sexual function. Verse 8b in 18 is the first clear usage of this idiom, but the structure of the verse makes this usage clear: "The sexual organs of your father's wife you shall not uncover, your father's sexual function it is." Verse 14 helps to clarify this particular usage of *'erwâ:* "the sexual function of your father's brother you shall not uncover, to his wife you shall not draw near, your aunt she is." Here the explanation is given in the second clause. To "not uncover the *'erwâ* of your father's brother" is defined as "to his wife you shall not draw near." Here, the *'erwâ* of a man means that a woman has been designated as his sexual partner; he has exclusive jurisdiction over her sexual function. Verse 16b demonstrates the jurisdiction of the brother over his wife's sexual function. Turning to verse 10, the idea of the grandfather having jurisdiction over his granddaughter's sexual function is consistent with these other occurrences of *'erwat* [of a man]. The pater familias, the father of the clan, would have jurisdiction over his granddaughter's sexual function until she is married. At that point, exclusive jurisdiction over the woman's sexual function passes to her husband.

The concept of exclusive male jurisdiction over a woman's sexual function is expressed alternatively in verse 18:15, but the use of *'erwâ* is consonant with the other occurrences of the second form. Mishnah's explanation of 18:7 supports this understanding of the second form of *'erwâ*. According to the interpretation standing in the Mishnah, "the one who has sexual relations with his mother is liable on her account because of her being the mother and because of her being the wife of the father."[24]

In chapter 20 *'erwâ* appears less frequently than in chapter 18 but reflects the two basic meanings we have seen before. Leviticus 20:17 includes a usage of *'erwâ* that is an apparent exception to the patterns noted in chapter 18. When discussing the possibility of a man having intercourse with his sister, it is employed in the expected manner—"he sees her sexual organs"—then immediately following that is the unexpected "and she sees his sexual organs." This verse is also exceptional in portraying the woman as an equal partner in prohibited sexual behavior.

That *'erwat* of a woman designated as inappropriate in its basic use means "sexual organs" is especially clear in the structure of 20:18b, part of the law against intercourse with a menstruant. The latter half of the verse begins "and he uncovers her sexual organs and her flow he has revealed; she uncovers the flow of her blood." The juxtaposition of "her nakedness" with "her source of menstruation" bolsters the conviction that this use of *'erwâ* means the sexual organs of the woman in most cases and the sexual organs of the man in one case.

In chapters 18 and 20 *'erwâ* and its nuances strengthen the idea that these laws are about intercourse along with male jurisdiction and exclusive claim over female reproductive potential. Concern for purity of descent can account in part for these intimations of male dominion over female sexual function.

"Flesh"

Other clues in the text hint at the concerns underlying these chapters. Verse 6 of chapter 18 constitutes a heading for the prohibitions that follow stating the general prohibition "Any man, to any flesh of his flesh, you shall not approach in order to uncover sexual organs, I am YHWH." *Šĕ'ēr bĕśārô*, or "flesh of his flesh," is a kinship term specifying close relationship, a meaning confirmed by the laws that follow.[25] Flesh refers to the relationship between the father and his sister (18:12), between the mother and her sister (18:13), and between a woman and her daughter or granddaughter (18:17). "His flesh" in 20:19 refers to the same relationships that are discussed in 18:12 and 13.

Leviticus 21:1–3 explains *šĕ'ēr* as members of the priest's immediate family. Leviticus 25:48–49 clarifies this issue. There, "after he has sold himself, redemption there will be for him. One of his brothers may redeem him. Or his uncle or the son of his uncle may redeem him, or (someone) from the flesh of his flesh, from his clan may redeem him, or if he has sufficient means he may redeem himself." "Flesh of his flesh" represents members of a clan, those kin who have the right or power of redemption after a "son of Israel" is forced to sell himself to a "resident alien" or "transient." The central concern of Lev. 25:47–54 is to prevent a "son of Israel" from becoming the permanent property of a "resident alien" or "transient." Nor can any of his descendants pass into bondage.

The larger context is the year of jubilee. Leviticus 25:8–54 is a legal discourse concerned with protecting the permanent property rights of the "sons of Israel." Verse 10 gives a clue that the larger discourse provides strategies to protect the permanent property rights of the individual clan. In the year of jubilee, "you shall return, each to his property, each to his clan, you shall return." It is no mistake that "property" and "clan" are connected in the verse, because the concepts are interwoven throughout vv. 8–54. Even if the

"son of Israel" becomes so poor he must sell himself to another "son of Israel," he will only serve until the year of jubilee, at which time "he will go
out from you, and his sons with him, and he will return to his clan and to the
property of his fathers he will return" (25:41, my translations). The clan is
tied to its own portion of land, and the laws of jubilee in 25:8–54 serve to
protect this system of patrilineal inheritance.

The passage 25:44–46, which immediately precedes the pericope con-
taining "flesh of his flesh," is concerned with the provision of servants for
the "son of Israel." The people from other nations or the transients and
their clans may become slaves for the son of Israel. Verse 46a instructs,
"You shall give them as an inheritance to your sons after you, to inherit as
property forever."

Numbers 27:1–11, a pericope Knohl attributes to the Holiness School,
employs šĕ'ēr in a context of inheritance laws, similar to the context and
concerns of Leviticus 25.[26] There, especially in vv. 7–11, the Holiness
School stipulates a ranking for rights of inheritance. If there is no son, the
inheritance of a dead man passes to his daughter; if no daughter, the brothers of the dead man inherit. If there are no brothers, the brothers of the
deceased's father inherit; if none of these exist, "you will give his inheritance to his flesh šĕ'ēr, the one close to him, from his clan. He will inherit
it, and it will be for the sons of Israel a statute and an ordinance just as
YHWH commanded Moses." A šĕ'ēr, then, is someone from the clan. It is
a term that occurs in the context of inheritance laws and in the laws of sexual prohibition. Its appearance in both places is significant.

Divine Punishment

A very helpful category of concepts for interpreting these laws of sexual
practice are the divine punishments ensuing upon their violation. An underlying rationale shaping this arrangement of laws becomes evident
through these punishments. In chapter 20 the people of the land are commanded to stone the person who "gives of his seed to Molech." But the text
provides for a divine punishment if the people of the land "indeed hide
their eyes from that man" (fail to punish him). YHWH says, "I will set my
face against that man and against his clan" (20:5). Note that the divine punishment includes the violator's clan. A variation of this punishment occurs
in 20:6: "I will set my face against that person." It is interesting that the divine punishment for a man misusing "his seed" results in a divine punishment against the entire clan.

In both verses, the phrase "I will set my face against" is followed by another divine punishment, that of kārēt, "cutting off." Verse 5 in chapter 20
gives the punishment: "I will cut him off . . . from the midst of their people." Remember that the preceding phrase, "I will set my face against that

man and against his clan," makes this a punishment that impacts the entire clan. Verse 6 indicates the basic form of the punishment, "I will cut him off from the midst of his people."

The most telling occurrence of this punishment is in verse 17, "They will be cut off before the eyes of the sons of their people." Here the verse explicitly states that the two violators of this sexual prohibition will not be seen by the "sons of their kin." Jacob Milgrom has outlined the possibilities for the meaning of *kārēt*, to be cut off, in *Leviticus 1—16*.[27] He mentions a form of extirpation, which would be death plus the destruction of the punished individual's line of descent. To Milgrom, *kārēt* is a punishment executed solely by the deity. That is correct, as far as it goes, but he does not follow the reasoning presented in verses 17–21 in chapter 20. The medieval Jewish exegete Rashi bases a quite reasonable argument on those verses. He cites verse 20:

> AND IF A MAN SHALL LIE WITH HIS AUNT . . . THEY SHALL DIE CHILDLESS—This verse is intended to teach that the "excision" mentioned above . . . consists in their . . . passing from this world childless: *'ryrym*. Translate this as the Targum renders it: *bl' wld*, childless. Similar is (Gen. XV. 2) "and I will pass away childless" *'ryry*. If he has children he will bury them (i.e., they will die during his lifetime); if he has no children when this sin is committed he will die childless (he will beget no children afterwards). That is why Scripture varies the expression in these two verses (this and the following) here stating *'ryrym ymtw*, "they shall die childless," and there *'ryrym yhyw*, "they shall be childless." The expression *'ryrym* implies: If he has any children at the time he commits the sin, he shall have none *remaining* when he dies because he will bury them during his lifetime; *'ryrym yhyw*, on the other hand, implies: If he has no children at the time when he commits the sin, he shall remain all his life just as he was then (Siphra; Jeb. 55a).[28]

Rashi's reasoning is impeccable. It is also in keeping with verse 17. If the offenders are "cut off from the eyes of the sons of their people," all trace of these people will be removed. So, at least in the Holiness Code, *kārēt* means premature death and the destruction of the offenders' line of descent.

The paranetic material in Lev. 18:24–30 and 20:22–24 shows how the concepts of YHWH's punishment, the land as an instrument of divine punishment, and the language of inheritance in connection with the land are intertwined. In 18:24–30, if the addressed persons violate any of the statutes in chapter 18, the land will become defiled, YHWH will visit its iniquities upon it, and the land will vomit out its inhabitants. Also, verse 29 assigns *kārēt* as punishment for violating any of the laws in 18:6–23. So the paranetic section 18:24–30 connects the destruction of the violator's lineage with expulsion from the land as divine punishment for failure to observe the laws of forbidden intercourse.

The paranetic section 20:22–24 similarly makes important conceptual connections. Violation of the statutes results in the land "vomiting out" the previous nations. The sons of Israel will inherit the land of the nations who violated these commandments. YHWH stresses their separation, their distinctiveness from other people.

Danna Nolan Fewell and David M. Gunn, in their book *Gender, Power, and Promise*, suggest a unifying subject for the laws of Leviticus 18, that of "men's seed."[29] This is a very helpful insight from a rich book. The "inappropriate disposition of seed" is the most successful unifying concept yet recommended for Leviticus 18. To take this cue a bit further, patrilineal inheritance of the land is the primary motivating factor that generates this arrangement of these laws of sexual practice: that and the concomitant preoccupation with purity of descent.

Conceptually, the spatial center for the Holiness Code is the land. In contrast, chapters 1—16 are spatially centered in the tent of meeting.[30] Though the land itself is never described as holy, it can be made unclean through the community's failure to follow the statutes given to Moses. Often the Holiness Code portrays the land as the potential means by which the community is expelled. In chapter 26 the land becomes the instrument of YHWH's blessing or curse. If the people walk in YHWH's statutes, the land will yield its produce and the people will dwell securely in the land (26:5). Part of the blessing is increased progeny, too, as shown by 26:9. But, in 26:19–20, the land becomes the vehicle of the curse. Loss of children is part of the curse in verse 22, but this aspect of the curse becomes particularly grisly in verse 29, "You will eat the flesh of your sons and the flesh of your daughters you will eat." The use of the term "flesh" here may be intended as an ironic reminder of the language of close kinship in 18:6 and 25:49.

Leviticus 17—26, the Holiness Code, is a complex document, weaving a texture of concepts, symbols, and signs. The text is marvelously persuasive; its use of rhetorical technique is sophisticated and effective. However, the rhetoric is not empty, nor is it full of devices created simply to persuade the reader. The Holiness Code is a fine tapestry with a variety of hues, but the interwoven value concepts are matters of urgent concern to the community: the protection of the system of patrilineal land tenure, purity of descent, the special status of the priests, and dwelling securely in the land. In a quite literal way, if their system of land tenure fails (a system based on patrilineal inheritance within the clan), the "sons of Israel" will find themselves to be landless. A clan's hold on the land is ensured by clear lines of descent and many pure descendants. The laws of jubilee can accomplish only so much in protecting a clan's hold. It seems that rules of inappropriate sexual intercourse serve to protect pure patrilineal descent. With the exception of the laws of "ghosts and familiar spirits" (20:6, 27), all these laws in chapters 18 and 20 seem to put a fence around pure patrilineal land inheritance.

Even the laws pertaining to "passing his seed to Molech" can be seen as a terrible violation of a system of patrilineal descent. If a pure male descendant is the most important element for maintaining a hold on the land, the worst violation of YHWH's covenant is this brazen destruction of the product of a pure, appropriate sexual union. Why laws forbidding certain partners for intercourse? Because of the potential for confusion of descent. There are also laws that constrain practices that do not promote the system. Intercourse with a menstruating woman is unlikely to produce a male heir; intercourse between two males most certainly will not; and the unproductive nature of intercourse with an animal in such a system is apparent. Even the law against cursing one's father or mother reinforces the boundaries between generations.

There are other influences discernible in these laws. A prohibition of intercourse with a menstruant is quite in keeping with the general awe of blood (Lev. 17:4, 10–14; 19:26). There is an element of abhorrence for sexual intercourse with the mother that is unrelated to concerns with purity of descent: "She is your mother!" (18:7). In addition, there are several other complex factors present in the text. The point is not to reduce these complex texts to one factor alone. However, patrilineal inheritance of the land is perhaps an organizing principle, an explanation for the distinctive arrangement of these laws in their literary context of the Holiness Code.

NOTES

1. Claude Lévi-Strauss, *The Elementary Structures of Kinship* (London: Eyre & Spottiswoode, 1969), 32.
2. James Muilenburg, "Form Criticism and Beyond," *JBL* 88 (1969): 7.
3. See James A. Sanders, *Torah and Canon* (Philadelphia: Fortress, 1972), *Canon and Community* (Philadelphia: Fortress, 1984), and *From Sacred Story to Sacred Text* (Philadelphia: Fortress, 1987); also Brevard S. Childs, *Introduction to the Old Testament as Scripture* (Philadelphia: Fortress, 1979), and *Old Testament Theology in a Canonical Context* (Philadelphia: Fortress, 1986).
4. Childs, *Introduction*, 78.
5. J. Cheryl Exum and David J. A. Clines, eds. *The New Literary Criticism and the Hebrew Bible*, JSOTSup 143 (Sheffield: Academic, 1993), 16.
6. Robert Polzin, *Moses and the Deuteronomist: A Literary Study of the Deuteronomic History* (New York: Seabury, 1980), 1–24.
7. Gerhard von Rad, *Studies in Deuteronomy* (London: SCM, 1953), 25–26.
8. Contra Henry T. C. Sun, "An Investigation into the Compositional Integrity of the So-Called Holiness Code (Leviticus 17–26)," (Ph.D. diss., Claremont Graduate School, 1990).
9. Max Kadushin, *A Conceptual Approach to the Mekilta* (New York: Jewish Theological Seminary, 1969) and *A Conceptual Commentary on Midrash Leviticus Rabbah: Value Concepts in Jewish Thought* (Atlanta: Scholars, 1987); Jacob Milgrom, *Studies in Levitical Terminology, I* (Berkeley: University of California, 1970), *Cult*

and Conscience (Leiden: Brill, 1976), and *Studies in Cultic Theology and Terminology* (Leiden: Brill, 1983). Milgrom makes two observations that are particularly appropriate here: "I assume that the Priestly Code makes sense. It is more than a pasticcio of laws, greater than the sum of its parts. In the main, it is a self-contained system—logical, coherent, and whole. A system is built on postulates but, in our case, they are nowhere stated. Instead, they are ensconced in the laws and rituals, especially in their technical vocabulary. Words have the power to condense concepts and, in aggregate, to comprise ideologies. The search for postulates must then begin with a study of terminology" (*Cult and Conscience*, 2). He also indicates that a sufficient number of these terminological studies can elucidate "the value system of the biblical cult, i.e., its theology" (*Studies in Cultic Theology and Terminology*, ix).

10. Karl Heinrich Graf, *Die geschichtlichen Bücher des Alten Testaments: Zwei historische-kritische Untersuchungen* (Leipzig: Weigel, 1866), 75–83. Graf bases his argument on the presence of characteristic phrases such as "I am YHWH" and "that person will be cut off from the midst of her/his people." Graf sees chapters 18—26 as the product of a deliberate arranging and shaping. According to him the finished document had been taken up as a whole into the Pentateuch. In addition to the evidence of idiomatic phrases, he stresses the introductory admonition of 18:2–5 and the closing blessings and curses of 26:3–45 as framework for the whole. This closing assumes that a larger collection of laws precedes it. Graf (75) suggests comparison with Deut. 28 and Ex. 23:22ff.

11. August Klostermann, "Ezekiel und das Heiligkeitsgesetz," *Zeitschrift für die Lutherische Theologie und Kirche* 38 (1877): 406–45.

12. In addition to Sun (see note 8), others have questioned the Holiness Code's previous existence as an independent unit. Among them are S. Küchler, *Das Heiligkeitsgesetz: Eine literarkritische Untersuchung* (Königsberg, 1929) and B. D. Eerdmanns, *Altestamentlichen Studien IV: Das Buch Leviticus* (Giessen, 1912), 831–32.

13. Israel Knohl, *The Sanctuary of Silence: The Priestly Torah and the Holiness School* (Minneapolis: Fortress, 1995).

14. Jacob Milgrom, *Leviticus 1—16: A New Translation with Introduction and Commentary.* AB 3 (New York: Doubleday, 1991), 13–42.

15. To clarify the use of terminology, "Holiness Code" in this chapter always refers to Leviticus 17—26 while "Holiness School" denotes all the material attributed by Knohl to the Holiness School.

16. Here I adopt the convention of representing the name of God as YHWH. Reverence restrains a Jewish person from uttering or writing the name of God. When reading the Tetragrammaton, I pronounce the word "*haššem*," which is Hebrew for "the name." The advantage of this convention is its acceptability for Jewish listeners and readers. In addition, this convention is inclusive in regards to gender.

17. The JPS translates similarly: "the Israelite people." However, the Vg and LXX renditions are *filiis Israhel* and *huiois Israël*," respectively. *Tg. Ps.-J, Tg. Onq., Tg. Neof.,* and the Syriac retain the *bny yśr'l* of the Hebrew.

18. Joanne Dupont notes problems for generic use of *běnê yiśrā'ēl* and raises the possibility that the phrase may be intended as an exclusive designation for the men of the community. She also notes the psychological impact that gram-

matical gender may have (see Joanne Dupont, "Women and the Concept of Holiness in the "Holiness Code" [Leviticus 17–26]: Literary, Theological, and Historical Context," Ph.D. diss., Marquette University, 1989, 198–99, 251, 257). For discussion about problems of masculine grammatical gender in English see Janice Moulton, "The Myth of the Neutral 'Man,' " *Sexist Language: A Modern Philosophical Analysis*, ed. Mary Vetterling-Braggin (Totowa, N.J.: Littlefield, 1981), 100–115; and Nancy A. Hardesty, *Inclusive Language in the Church* (Atlanta: John Knox, 1987). Since it is risky to draw parallels in such vastly different languages, a study of gender in the grammatical structure of biblical Hebrew would be very useful. Robert Hodge and Gunther Kress describe a gender system as "a classification of reality . . . inscribing an ideology of sex roles and sex identities into the language itself" (*Social Semiotics* [Ithaca, N.Y.: Cornell, 1988], 98). Their insights about gender markers in Latin hint at the fruitfulness of such a study for biblical Hebrew.

19. The following verses use second-person masculine plural forms of address: 18:3, 4, 5, 24, 26, 28 (technically v. 28 uses a Piel infinitive construct with a second-person plural suffix, but the effect is the same), 30; 20:7, 8, 14 (here it is uncertain whether the actual verb form is 2d m. s. imperfect or 3d f. s. imperfect, but its phrase *bětôkkem* creates the effect of a second-person plural address), 22, 23, 24, 25, 26.

20. There are variations on these idioms, such as those used in 18:6, 14, 17, 18, 19, 20, 23 and 20:10, 16. All denote sexual intercourse. The idiom *yiqqaḥ*, if followed by anything other than the expected *'iššâ*, apparently indicates sexual intercourse in this context rather than marriage (see 20:17 and 20:21). Leviticus 20:16 is no exception to this last point. Mishnah's *Keritot* 1:1 shows that Leviticus 18 is understood to be about sexual intercourse. Mishnah employs its own idiom: "prohibited sexual partner, *habbā' 'al*."

21. Dupont, "Women," 110, 119. She does allow that casual sexual intercourse is also prohibited by vv. 17–20, and does allude to "confusing blood relationship" in vv. 17–18, but stops short in making a case for conceptual coherence throughout chapter 18.

22. Apart from its use as "seed for sowing," *zera'* in the Pentateuch is always used to denote "progeny" or "semen." These concepts are often closely affiliated (Lev. 18:20, 21; 22:4).

23. Early Jewish sources support this interpretation. The Mishnah refers to these laws as "prohibited relationships" (or "prohibited sexual partners"). See *m. Meg* 4:9; *m. Ker.* 2:4. This same plural use is found in the CD 5,9 in the phrase "law of forbidden relationships." This later metaphorical usage also appears in the singular in *m. Hag* 1:7, "one who has intercourse with a woman who is a prohibited sexual partner." For a similar singular usage see *m. Yebam.* 2:3; *'erwâ* denotes "sexual organs" or "sexual function" in the Holiness Code but takes on the meaning of "prohibited sexual relationship" in the later material. This metaphorical usage shows that the early Jewish interpreters understood Leviticus 18 in a similar light.

24. *M. Sanh.* 7:4. All Mishnah citations are based on Chanoch Albeck, *Shishah Sidrei Mishnah* (Jerusalem: Mosad Beyalik, 1952–59).

25. *šě'ēr* has a cognate in Akkadian, *šī r*, that also indicates "flesh." Ugaritic also has a cognate. The versions have interpreted the phrase *šě'ēr běśārô* as near kin *Tg. Ps.-J.*

26. Knohl, *The Sanctuary*, 100.
27. Milgrom, *Leviticus 1—16*, 457–60.
28. Rashi, *Leviticus: Pentateuch with Targum Onkelos, Haphtaroth and Rashi's Commentary*, trans. M. Rosenbaum and A. Silbermann (Jerusalem: Silbermann, 1965), 93b–94.
29. Danna Nolan Fewell and David M. Gunn, *Gender, Power, and Promise: The Subject of the Bible's First Story* (Nashville: Abingdon, 1993), 106.
30. Milgrom describes the Holiness Code's preoccupation with the land and the distinction from the Priestly material: "For P, spatial holiness is limited to the sanctuary; for H, it is coextensive with the promised land" (Jacob Milgrom, "Leviticus: Introduction," *The HarperCollins Study Bible* [New York: HarperCollins, 1993], 152.) There is no explicit statement in chapters 17—26 that attributes holiness to the land. The land can become "unclean," but "unclean" is opposed to "clean" in the Holiness Code's conceptual framework. Something that is clean can become "unclean," but this does not imply that the land is holy.

7

Same-Sex Sexual Relations in Antiquity and Sexuality and Sexual Identity in Contemporary American Society

Herman C. Waetjen

Taxonomic classification, the typing or categorizing of human beings, was governed in earlier times by the natural fact of sex. Genitals determined gender. Accordingly, humankind was divided into two types of human beings, male and female. The earliest literary texts of antiquity not only bear witness to this binary differentiation; they also evince them to be the dominant taxonomy by which other binary differentiations were symbolized in ancient cultures. The fertility of people and land appears to have been the primary determinant of the social construction of reality. It was the logocentric order of meaning that constituted the foundation of life, language, and world, and religion—namely, the temple and its priesthood—served as its guardian.

The Sumerian cycle of Inanna, two thousand years older than the Bible, transmits this dualistic ordering of reality determined by the binary differentiation of male and female. Already, at the very beginning,

> When heaven had moved away from earth,
> And earth had separated from heaven,[1]

their differentiation is based on the natural fact of sex. The male sky god, An, sets sail for the underworld, and in his fierce sexual encounter with Ereshkigal, the goddess of the underworld, a *huluppu* tree is spawned and planted on the bank of the Euphrates. It is the tree of life, anchored in the underworld and growing heavenward. Because of its procreation by An and Ereshkigal, it is the embodiment of the dual forces of the universe: consciousness and unconsciousness, light and darkness, sun and moon, life and death, male and female. Inanna, the "Queen of Heaven" (also known as Ishtar), who was born of divine parents, appears out of nowhere, plucks the tree from the river, and plants it in her holy garden. As she cares for it, her consciousness grows and expands, and her wishes and fears gradually emerge. She wants both a throne and a bed, rule and womanhood. A snake, a bird, and Lilith appear, giving embodiment to her wishes and fears. Unable to tame these creatures, she seeks help from her peers. Gilgamesh, the young king of Uruk, kills the snake, enters Inanna's garden, and, although a divine mortal, shares the *huluppu* tree with her. Eventually he uproots the tree, and from its wood both a throne and a bed are constructed. Inanna will sit on the throne and lie on the bed; accordingly, her understanding of the mysteries of life and death will grow, particularly as she enters into a courtship with Dumuzi (in later tradition, Tammuz), experiences sexual relations with him, and concomitantly promotes the fertility of land and people.[2]

The same taxonomy determines the creation myths of Genesis 1—2, but in contrast to the epic of Inanna and other earlier Mesopotamian myths it does not serve as the foundation of the social construction of reality and its system of binary differentiations in ancient Israel. The creation and its cosmic order do not originate from a primordial struggle between the binary realities of male and female, nor are women identified with nature while men are representative of culture. Nevertheless, gender differentiation is a structural reality of creation and is therefore determinative of life in society. Although the man is created first in the earlier myth of Genesis 2, he does not find companionship with the animals who share the garden of Eden with him. When he is confronted with the "helpfulness" that is embodied in the woman whom YHWH fashioned from a chunk of flesh and bone taken from him, he—in contrast to Enkidu of the Gilgamesh epic— acknowledges (Gen. 2:23),

> This at last is bone of my bones and flesh of my flesh;
> this one shall be called *ishshah,* for out of *ish* this one was taken.

Consequently *ish* ("man") and *ishshah* ("woman") belong together. The male may be prior to the female, but he was formed out of the clay of the earth while she was created from his flesh and bone. Because of this common physicality, which they share in their heterosexual difference, they are able to enjoy sexual union with each other. The patriarchal prejudice of the myth, however, attributes the actualization of that union to the initiative of the male: "Therefore a man leaves his father and his mother and cleaves to his wife, and they become one flesh" (Gen. 2:24, my trans.). Whether they recognized their sexual difference from the outset or whether they became aware of it after they had partaken of the fruit of the knowledge of good and evil is irrelevant to the basic premise of gender differentiation that is implicit in the myth.[3]

The Priestly account of creation in Gen. 1:1–2:3 culminates (1:26–28) in the creation of the godlike humanity of *adam,* who from the beginning is both male and female.

> And God said, "Let us make *adam* in our image, according to our
> likeness, and let them rule over the fish of the sea and over the birds

of the heaven and over cattle and over the whole earth." And God created the *adam* in his image; in the image of God he created him, male and female he created them. And God blessed them, and God said to them, "Be fruitful and grow large and fill the earth."

Adam, the human being, on the one hand, is unlike all the other creatures God brought into being. As Ps. 8:5 stipulates, *adam* is "little less than God" and therefore is designated to govern the creation on behalf of the Creator. Divine likeness is essential to the fulfillment of this commission in order to enable the earth to sustain life. But *adam* as a humanity of two genders is also like all other created life. Constituted as male and female, humanity is also commissioned to fulfill the divine mandate of procreation: "Be fruitful and grow large and fill the earth." As Phyllis Bird writes,

> *Adam* is creature who . . . is given the power of reproduction through the word-act of creation, receiving it in the identical words of blessing addressed first to the creatures of sea and sky (v. 22). It is in relation to this statement that the specification, "male and female he created them" must be understood. The word of sexual differentiation anticipates the blessing and prepares for it."[4]

Accordingly, the integrity of this primordially established differentiation of male and female is guarded by the Holiness Code of Leviticus 17—26. There can be no compromise of sexual identity. Created as a male, a man must remain pure and unblemished in his nature of maleness. To surrender it sexually by assuming the role of the opposite sex is a desecration of the divine order of creation.[5] Same-sex sexual relations, therefore, are forbidden, explicitly at least to men. "You shall not lie with a male as with a woman; it is an abomination" (Lev. 18:22, NRSV), or literally, according to the Hebrew text, "And [with] the male you shall not cohabit the cohabitings [with] a woman; it is an abomination."

Death is the sentence which the Holiness Code pronounces on such a desecration of the divinely created order of male and female. "And a man who cohabits [with] a male the cohabitings (with) a woman, the two have done an abomination. They shall be put to death" (Lev. 20:13).

Determined by the creation myths of Genesis 1—2, Israelite culture and socialization propagated the binary differentiation of male and female. Physiology established gender identity, and sexual practice conformed to or violated "conventionally defined gender roles." All inversions were denounced as abominations.

Early Christianity inherited and transmitted this ideology. The New Testament Gospels preserve traditions in which Jesus affirms the gender differentiation of the Genesis creation myths. In the more radical Marcan tradition (10:2–9), Jesus rejects the Mosaic legislation on divorce because of its compromise of the divine order of creation by making concessions to human weaknesses that promote separation. "But from the beginning he made them male and female. On account of this a human being will leave his father and mother, and the two will become one flesh" (Mark 10:6–7).

God's will is expressed in the realization of union between the two sexes. The separation of divorce not only annuls the original design of creation but also the eschatological reality of the rule of God and its reconstitution of all things which Jesus is inaugurating. The binary differentiation of male and female is intrinsic to the restructuring of the moral order.

This conflict tradition on divorce was adopted by the evangelist Matthew, but the narrative structure of the story was revised so Jesus himself could negate the Mosaic legislation of Deuteronomy by means of the Mosaic traditions of Genesis. By citing the foundational texts of Israel's scriptural heritage, Jesus can add his messianic authority to the divine order of creation. "Do you not know that the creator from the beginning made them male and female?" (Matt. 19:4).

After acknowledging the binary realities of male and female on the basis of Gen. 1:27, Jesus endorses the corresponding divine will of Gen. 2:24. "On account of this a human being will leave father and mother and be joined to his woman and the two will be one flesh" (Matt. 19:5).

Nevertheless, the order of creation and its fulfillment in the heterosexual relationship of male and female cannot always be realized. The exacting ideal of Jesus' teaching elicits the alternative of singleness from the disciples: "If such is the case of the man with the woman, it is better not to marry." Jesus validates such an option, but with an admission of its severity (Matt. 19:11–12):

> Not all grasp this word, but to whom it is given. For there are eunuchs who became thus from the mother's womb, and there are eunuchs who were castrated by human beings, and there are eunuchs who castrated themselves on account of the rule of the heavens.

Although the divine order of creation may accentuate gender differentiation for sexual union and procreation, the absence of male genitals, as well as the commitment to celibacy, do not preclude the realization of human integrity and wholeness promoted by the rule of God.[6]

There are no implications here regarding same-sex unions. Moreover, no explicit or implicit teaching of Jesus on this matter has been transmitted by the Gospels. Speculation may be futile, but on the basis of the tradition that has been preserved it is reasonable to assume that his orientation as a Jew was determined by the created order of male and female.

It is in other writings of the New Testament, specifically 1 Corinthians, Romans, and 1 Timothy, that the issue of same-sex sexual relations emerges. Although all three are attributed to the apostle Paul, only 1 Corinthians and Romans are generally considered to be authentic.[7] The text of 1 Cor. 6:9–10 denominates the two types of individuals who engage in pederasty. In Rom. 1:26–27, Paul includes same-sex unions among women and men in his analysis of the universal condition of *hamartia* ("sin") and its downward-spiraling movement into living death. The addressees of these letters live and participate in a social construction of reality in which homoeroticism was expressed in the form of pederasty and perhaps also lesbianism.[8]

In the *Symposium*, Plato parodies a trinal taxonomy of human beings by presenting an intoxicated Aristophanes, who contends that originally "there were three kinds of human beings, not two as now, male and female; there was a third kind as well which had equal shares of the other two, and whose name survives though the thing itself has vanished."[9] It is "androgynon" or the androgynous, a "unity composed of both sexes and sharing equally in male and female." Originally, according to Aristophanes, these three types were "round all over," "globular in shape," reflecting their origin as the offspring of the sun (the male), the earth (the female), and the moon (the androgynous being). Each had four arms and four legs, four ears, two sets of genitals, only one head but with two faces, each looking in the opposite direction. They were powerful creatures and "so lofty in their notions that they even conspired against the gods."[10] Zeus refused to destroy them, but in order to limit their power he sliced them in two, and, with the assistance of Apollo, pulled their skin over the exposed flesh and "tied it up in the middle of the belly, so making what we know as the navel."

Each half, as a result of this separation, would search for its counterpart and from the moment of reunion would concentrate all its energies on enfolding the other in a perpetual embrace in an effort to recover original wholeness. Ignoring their bodily needs in this desperate condition, many of them eventually died of starvation. Those who survived would look for others who belonged to the same sex and perpetuate the struggle for their primordial unity. In his pity Zeus

> moved their privy parts to the front . . . to be used for propagating on each other—in the female members by means of the male; so that if in their embracements a man should happen on a woman there might be conception and continuation of their kin; and also, if male met with male they might have some satiety of their union and a relief, and so might turn their hands to their labors and their interest in ordinary life.[11]

Consequently, the two halves of each type that was cut in two would naturally search for each other and express their reunion in sexual relations. The androgynous, of course, would be heterosexual, the male half uniting with the female half or vice versa. Of them, Aristophanes observes, "Our adulterers are mostly descended from that sex, whence likewise are

derived our man-courting women and adulteresses." Female halves, having "no great fancy for men," will search for their female counterparts. And
last:

> Men who are sections of the male pursue the masculine, and so
> long as their boyhood lasts they show themselves to be slices of the
> male by making friends with men and delighting to lie with them
> and to be clasped in men's embraces; these are the finest boys and
> striplings, for they have the most manly nature. Some say they are
> shameless creatures, but falsely: for their behavior is due not to
> shamelessness but to daring, manliness, and virility, since they are
> quick to welcome their like.[12]

The surprise here is the objective of the search in which the sliced male
halves engage: not for same-sex unions with age-matched counterparts, but
with boys. David M. Halperin has observed that

> although his genetic explanation of the diversity of sexual object-
> choice among human beings would seem to require that there be
> some adult males who are sexually attracted to other adult males,
> Aristophanes appears to be wholly unaware of such a possibility,
> and in any case he has left no room for it in his taxonomic scheme.[13]

Halperin concludes:

> No age-matched couples figure among their latter-day offspring,
> however: in the real world of classical Athens—at least as Aristo-
> phanes portrays it—reciprocal erotic desire among males is un-
> known.[14]

and again:

> Those Athenians who allegedly descend from a mythical all-male
> ancestor are not defined by Aristophanes as male homosexuals but
> as willing boys when they are young and as lovers of youths when
> they are old. Despite Boswell, then, neither the concept nor the
> experience of "homosexuality" is known to Plato's Aristophanes.[15]

In an earlier speech of Plato's *Symposium*, Pausanias reinforces this pederastic paradigm of same-sex sexual relations in Greek culture, but at the
same time he offers a more idealistic perspective. Love is to be praised, but
since there are two Loves, the Popular Aphrodite and the Heavenly
Aphrodite, the one that is superior and therefore also authentic must first
be identified. The Love that belongs to the former Aphrodite is evident in

> the meaner sort of men, who, in the first place, love women as well
> as boys; secondly, where they love, they are set on the body more
> than the soul; and thirdly, they choose the most witless people they
> can find, since they look merely to the accomplishment and care
> not if the manner be noble or not.[16]

The other Love, according to Pausanias,

> springs from the Heavenly goddess who, first, partakes not of the female but only of the male; and secondly, is the elder, untinged with wantonness. . . . They love boys only when they begin to acquire some mind—a growth associated with that of down on their chins. For I perceive that those who begin to love them at this age are prepared to be always with them and share all with them as long as life shall last: they will not take advantage of a boy's green thoughtlessness to deceive him and make a mock of him by running straight off to another.[17]

It is this kind of sexual inversion that expresses itself in pederasty that is condemned by Paul in 1 Cor. 6:9–10.

> Or do you not know that unjust individuals will not inherit the rule of God? Do not be deceived! Neither prostitutes nor idolaters nor adulterers nor soft ones *(malakoi)* nor pederasts *(arsenokoitai)* nor thieves nor greedy people nor drunkards nor abusive persons nor swindlers will inherit the rule of God.

Participation in God's rule, according to the apostle, is a present possibility, but it excludes those who perpetrate injustice of one kind or another. All these types he has named do injury to others or to themselves or both. Among them are the *malakoi* and the *arsenokoitai*. Although these two words are translated and therefore also interpreted differently, their juxtaposition, in the light of the distinctive kind of same-sex sexual relations to which the literature and art of the Mediterranean world of antiquity bear witness, indicates that they refer to those who involved themselves in pederasty. *Malakoi*, an adjective that literally means "soft ones" or "unmanly ones," most likely refers to boys or young men between the ages of eleven and seventeen, who because they had not yet grown a beard or pubic hair bore a likeness to young women and were attractive to older men.[18] *Arsenokoitai*, on the other hand, is a word that appears to have no prior history in the Greek language and, as is generally surmised, may have been coined by the apostle himself by combining *arsen* (male) and *koitos* (bed), two words that are contiguous in Lev. 18:22 and especially in 20:13.

Very likely the pederastic ideal that Pausanias articulated in the *Symposium* was seldom achieved. Power and exploitation usually characterized the nature of that relationship.[19] The youth (designated the *eromenos* in the Greek texts) was required to be submissive and passive, while the older man (the *erastes*) initiated the coitus and enjoyed the self-gratification it offered. Generally the relationship was terminated by the latter when the youth showed signs of reaching adulthood by growing a beard.[20] The older man would search for a new *eromenos* or *malakos*, while the young man, who had reached adulthood, would eventually assume the role of the *erastes* and initiate sexual relations with a youth. Accordingly, the cycle of pederasty would continue.[21]

In view of the other types of individuals that are named alongside the *malakoi* and the *arsenokoitai*, it seems doubtful that Paul is excluding both youth and adult male from participation in the rule of God on the basis of the stipulations of the purity code of Leviticus 18 and 20. Rather, all of them—prostitutes, idolaters, adulterers, thieves, greedy people, drunkards, abusive persons, and swindlers, as well as the "soft ones" and their adult male lovers—engage in activities that are destructive to the humanity of others or themselves. All of them are either victimizers, dominating and exploiting others, or victims who for one reason or another allow themselves to be dominated and dehumanized. As long as they continue in their injustice, oppression, and enslavement, they are incapable of receiving the gifts that the rule of God imparts: transcendence into freedom, possibility, and the fullness of life.

It is the eschatological reality of God's rule, constituted by Jesus' resurrection from the dead, that determines Paul's ethical teaching. "For neither is circumcision anything nor uncircumcision but a new creation. Peace and mercy on those who adhere to/follow this measuring stick *(kanōn)*" (Gal. 6:15–16).

Circumcision and uncircumcision, the clean and the unclean: all such dualistic realities structured by the purity code have been superseded by "the ministry of justice" (2 Cor. 3:9). All pollution systems that divide the world into the binary oppositions of the sacred and the secular have been abrogated. The moral order of the new creation and its ministry of justice is the emerging reality of "the One and the Many": that is, the Body of Christ. "For even as the body is *one* and has *many* members, and all the members of the body being *many* are *one* body, so also the Christ" (1 Cor. 12:12, my emphasis).

The spontaneous outcome of participating in this Body of the One and the Many, the new creation, the eschatological rule of God, manifests itself in doing justice, "ruling in life" (Rom. 5:17), and being fully alive (2 Cor. 3:18). This excludes those who engage in pederasty, as well as the other types who are named by the apostle in 1 Cor. 6:9–10.

The text of Rom. 1:26–27 is embedded in 1:18–32, the opening statement of a lengthier diagnosis of the human condition. Impiety and injustice, according to Paul, are the ultimate cause of the universal infection of sin. Impiety, the transgressions of the first table of the Law, induces injustice, transgressions of the second table of the Law, and both bring their own moral retribution. The disavowal of God produces futile reasonings and a senseless heart, which in turn engender idolatry. The resulting condition of alienation from God coincidentally produces alienation from self, and in this circumstance of exile "the wrath of God" is actualized and human beings are handed over to the consequences of their actions.

> Wherefore God delivered them up in the lusts of their hearts unto *uncleanness* to dishonor their bodies among themselves. Who exchanged the truth of God for the lie and worshiped and served the creature in place of the Creator, who is blessed forever (Rom. 1:24–25).

It is in this analytical context that the apostle acknowledges the condemnation that the Levitical code pronounces on the desecration of the human body by compromising its gender. The disease of estrangement generates "passions of dishonor." "For," as he continues (Rom. 1:26–27),

> their females exchanged their natural intercourse for the one contrary to nature; likewise also the males, leaving the natural use of the female, were consumed in their lust for one another, males with males working that which is shameful and receiving in themselves the due penalty for their error.

For Paul, as for his contemporaries, sex is a natural fact and establishes gender identity. The sexual inversion of the binary differentiation of male and female, therefore, is not only dishonorable, it is a symptom of alienation and idolatry that produces its own retribution. "The due penalty of their error," to use Paul's phrase, must be another instance of "the wrath of God," in this case being delivered up or fated to a worthless consciousness that diffuses into society the living death to which it is doomed.

Very little is said of the same-sex sexual relations of women in the literature and art of antiquity; it was "a taboo subject."[22] As already noted, it was acknowledged by Aristophanes in the *Symposium*. Plato refers to it in *The Laws*, along with the same-sex sexual relations of men, but with the identical judgment expressed by the apostle Paul in the use of the prepositional phrase *para physin* (contrary to nature).[23] The evidence that Sappho of Lesbos offers in her poetry is "fragmentary" and "fragile and ambiguous."[24] The correlate words "lesbian" and "lesbianism" that are current today are avoided by K. L. Dover in his discussion of "Women and Homosexuality" because of their adverse use in Greek society. The extravagant and uninhibited language that was employed to express relations between women and girls "hardly suffices to tell us whether Sappho, the girls of Lesbos, and the members of Alkman's choruses sought to induce orgasms in one another by bodily contact."[25]

There is no differentiation between the *malakoi*, the boy pederasts, and the *arsenokoitai*, the adult pederasts, in this general reference of Rom. 1:27 to male same-sex unions. But it should not be assumed that this lack of specification also encompasses the practice of same-sex sexual relations between male adults of more or less the same age. As already stated, no evidence of male age-matched couples engaging in sexual activities is to be found in antiquity.

Paul's analysis of the causes and effects of the human disease of sin that permeates society extends beyond Rom. 1:18–32 and includes 2:1–3:20. His summation is finally pronounced in 3:9, "For we already charged all both Jews and Greeks to be under sin *(hamartian),*" and is supported by a series of texts drawn from the Septuagint. Romans 1:18–3:20, therefore, is the indispensable grounding for the subsequent explication of the Christ event and the salvation or healing of the human infection it inaugurates (Rom. 5:1–21). Accordingly, an entirely different purpose underlies the reference to sexual inversion in Rom. 1:26–27. Consequently, it has no relevance for the ethics of the eschatological reality of God's rule.

In the Mediterranean world of antiquity in which Paul and the other writers of the biblical texts participated, gender was determined on the basis of the natural fact of sex, and the attendantly established taxonomy of male and female served as the basis of social and cultural relations. In spite of various significant changes that have occurred in modern times, however, both the identification of sex and gender and its concomitant binary differentiation of male and female are presupposed to be foundational for structuring the social and cultural conventions of today. In actuality neither of them can or should be normative any longer. Their validity has been canceled once and for all by the paradigm shift that has occurred in the last 150 years.

Sexual identity, as well as sexual role, is no longer defined on the basis of genitals. The modern invention of sexuality has superseded the natural fact of sex and has been constituted as a "principle of the self."[26] Originating as a cultural production from the sciences of physiology, anatomy, and psychology, sexuality individuates human beings according to their sexual predilection and thereby establishes sexual identity apart from the taxonomy of male and female and its conventionally defined roles.[27] As Halperin contends,

> Sexuality . . . turns out to be something more than an endogenous principle of motivation outwardly expressed by the performance of sexual acts; it is a mute power subtly and deviously at work throughout the wide range of human behaviors, attitudes, tastes, choices, gestures, styles, pursuits, judgment, and utterances. Sexuality is thus the inmost part of an individual human nature. It is the feature of a person that takes longest to get to know well, and knowing it renders transparent and intelligible to the knower the person to whom it belongs. Sexuality holds the key to unlocking the deepest mysteries of the human personality: it lies at the center of the hermeneutics of the self.[28]

Homosexuality and heterosexuality, therefore, are modern orientations that presuppose the sociocultural constructs of sexuality. Both terms in fact originated a little more than one hundred years ago. Charles Gilbert Chaddock, "an early translator" of Krafft-Ebing's classic medical handbook of sexual deviance, the *Psychopathia Sexualis*, is credited by the *Oxford English Dictionary* with having introduced "homo-sexuality into the English language in 1892, in order to render a German cognate twenty years its senior."[29] The word "heterosexuality" evidently appeared eight years later.

Consequently, none of the texts of the Bible's two testaments that deal with sexual deviance can or should be related to what today is being called "homosexuality." Moreover, as a result of the inauguration of the rule of God and its eclipse of the Levitical purity code, all pollution systems and their attendant ethical norms have been canceled. Heterosexual and homosexual, therefore, must not be constituted as a binary opposition in which the former is affirmed as "clean" while the latter is rejected as "unclean." Given the realities of sexuality as conceptualized, experienced, and institutionalized human nature, both homosexuality and heterosexuality may be represented in the body of Christ, the new creation of the One and the Many. This implies, of course, that both are subject to the ethical norms of God's rule and therefore are expected to give embodiment to the new humanization that it makes possible.

Another aspect of the paradigm shift in human sexuality is the growing acknowledgment of the realities of *intersex*. The taxonomy of female and male is inadequate to account for the many gradations between these binary categories. Anne Fausto-Sterling identifies three major subgroups: true hermaphrodites who possess one testis and one ovary, male pseudohermaphrodites who have testes and some aspects of the female genitalia but no ovaries, and female pseudohermaphrodites who have ovaries and some aspects of the male genitalia but lack testes.[30] Moreover, she contends that "sex is a vast, infinitely malleable continuum that defies the constraints of even five categories."[31] It is conjectured that at least 4 percent of all births are intersexual. Society, however, determined by the ideology of gender based on genitals, and apprehensive and insecure with the ambiguities of intersex, forces them into one or the other of the two prevailing genders and, by enlisting the services of the legal and medical communities, erases the intersexual gradations. But as Martine Rothblatt argues, "If there are no hard and fast sex types, then there can be no apartheid of sex."[32]

Today the binary differentiation of male and female is being subverted by science and technology. Human beings, therefore, can no longer be viewed as simply sex types belonging to one of the two categories of the heterosexual taxonomy. Individuated as a self by the constitutive principle of their sexuality, they give expression to "a wide range of human behaviors, attitudes, tastes, choices, gestures, styles, pursuits, judgments, and utterances," as

Halperin has specified.[33] Accordingly, the baptismal formula used by the apostle Paul, which negates the fundamental binary differentiations of the ancient world, is equally pertinent today, especially the last of the three. "There is neither Jew nor Greek, neither slave nor free, *neither male and female*. For you are all *one* in Christ Jesus" (Gal. 3:28).

In the new creation all pollution systems, which separated human beings from each other and discriminated against those categorized as unclean and therefore sinful, are invalid. Consequently, if all binary oppositions have been transcended, especially the binary realities of male and female—which for Paul is a differentiation and not an opposition like "slave or free" or "Jew or Greek"—the actuality of many individuated selves of human beings, regardless of their sexual or intersexual physiology, regardless of their homo- or heterosexuality, can be united as one body to constitute the New Humanity of Christ Jesus. This is the vision derived from the writings of the apostle Paul, which the church of today can begin to actualize and thereby fulfill its destiny as the pioneer of a new moral order.

The parable of the Good Samaritan in Luke 10:25–37 not only subverts the binary opposition between the Jew and the Samaritan, the clean and the unclean, it also provides an illustration of the ethics of transcending any and every pollution system in order to minister to the needs of others, regardless of race, sex, or class. But the paradigm shift of the ground from which ethical responses originate, which the context of the parable transmits, makes the parable even more apposite for the critical issue of living a life in a world of the One and the Many without the defenses of a pollution system. The lawyer's question, "Who is my *plesion*?"— meaning "next one" and not "neighbor"—poses the problem of drawing lines in order to determine who is to be admitted into my world for relationships and the help and support those relationships may necessitate. Jesus responds, not only by telling the story of the Good Samaritan, but at the conclusion by substituting a reformulation of the original question: "Who of the three was a *plesion*, a next one, to the one who fell among bandits?" In other words, the new question is: To what fellow human being can I be a "next one"? Instead of drawing lines in order to build an ordered and safe world, the challenge is to act for and with those who are in trouble, disadvantaged, or marginalized. As T. W. Manson phrased it, "Love does not begin by defining its objects; it discovers them."[34]

> . . . . Ach, wir
> Die wir den Boden bereiten wollten für Freundlichkeit
> Konnten selber nicht freundlich sein.

> . . . . Alas, we
> Who wished to lay the foundations of kindness
> Could not ourselves be kind.[35]

NOTES

1. Diane Wolkstein and Samuel Noah Kramer, *Inanna, Queen of Heaven and Earth: Her Stories and Hymns from Sumer* (New York: Harper, 1983), 4.
2. Wolkstein and Kramer, *Inanna*, 7–49, 136–55.
3. Robert B. Coote and David R. Ord, *The Bible's First History: From Eden to the Court of David with the Yahwist* (Philadelphia: Fortress, 1989), 59. For their views on the attempted homosexual rape of Abraham's two divine visitors by the men of Sodom, see 127–31.
4. Phyllis A. Bird, "Male and Female He Created Them": Gen. 1:27b in the Context of the Priestly Account of Creation," *HTR* 74, no. 2 (1981): 147. Also 148, "*Unlike* God, but *like* the other creatures, *adam* is characterized by sexual differentiation."
5. Victor Paul Furnish, "The Bible and Homosexuality: Reading the Tests in Context," *Homosexuality in the Church: Both Sides of the Debate*, ed. Jeffrey S. Siker (Louisville, Ky.: Westminster John Knox, 1994), 20; Juergen Becker, "Zum Problem der Homosexualität in der Bibel," *Annäherungen. Zur urchristlichen Theologiegeschichte und zum Umgang mit ihren Quellen* (Berlin: de Gruyter, 1995), 398–401. Becker attributes the practice of "homosexuality" in Israel to the imitation of Canaanite fertility cult prostitution and claims that it is implied in 1 Kings 15:12; 22:47; 2 Kings 23:7.
6. Herman C. Waetjen, *The Origin and Destiny of Humanness: An Interpretation of the Gospel according to Matthew* (San Rafael, Calif.: Crystal, 1976), 194.
7. 1 Tim. 1:10 is omitted because it has nothing to contribute to the direction of this discussion. In contrast to Gal. 3:19 and Rom. 3:30, its pseudonymous author maintains that the law is laid down for various types of ungodly people, among whom are named *arsenokoitai* ("pederasts"), the same word that Paul employs—and perhaps coined—in 1 Cor. 6:9.
8. Aristotle, however, is oriented toward a taxonomy of male and female. See *De Generatione Animalium* I, 730a–731a; also *Historia Animalium* 1.2.489a, 10–14, where Aristotle defines "male" as emitting into another and "female" as emitting into itself in order to ground difference in anatomy and physiology. For a discussion of these and other texts, see Thomas Laqueur, *Making Sex: Body and Gender from the Greeks to Freud* (Cambridge: Harvard, 1992), especially the chapter entitled "Destiny Is Anatomy," 25–62.
9. Plato, *Symposium*, 189 D–E.
10. *Symposium*, 190 B.
11. *Symposium*, 191 B, C, D.
12. *Symposium*, 192 A.
13. David M. Halperin, *One Hundred Years of Homosexuality and Other Essays on Greek Love* (New York: Routledge, 1990), 20–21. For a discussion of sexual desire and friendship between Gilgamesh and Enkidu and David and Jonathan, see chap. 4, "Heroes and Their Pals."
14. Halperin, *One Hundred Years*, 21.
15. Ibid.; also 161, n. 32. For Boswell's view, see John Boswell, *Christianity, Social Tolerance, and Homosexuality: Gay People in Western Europe from the Beginning of the Christian Era to the Fourteenth Century* (Chicago: University Press, 1980).
16. *Symposium*, 181 B.
17. *Symposium*, 181 C.

18. K. J. Dover, *Greek Homosexuality* (Cambridge: Harvard, 1989), 79–80; Halperin, *One Hundred Years*, 22–24; Robin Scroggs, *The New Testament and Homosexuality: Contextual Background for Contemporary Debate* (Philadelphia: Fortress, 1983), 24–28.

19. Halperin, *One Hundred Years*, 30, "Sexual 'activity,' moreover, is thematized as domination: the relation between the 'active' and 'passive' sexual partner is thought of as the same kind of relation as that obtaining between social superior and social inferior." See also Dover, *Greek Homosexuality*, 100–109, and Eva Cantarella, *Bisexuality in the Ancient World* (New Haven: Yale, 1992).

20. Halperin, *One Hundred Years*, 88, "In particular, Greek men seem to have regarded the presence of hair upon the cheeks, thighs, and hindquarters of maturing youths with intense sexual distaste."

21. Dover, *Greek Homosexuality*, 16, 57–59, 91–100.

22. Ibid., 182. Also 171–84.

23. Compare Plato, *The Laws* I 636c, trans. R. G. Bury, Loeb Classical Library (Cambridge: Harvard, 1961), with Rom. 1:26.

24. Dover, *Greek Homosexuality*, 181.

25. Ibid., 181–82.

26. Halperin, *One Hundred Years*, 24.

27. Ibid., 25.

28. Ibid., 26.

29. Ibid., 15. See especially 155, n. 2.

30. Anne Fausto-Sterling, "The Five Sexes: Why Male and Female Are Not Enough," *The Sciences* (March/April 1993): 21.

31. Ibid. At the conclusion of her article, on page 24, Fausto-Sterling imagines another world in which "patient and physician, parent and child, male and female, heterosexual and homosexual—all these oppositions and others would have to be dissolved as sources of division. A new ethic of medical treatment would arise, one that would permit ambiguity in a culture that had overcome sexual division."

32. Martine Rothblatt, *The Apartheid of Sex: A Manifesto on the Freedom of Gender* (New York: Crown, 1995), 19.

33. Halperin, *One Hundred Years*, 26.

34. T. W. Manson, *The Sayings of Jesus* (London: SCM, 1937), 261.

35. Bertolt Brecht, "An die Nachgeborenen," *Selected Poems*, trans. H. R. Hayes (New York: Harcourt Brace Jovanovitch, 1987), 176–77.

8

Arsenokoitês and *Malakos:*
Meanings and Consequences

Dale B. Martin

The New Testament provides little ammunition to those wishing to condemn modern homosexuality. Compared to the much more certain condemnations of anger, wealth (sometimes anything but poverty), adultery, or disobedience of wives and children, the few passages that *might* be taken as condemning homosexuality are meager. It is not surprising, therefore, that the interpretation of two mere words has commanded a disproportionate amount of attention. Both words, *arsenokoitês* and *malakos*, occur in a vice list in 1 Cor. 6:9, and *arsenokoitês* recurs in 1 Tim. 1:10. Although the translation of these two words has varied through the years, in the twentieth century they have often been taken to refer to people who engage in homosexual, or at least male homosexual, sex, and the conclusion sometimes then follows that the New Testament or Paul, condemns homosexual "activity."

Usually the statement is accompanied by a shrugged-shoulder expression, as if to say, I'm not condemning homosexuality! I'm just reading the Bible. It's there in the text. Such protestations of objectivity, however, become untenable when examined closely. By analyzing ancient meanings of the terms, on the one hand, and historical changes in the translation of the terms on the other, we discover that interpretations of *arsenokoitês* and *malakos* as condemning modern homosexuality have been driven more by ideological interests in marginalizing gay and lesbian people than by the general strictures of historical criticism.

In the end, the goal of this chapter is not mere historical or philological accuracy. By emphasizing the ideological contexts in which interpretation has taken place and will always take place, I intend to challenge the objectivist notion that the Bible or historical criticism can provide contemporary Christians with a reliable *foundation* for ethical reflection. Neither a simple reading of "what the Bible says" nor a professional historical-critical reconstruction of the ancient meaning of the texts will provide a prescription for contemporary Christian ethics. Indeed, the naive attempts by conservative Christians, well-meaning though they may be, to derive their ethics from a "simple" reading of the Bible have meant merely that they impute to the Bible their own destructive ideologies.[1] The destruction is today nowhere more evident than in the church's mistreatment of lesbian and gay Christians.

Arsenokoitês

From the earliest English translations of the Bible, *arsenokoitês* has suffered confusing treatment. Wyclif (in 1380) translated it as "thei that don leccherie with men" and until the twentieth century similar translations prevailed, primarily "abusars of them selves with the mankynde" (Tyndale 1534; see also Coverdale 1535, Cranmer 1539, Geneva Bible 1557, KJV 1611, ASV 1901; the Douai-Rheims version of 1582 was a bit clearer: "the liers vvith mankinde"). A curious shift in translation occurred in the mid-twentieth century. Suddenly, the language of psychology and "normalcy" creeps into English versions. Although some still use archiac terms, like "sodomite" (JB 1966, NAB 1970, NRSV 1989), several influential versions substitute more modern concepts like "sexual perverts" (RSV 1946, REB 1992) or terms that reflect the nineteenth century's invention of the category of the "homosexual," such as the NIV's (1973) "homosexual offenders." Some translations even go so far as to collapse *arsenokoitês* and *malakos* together into one term: "homosexual perverts" or "homosexual perversion" (TEV 1966, NEB 1970). Modern commentators also offer a variety of interpretations. Some explain that *malakos* refers to the "passive" partner in male-male anal intercourse and *arsenokoitês* the "active" partner, thus the two disputable terms being taken care of mutually.[2] Some simply import wholesale the modern category and translate *arsenokoitês* as "male homosexual."[3] Others, in an attempt, I suppose, to separate the "sin" from the "sinner," have suggested "practicing homosexuals."[4]

Between the end of the nineteenth and the middle of the twentieth century, therefore, the translation of *arsenokoitês* shifted from being the reference to an action that any man might well perform, regardless of orientation or disorientation, to refer to a "perversion," either an action or a propensity taken to be self-evidently abnormal and diseased. The shift in translation, that is, reflected the invention of the category of "homosexuality" as an abnormal orientation, an invention that occurred in the nineteenth century but gained popular currency only gradually in the twentieth.[5] Furthermore, whereas earlier translations had all taken the term (correctly) to refer to men, the newer translations broadened the reference to include people of either sex who could be diagnosed as suffering from the new modern neurosis of homosexuality. Thorough historical or philological evidence was never adduced to support this shift in translation. The interpretations were prompted not by criteria of historical criticism but by shifts in modern sexual ideology.

As the debate over homosexuality and the Bible has become more explicit, various attempts have been made to defend the interpretation of *arsenokoitês* as a reference to male-male or homosexual sex in general. A common error made in such attempts is to point to its two parts, *arsên* and *koitês*, and say that "obviously" the word refers to men who have sex with men.[6] Scholars sometimes support this reading by pointing out that the two words occur together, though not joined, in Greek translations of the Hebrew Bible and in Philo in a context in which he condemns male homosexual sex.[7] Either Paul, it is suggested, or someone before him simply combined the two words together to form a new term for men who have sex with men.

This approach is linguistically invalid. It is highly precarious to try to ascertain the meaning of a word by taking it apart, getting the meanings of its component parts, and then assuming, with no supporting evidence, that the meaning of the longer word is a simple combination of its component parts. To "understand" does not mean to "stand under." In fact, nothing about the basic meanings of either "stand" or "under" has any direct bearing on the meaning of "understand." This phenomenon of language is sometimes even more obvious with terms that designate social roles, since the nature of the roles themselves often changes over time and becomes separated from any original reference. None of us, for example, takes the word "chairman" to have any *necessary* reference to a chair, even if it originally did. Thus, all definitions of *arsenokoitês* that derive its meaning from its components are naive and indefensible. Furthermore, the claim that *arsenokoitês* came from a combination of these two words and *therefore* means "men who have sex with men" makes the additional error of defining a word by its (assumed) etymology. The etymology of a word is its history, not its meaning.[8]

The only reliable way to define a word is to analyze its use in as many different contexts as possible. The word "means" according to its function, according to how particular people use the word in different situations. Unfortunately, we have very few uses of *arsenokoitês* and most of those occur in simple lists of sins, mostly in quotations of the biblical lists, thus providing no explanation of the term, no independent usage, and few clues from the context about the term's meaning. But having analyzed these different occurrences of *arsenokoitês*, especially cases where it occurs in vice lists that do *not* merely quote 1 Cor. 6:9 or 1 Tim. 1:10, I am convinced that we can make some guarded statements.

As others have noted, vice lists are sometimes organized into groups of "sins," with sins put together that have something to do with one another.[9]

First are listed, say, vices of sex, then those of violence, then others related to economics or injustice. Analyzing the occurrence of *arsenokoitês* in different vice lists, I noticed that it often occurs not where we would expect to find reference to homosexual intercourse—that is, along with adultery *(moicheia)* and prostitution or illicit sex *(porneia)*—but among vices related to economic injustice or exploitation. Though this provides little to go on, I suggest that a careful analysis of the actual context of the use of *arsenokoitês*, free from linguistically specious arguments from etymology or the word's separate parts, indicates that *arsenokoitês* had a more specific meaning in Greco-Roman culture than homosexual penetration in general, a meaning that is now lost to us. It seems to have referred to some kind of economic exploitation by means of sex, perhaps but not necessarily homosexual sex.

One of the earliest appearances of the word (here the verb) occurs in *Sibylline Oracle* 2.70–77.[10] Although the date of this section of the oracle—indeed, of the finished oracle itself—is uncertain, there is no reason to take the text as dependent on Paul or the New Testament. The oracle probably provides an independent use of the word. It occurs in a section listing acts of economic injustice and exploitation; in fact, the editors of the English translation here quoted (J. J. Collins) label the section "On Justice":

> (Never accept in your hand a gift which derives from unjust deeds.)
> Do not steal seeds. Whoever takes for himself is accursed (to generations of generations, to the scattering of life.
> Do not *arsenokoitein*, do not betray information, do not murder.)
> Give one who has labored his wage. Do not oppress a poor man.
> Take heed of your speech. Keep a secret matter in your heart.
> (Make provision for orphans and widows and those in need.)
> Do not be willing to act unjustly, and therefore do not give leave to one who is acting unjustly.

The term occurs in a list of what we might call "economic sins," actions related to economic injustice or exploitation: accepting gifts from unjust sources, extortion, withholding wages, oppressing the poor. "Stealing seeds" probably refers to the hoarding of grain; in the ancient world, the poor often accused the rich of withholding grain from the market as a price-fixing strategy.[11] I would argue that other sins here mentioned that have no necessary economic connotation probably do here. Thus the references to speech and keeping secrets may connote the use of information for unjust gain, like fraud, extortion, or blackmail; and "murder" here may hint at motivations of economic gain, recalling, for example, the murder of Naboth by Jezebel (1 Kings 21). In any case, no other term in the section refers to sex. Indeed, nothing in the context (including what precedes and follows this quotation) suggests that a sexual action in general is being referred to at all. If we take the *context* as indicating the *meaning*, we should assume that *arsenokoitein* here refers to some kind of economic exploitation, probably by sexual means: rape or sex by economic coercion, prostitution, pimping,or something of the sort.

This suggestion is supported by the fact that a list of sexual sins does occur elsewhere in the same oracle, which is where we might expect to find a reference to male-male sex (2.279–82). The author condemns "defiling the flesh by licentiousness," "undoing the girdle of virginity by secret intercourse," abortion, and exposure of infants (the last two often taken to be means of birth control used by people enslaved to sex; such people proved by these deeds that they had sex purely out of lust rather than from the "nobler" motive of procreation). If the prohibition against *arsenokoitein* was taken to condemn homosexual intercourse in general, one would expect the term to occur here, rather than among the terms condemning unjust exploitation.[12]

A similar case exists in the second-century *Acts of John.* "John" is condemning the rich men of Ephesus:

> You who delight in gold and ivory and jewels, do you see your loved (possessions) when night comes on? And you who give way to soft clothing, and then depart from life, will these things be useful in the place where you are going? And let the murderer know that the punishment he has earned awaits him in double measure after he leaves this (world). So also the poisoner, sorcerer, robber, swindler, and *arsenokoitês*, the thief and all of this band. . . . So, men of Ephesus, change your ways; for you know this also, that kings, rulers, tyrants, boasters, and warmongers shall go naked from this world and come to eternal misery and torment (section 36; Hennecke-Schneemelcher).

Here also, *arsenokoitês* occurs in a list of sins related to economics and injustice: delighting in wealth, robbery, swindling, thievery. Note also the list of those who prosper by their power over others: kings, rulers, tyrants, boasters, warmongers. The emphasis throughout the section is on power, money, and unjust exploitation, not sex.

As was the case in the *Sybilline Oracle,* "John" *does* denounce sexual sins elsewhere in the text, and the word *arsenokoitês* is absent (section 35). If this author took *arsenokoitês* to refer generally to homosexual sex or penetration, we would expect him to mention it among the other sexual sins, rather than in the section condemning the rich for economic exploitation. Thus, here also *arsenokoitês* probably refers to some kind of economic exploitation, again perhaps by sexual means.

Another second-century Christian document offers corroborative, though a bit less obvious, evidence. Theophilus of Antioch, in his treatise addressed *To Autolychus*, provides a vice list.[13] First come the two sexual sins of adultery and fornication or prostitution.[14] Next come three economic sinners: thief, plunderer, and defrauder (or robber). Sixth is *arsenokoitês*. The next group includes savagery, abusive behavior, wrath, and jealousy or envy, all of which the ancients would recognize as sins of "passion": that is, uncontrolled emotion. Next come instances of pride: boastfulness and conceit or haughtiness. I take the next term, *plêktês* ("striker") to denote someone who thinks he can go around hitting people as if they were his slaves. Then occurs the term "avaricious," or "greedy." Finally are two phrases related to the family: disobedience to parents and selling one's children. These last three may all have been taken as belonging to the category of greed, surely in the case of selling one's children and also perhaps in the reference to parents, if the particular action is understood as a refusal to support one's parents in their old age.

Arsenokoitês is separated from the sexual sins by three terms that refer to economic injustice. Would this be the case if it was understood as a condemnation of simple male homosexual intercourse? Furthermore, as Robert Grant notes, Theophilus takes these terms, with the exceptions of *phthoneros* and *hyperoptês*, from vice lists in the Pauline corpus. Therefore, it is notable that Theophilus places *arsenokoitês* in a different position. Grouping it with economic sins, I suggest, reflects his understanding of the social role to which it referred and his rhetorical goal of grouping the vices by category.

Later in the same work, *arsenokoitia* occurs in another list: again adultery and *porneia* come first, then *arsenokoitia*, followed by greed *(pleonexia)* and *athemitoi eidôlolatreia*, referring to idolatry. This list is not very helpful, since the term could here be taken as a sexual vice, grouped with the two preceding terms, or as an economic vice, grouped with the following. One possible explanation is that it is both: it is economic exploitation by some sexual means.[15]

There are two texts in which one might reasonably take *arsenokoitia* as referring to homosexual sex. In each case, however, I believe a careful reading encourages more cautious conclusions. The first occurs in Hippolytus's *Refutation of All Heresies* 5.26.22–23. Hippolytus claims to be passing along a Gnostic myth about the seduction of Eve and Adam by the evil being Naas. Naas came to Eve, deceived her, and committed adultery with her. He then came to Adam and "possessed him like a boy (slave)." This is how, according to the myth, *moicheia* (adultery) and *arsenokoitia* came into the world. Since *arsenokoitia* is in parallel construction with *moicheia*, it would be reasonable for the reader to take its reference as simply homosexual penetration. We should note, nonetheless, the element of deception and fraud here. The language about Naas's treatment of Adam, indeed, which could be read "taking or possessing him like a slave," could connote exploitation and even rape. Certainly the context allows a reading of *arsenokoitia* to imply the unjust and coercive use of another person sexually.

The second debatable use of the term occurs in a quotation of the second- to third-century writer Bardesanes found in Eusebius's *Preparation for the Gospel.*[16] Bardesanes is remarking that the peoples who live east of the Euphrates River take the charge of *arsenokoitia* very seriously: "From the Euphrates River all the way to the ocean in the East, a man who is derided as a murderer or thief will not be the least bit angry; but if he is derided as an *arsenokoitês,* he will defend himself to the point of murder. [Among the Greeks, wise men who have lovers (*erômenous echontes,* males whom they love; "favorites") are not condemned]" (my trans.).

On the surface, this passage appears to equate "being an *arsenokoitês*" and "having a favorite." But there are complicating factors. In the first place, the text seems to have gone through some corruption in transmission. The sentence I have given in brackets does not occur in the Syriac fragments of Bardesanes's text or in the other ancient authors who seem to know Bardesanes's account, leading Jacoby, the editor of the Greek fragments, to suggest that Eusebius himself supplied the comment.[17] Thus Eusebius's text would provide evidence only that he or other late-Christian scribes wanted to equate *arsenokoitês* with "having a favorite." This fourth-century usage would therefore be less important for ascertaining an earlier, perhaps more specific, meaning of the term. Furthermore, we should note that the phrases occur in Eusebius in a parallel construction, but this does not necessarily mean that the second phrase is a defining gloss on the first. The point *could* be that "wise men" among the Greeks are not condemned for an action that is *similar* to one found offensive to Easterners. The *equation* of the terms is not absolutely clear. I offer these thoughts only as speculations meant to urge caution, but caution is justified. Especially since this text from Eusebius is the *only* one that might reasonably be taken to equate *arsenokoitia* with simple homosexual penetration, we should be wary of saying that it always does.[18]

I should be clear about my claims here. I am not claiming to know what *arsenokoitês* meant, I am claiming that *no one* knows what it meant. I freely admit that it could have been taken as a reference to homosexual sex.[19] But given the scarcity of evidence and the several contexts just analyzed, in which *arsenokoitês* appears to refer to some particular kind of economic exploitation, no one should be allowed to get away with claiming that "of course" the term refers to "men who have sex with other men." It is certainly possible, I think probable, that *arsenokoitês* referred to a particular role of exploiting others by means of sex, perhaps but not necessarily by homosexual sex. The more important question, I think, is why some scholars are certain it refers to simple male-male sex in the face of evidence to the contrary. Perhaps ideology has been more important than philology.

Malakos

The translations and interpretations of *malakos* provide an even clearer case of ideological scholarship. For one thing, in contrast to the case with *arsenokoitês*, in which we have too few occurrences of the term to make confident claims, we possess many occurrences of *malakos* and can be fairly confident about its meaning. Moreover, the changes in translation of *malakos* provide an even clearer record of how interpretive decisions have changed due to historical shifts in the ideology of sexuality.

Early English translations render *malakos* by terms that denote a general weakness of character or degeneracy, usually "weaklinges" (Tyndale 1534, Coverdale 1535, Cranmer 1539; see also Wyclif 1380, "lechouris ayens kynde," and Geneva Bible 1557, "wantons"). From the end of the sixteenth century to the twentieth, the preferred translation was "effeminate" (Douai-Rheims 1582, KJV 1611, ASV 1901). As was the case with *arsenokoitês*, however, a curious shift takes place in the mid-twentieth century. The translation of *malakos* as "effeminate" is universally rejected and some term that denotes a particular sexual action or orientation is substituted. The JB (1966) chooses "catamite," the NAB (1970) renders *arsenokoitês* and *malakos* together as "sodomite," others translate *malakos* as "male prostitute" (NIV 1973, NRSV 1989), and again some combine both terms and offer the modern medicalized categories of sexual, or particularly homosexual, "perversion" (RSV 1946, TEV 1966, NEB 1970, REB 1992). As was the case with *arsenokoitês*, no real historical or philological evidence has been marshaled to support these shifts in translation, especially not that from the "effeminacy" of earlier versions to the "homosexual perversion" of the last fifty years. In fact, all the historical and philological evidence is on the side of the earlier versions. The shift in translation resulted not from the findings of historical scholarship but from shifts in sexual ideology.

This hypothesis is easy to support because *malakos* is easy to define. Evidence from the ancient sources is abundant and easily accessible. *Malakos* can refer to many things: the softness of expensive clothes, the richness and delicacy of gourmet food, the gentleness of light winds and breezes. When used as a term of moral condemnation, the word still refers to something perceived as "soft": laziness, degeneracy, decadence, lack of courage, or, to sum up all these vices in one ancient category, the feminine. For the ancients, or at least for the men who produced almost all our ancient literature, the connection was commonsensical and natural. Women are weak, fearful, vulnerable, tender. They stay indoors and protect their soft skin and nature: their flesh is moister, more flaccid, and more porous than male flesh, which is why their bodies retain all that excess fluid that must be expelled every month. The female is quintessentially penetrable; their pores are looser than men's. One might even say that in the ancient male ideology women exist to be penetrated. It is their purpose *(telos)*. And their "softness" or "porousnes" is nature's way of inscribing on and within their bodies this reason for their existence.[20]

And so it was that a man who allowed himself to be penetrated—by either a man or a woman—could be labeled a *malakos*. But to say that *malakos meant* a man who was penetrated is simply wrong. In fact, a perfectly good word existed that seems to have had that narrower meaning: *kinaedos. Malakos*, rather, referred to this entire complex of femininity.[21] This can be recognized by looking at the range of ways men condemned other men by calling them *malakoi*.

As I mentioned, a man could, by submitting to penetration, leave himself open to charges of *malakia*.[22] But in those cases, the term refers to the effeminacy of which the penetration is only a sign or proof; it does not refer to the sexual act itself. The category of effeminate men was much broader than that. In philosophical texts, for example, *malakoi* are those people who cannot put up with hard work. Xenophon uses the term for lazy men.[23] For Epictetus and the Cynic Epistles, the term refers to men who take life easy rather than enduring the hardships of philosophy.[24] In Dio Cassius, Plutarch, and Josephus, cowards are *malakoi*.[25] Throughout ancient literature, *malakoi* are men who live lives of decadence and luxury.[26] They drink too much wine, have too much sex, love gourmet food, and hire professional cooks. According to Josephus, a man may be accused of *malakia* if he is weak in battle, enjoys luxury, or is reluctant to commit suicide (*War* 7.338; *Antiquities* 5.246; 10.194). Dio Chrysostom says that the common crowd might stupidly call a man *malakos* just because he studies a lot—that is, a bookworm might be called a sissy (66.25).

The term *malakos* occurs repeatedly in the Pseudo-Aristotelian *Physiognomy*, a book that tells how to recognize someone's character by body type and body language, including whether a man is *really* effeminate even if he outwardly appears virile. The word never refers specifically to penetration in homosexual sex (although men who endure it are discussed in the book). Rather, it denotes the feminine, whether the reference is to feet, ankles, thighs, bones, flesh, or whatever (see esp. chap. 6 passim). It always represents the negative female characteristic to which the positive masculine characteristic is contrasted. For example, if a man has weak eyes, it means one of two things: either he is *malakos* and *thêlu* or he is a depressive and lacks spirit (808a10). Each option contains a pair of synonyms: just as "depressive" and "lacking spirit" *(katêphês, athymos)* are synonyms, so are *malakos* and *thêlu*, both referring to effeminacy. *Malakia*, therefore, was a rather broad social category. It included, of course, penetrated men, but many others besides. To put it simply, all penetrated men were *malakoi*, but not all *malakoi* were penetrated men.[27]

In fact, *malakos* more often referred to men who prettied themselves up to further their *heterosexual* exploits. In Greco-Roman culture, it seems generally to have been assumed that both men and women would be attracted to a pretty-boy. And boys who worked to make themselves more attractive, whether they were trying to attract men *or* women, were called effeminate. An old hag in a play by Aristophanes drags off a young man, saying, "Come along, my little softie" *(malakiôn)*, although she has perfectly heterosexual things in mind *(Ecclesiazusae* 1058). The Roman playwright Plautus uses the Latin transliteration *malacus* to indicate effeminate men. But whereas in one comedy the term is *cinaedus malacus*, referring to a penetrated man, in another it is *moechus malacus*, referring to a man who seduces other men's wives *(Miles Gloriosus* 3.1 [1.668]; *Truculentus* 2.7.49 [1.610]).

In the ancient world, effeminacy was implicated in heterosexual sex as much as homosexual—or more so.[28] When Diogenes the Cynic sees a young man prettied up, he cannot tell whether the boy is trying to attract a man or a woman; in either case the boy is equally effeminate (Diogenes Laertius 6.54; the term *malakos* does not occur here, but effeminacy is the subject).[29] Chariton in his novel *Chaereas and Callirhoe* provides a typical portrait of an effeminate man (1.4.9): he has a fresh hairdo, scented with perfume; he wears eye makeup, a soft *(malakon)* mantle, and light, swishy slippers; his fingers glisten with rings. Only a modern audience would find it strange that he is off to seduce not a man but a maiden.[30] When the author of the Pseudo-Aristotelian *Physiognomy* wants to portray the "Charitable Type" of man, he makes him typically effeminate—and very heterosexual. Such men, he says, are delicate, pale, with shining eyes and wrinkled noses; they cry a lot, are "reminiscent," warmhearted, and with nice dispositions. They are particularly fond of women, with whom they have lots of sex, and they tend to produce female children (808a34).

Ancient sexist ideology was quite different from modern sexist—and heterosexist—ideology. The ancients operated with an axis that represented masculinity at one end and femininity at the other. All people theoretically could be assigned a particular place on the axis. The ancients could also assume, rather less often or obviously, an axis on which men-who-love-boys occupied one end and men-who-love-women the other, with most men assumed to fall somewhere in the middle as naturally omnisexual. To some extent, therefore, we can recognize analogies to the modern axes of masculine–feminine and heterosexual–homosexual. But whereas in modern ideology the two axes are usually collapsed together, with queer men of all sexual positions considered feminine and straight guys masculine (and even more masculine the lustier they are), the two axes had no relation to one another in the ancient ideology. A man could be branded as effeminate whether he had sex with men or with women. Effeminacy had no relation to the sex of one's partner but to a complex system of signals with a much wider reference code. Thus it would never have occurred to an ancient person to think that *malakos* or any other word indicating the feminine *in itself* referred to homosexual sex at all. It could just as easily refer to heterosexual sex.[31]

This can be demonstrated by analyzing those famous texts in which men argue about whether the love of women is inferior or superior to the love of boys. Each side accuses the other of effeminacy and can claim some logical grounds for doing so. In Plato's *Symposium*, where Aristophanes is made to relate his fanciful myth about the origins of the different kinds of loves, man for man, man for woman, and woman for woman, it is taken as natural that male–male love is the most "manly" *(andreiotatoi)* of all three (192A). In the *Symposium* no one attempts to argue the opposite, more difficult case. In Plutarch's *Dialogue on Love (Moralia* 748E–771E), the man defending the love of women does accuse the penetrated man of *malakia* and *thêlutês,* but the speaker advocating the love of boys is given the stronger case. He says that the love of *females* is, of course, more effeminate (750F); the love of women is "moist" *(hygron),* "housebound," "unmanly" *(anandrois),* and implicated in *ta malaka,* "softness" (751A–B). Men who fall in love with women demonstrate their effeminacy *(malakia)* and weakness *(astheneia,* 753F; 760D) by the fact that they are controlled by women.

Similar mutual insults are exchanged in the Pseudo-Lucianic *Affairs of the Heart.* The man advocating the love of women is portrayed by the author as the more effeminate. He is said to be skilled in the use of makeup, presumably, the narrator comments, in order to attract women, who like that kind of thing (9). True, in his own turn, the "woman lover" complains that the penetrated man in homosexual sex is feminized; it is masculine to ejaculate seed and feminine to receive it (28, 19; note *malakizesthai*). But the man advocating the love of boys counters that *heterosexual* sex taints a man with femininity, which is why men are so eager to take a bath after copulating with women (43). Male love, on the other hand, is manly, he says, associated with athletics, learning, books, and sports equipment, rather than with cosmetics and combs (9, 44).[32]

I cite these texts not to celebrate homosexual love. What strikes me about them is rather their rank misogyny.[33] But that is just the point. The real problem with being penetrated was that it implicated the man in the feminine, and *malakos* referred not to the penetration per se but to the perceived aspects of femaleness associated with it. The word *malakos* refers to the entire ancient complex of the devaluation of the feminine. Thus people could use *malakos* as an insult directed against men who love women too much.[34]

At issue here is the ancient horror of the feminine, which can be gruesomely illustrated by an example from Epictetus. In one of his especially "manly" moments, Epictetus praises an athlete who died rather than submit to an operation that would have saved his life by amputating his diseased genitals (1.2.25–26). Whereas we might think the paramount issue would be the man's wish to avoid an excruciatingly painful operation, the issue for Epictetus is the man's manly refusal to go on living if he must do so without his masculine equipment—the things that set him apart from despised femininity. It is better to die than be less than a man. Or, perhaps more to the point, any sensible person would rather be dead than be a woman.

There is no question, then, about what *malakos* referred to in the ancient world. In moral contexts it always referred either obviously or obliquely to the feminine. There is no historical reason to take *malakos* as a specific reference to the penetrated man in homosexual intercourse.[35] It is even less defensible to narrow that reference down further to mean "male prostitute."[36] The meaning of the word is clear, even if too broad to be taken to refer to a single act or role. *Malakos* means "effeminate."

Why has this obvious translation been universally rejected in recent English versions? Doubtless because contemporary scholars have been loath to consider effeminacy a moral category but have been less hesitant in condemning gay and lesbian people. Today, effeminacy may be perceived as a quaint or distasteful personal mannerism, but the prissy church musician or stereotyped interior designer is not, merely on the basis of a limp wrist, to be considered fuel for hell. For most English-speaking Christians in the twentieth century, effeminacy may be unattractive, but it is not a sin. Their Bibles could not be allowed to condemn so vociferously something that was a mere embarrassment. So the obvious translation of *malakos* as "effeminate" was jettisoned.

Consequences

Being faced with a Pauline condemnation of effeminacy hardly solves the more important hermeneutical issues. Suppose that we wanted to be historically and philologically rigorous and restore the translation "effeminate" to our Bibles. What do we then tell our congregations "effeminacy" means? As I have already illustrated in part, in the ancient world a man could be condemned as effeminate for, among many other things, eating or drinking too much, enjoying gourmet cooking, wearing nice underwear or shoes, wearing much of anything on his head, having long hair, shaving, caring for his skin, wearing cologne or aftershave, dancing too much, laughing too much, or gesticulating too much. Keeping one's knees together is effeminate, as well as swaying when walking, or bowing the head. And of course there were the sexual acts and positions: being penetrated (by a man *or* a woman), enjoying sex with women too much, or masturbating.[37] The list could go on—and that contributed to the usefulness of the word as a weapon. It was a malleable condemnation.

Naturally, many of these things do not make a man effeminate today. If in trying to be "biblical," then, we attempt to "take seriously" Paul's condemnation, do we condemn what Paul and his readers are likely to have considered effeminate—that is, take the historical route? Or do we condemn only those things that *our* culture considers effeminate? And what might that be? Taking piano lessons? ballet dancing? singing falsetto in the men and boys' choir? shaving one's body hair for anything but a swim meet or a bicycle race? being a drag queen? having a transsexual operation? camping it up? or wearing *any* article of "women's clothes" (unless you are a TV talk show host trying to make a point)? refusing to own a gun? driving an automatic transmission instead of a stick shift? drinking tea? actually requesting sherry? Or do we just narrow the category to include only those people most heterosexist Christians would really like to condemn: "gays" and "manly men" who are careless enough to get caught?

Condemning penetrated men for being effeminate would also implicate us in a more elusive and pervasive problem: the misogyny of degrading the penetrated. The ancient condemnation of the penetrated man was possible only because sexist ideology had already inscribed the inferiority of women into heterosexual sex. To be penetrated was to be inferior because women were inferior. Let us also be clear that our modern culture has in no way liberated itself from this sexism. This should be obvious every time a frat boy says "This sucks!" or "Fuck you!"—thus implicating both his girlfriend and possibly his roommate in the despised role of the penetrated. The particular form taken by modern heterosexism is derived largely from sexism. People who retain Paul's condemnation of effeminacy as ethical grounding for a condemnation of contemporary gay sex must face the fact that they thereby participate in the hatred of women inherent in the ancient use of the term.

In the face of such confusion and uncertainty, no wonder modern heterosexist scholars and Christians have shrunk from translating *malakos* as "effeminate." I myself would not advocate reading a condemnation of effeminacy out loud in church as the "word of the Lord." But to mask such problems and tell our fellow Christians that the word "really" refers just to boy prostitutes or, worse, "passive homosexuals" is by this time just willful ignorance or dishonesty.

Some scholars and Christians have wanted to make *arsenokoitês* and *malakos* mean both *more* and *less* than the words actually mean, according to the heterosexist goals of the moment. Rather than noting that *arsenokoitês* may refer to a specific role of exploitation, they say it refers to all "active homosexuals" or "sodomites" or some such catch-all term, often broadening its reference even more to include all homosexual eroticism. And rather than admitting the obvious, that *malakos* is a blanket condemnation of all effeminacy, they explain that it refers quite particularly to the penetrated man in homosexual sex. Modern scholars have conveniently narrowed down the wide range of meanings of *malakia* so that it now condemns one group: gay men—in particular, "bottoms." In order to use 1 Cor. 6:9 to condemn contemporary homosexual relationships, they must insist that the two words mean *no more* but also *no less* than what *they* say they mean. It should be clear that this exercise is driven more by heterosexist ideology than historical criticism.

My goal is not to deny that Paul condemned homosexual acts but to highlight the ideological contexts in which such discussions have taken place. My goal is to dispute appeals to "what the Bible says" as a foundation for Christian ethical arguments. It really is time to cut the Gordian knot of fundamentalism. And do not be fooled: any argument that tries to defend its ethical position by an appeal to "what the Bible says" without explicitly acknowledging the agency and contingency of the interpreter is fundamentalism, whether it comes from a right-wing Southern Baptist or a moderate Presbyterian. We must simply stop giving that kind of argument any credibility. Furthermore, we will not find the answers merely by becoming better historians or exegetes. The test for whether an interpretation is Christian or not does not hang on whether it is historically accurate or exegetically nuanced. The touchstone is not the historically reconstructed meaning in the past, nor is it the fancifully imagined, modernly constructed intentions of the biblical writers.[38] Nor can any responsible Christian—after the revolutionary changes in Christian thought in the past twenty years, much less in the past three hundred—maintain that Christian interpretations are those conforming to Christian tradition. The traditions, all of them, have changed too much and are far too open to cynical manipulation to be taken as foundations for gauging the ethical value of a reading of scripture.

The only recourse in our radical contingency is to *accept* our contingency and look for guidance within the discourse that we occupy and that forms our very selves. The best place to find criteria for talking about ethics and interpretation will be in Christian discourse itself, which includes scripture and tradition but not in a "foundational" sense. Nor do I mean that Christian discourse can itself furnish a stable base on which to secure ethical positions; it is merely the context in which those positions are formed and discussed. Conscious of this precarious contingency, and looking for guiding lights within the discourse, I take my stand with a quotation from an impeccably traditional witness, Augustine, who wrote: "Whoever, therefore, thinks that he understands the divine Scriptures or any part of them so that it does not build the double love of God and of our neighbor does not understand it at all" (*Christian Doctrine* 1.35.40).

By this light, any interpretation of scripture that hurts people, oppresses people, or destroys people cannot be the right interpretation, no matter how traditional, historical, or exegetically respectable. There can be no debate about the fact that the church's stand on homosexuality has caused oppression, loneliness, self-hatred, violence, sickness, and suicide for millions of people. If the church wishes to continue with its traditional interpretation it must *demonstrate*, not just claim, that it is more loving to condemn homosexuality than to affirm homosexuals. Can the church *show* that same-sex loving relationships damage those involved in them? Can the church give compelling reasons to believe that it really would be better for all lesbian and gay Christians to live alone, without the joy of intimate touch, without hearing a lover's voice when they go to sleep or awake? Is it really better for lesbian and gay teenagers to despise themselves and endlessly pray that their very personalities be reconstructed so that they may experience romance like their straight friends? Is it really more loving for the church to continue its worship of "heterosexual fulfillment" (a "nonbiblical" concept, by the way) while consigning thousands of its members to a life of either celibacy or endless psychological manipulations that masquerade as "healing"?

The burden of proof in the last twenty years has shifted. There are too many of us who are not sick, or inverted, or perverted, or even "effeminate," but who just have a knack for falling in love with people of our own sex. When we have been damaged, it has not been due to our homosexuality but to your and our denial of it. The burden of proof now is not on us, to show that we are not sick, but rather on those who insist that we would be better off going back into the closet. What will "build the double love of God and of our neighbor?"

I have tried to illustrate how all appeals to "what the Bible says" are ideological and problematic. But in the end, all appeals, whether to the Bible or anything else, must submit to the test of love. To people who say this is simplistic, I say, far from it. There are no easy answers. "Love" will not work as a foundation for ethics in a prescriptive or predictable fashion either—as can be seen by all the injustices, imperialisms, and violence committed in the name of love. But rather than expecting the answer to come from a particular method of reading the Bible, we at least push the discussion to where it ought to be: into the realm of debates about Christian love, rather than into either fundamentalism or modernist historicism.

We ask the question that must be asked: "What is the loving thing to do?"

NOTES

I wish to thank Elizabeth A. Clark and Anthony Neil Whitley for assistance in the research for this chapter.

1. For a similar ideological analysis of modern interpretations of Romans 1 and homosexuality, see my "Heterosexism and the Interpretation of Romans 1:18–32," *Biblical Interpretation* 3 (1995), forthcoming.

2. So most of the commentaries. See also Else Kähler, "Exegese zweier neutestamentlicher Stellen (Römer 1.18–32; 1 Korinther 6.9–11). *Problem der*

Homophilie in medizinischer, theologischer, und juristischer Sicht, ed. Th. Bovet (Bern and Tübingen: Paul Haupt, 1965), 33; Jürgen Becker, "Zum Problem der Homosexualität in der Bibel," *ZEE* 31 (1987):51.

3. William F. Orr and James Arthur Walker, *I Corinthians* (Garden City, N.Y.: Doubleday, 1976), 199. While not tying *arsenokoitês* to *malakos* directly, Wolfgang Schrage says that the former should *not* be taken to refer to pederasty alone but to all homosexual relations, this on the basis of Romans 1 (*Der erste Brief an die Korinther* [Zurich: Benziger, 1991], 1.432). Of course, unless we can be certain that *arsenokoitês* refers simply to homosexual relations in general, an appeal to Romans 1 is irrelevant.

4. "Practicing homosexuals" was suggested several years ago for a Catholic lectionary translation. I do not know if the suggestion was finally adopted or published. The arguments by John Boswell (*Christianity, Social Tolerance, and Homosexuality* [Chicago: University Press, 1980]), while useful as a corrective to many overly confident claims that *arsenokoitês* "of course" means a "male homosexual," are I believe flawed by overstatement and occasional interpretive errors. On the other hand, some of those arguing against Boswell seem not completely to understand *his* arguments, make textual mistakes of their own, and operate from uncritical linguistic assumptions (e.g., David F. Wright, "Homosexuals or Prostitutes? The Meaning of ARSENOKOITAI [1 Cor. 6:9, 1 Tim. 1:10]," *VC* 38 [1984]:125–53; see my comments on Wright in following notes). To enter into a detailed tit-for-tat with Boswell, Wright, or other individual treatments of the issue would result in a quagmire. I will, instead, offer my reading with an occasional note on those of others.

5. The history of the invention of "homosexuality" as a psychological, indeed medical, category is now well known. See e.g., Michel Foucault, *The History of Sexuality I: An Introduction* (New York: Random, 1978); and David M. Halperin, *One Hundred Years of Homosexuality* (New York: Routledge, 1990); for a comparison with ancient concepts see Martha Nussbaum, "Therapeutic Arguments and Structures of Desire," *Differences* 2 (1990):46–66, esp. 49.

6. See note 2 and William. L Petersen "Can ARSENOKOITAI Be Translated by 'Homosexuals'?" *VC* 40 (1986):187–91.

7. David Wright, "Homosexuals or Prostitutes?" *VC* 38 (1984):129; Robin Scroggs, *The New Testament and Homosexuality* (Philadelphia: Fortress, 1983), 85–86.

8. See James Barr, *The Semantics of Biblical Language* (London: Oxford, 1961), 107–10.

9. Anton Vögtle, *Die Tugend- und Lasterkataloge im Neuen Testament* (Münster: Aschendorffschen Buckdruckerei, 1936), 13–18; for comparative texts, see Ehrhard Kamlah, *Die Form der katalogischen Paränese im Neuen Testament* (Tübingen: Mohr/Siebeck, 1964).

10. The dates for the document and its different sections are uncertain. This section of the oracle quotes Pseudo-Phocylides (excepting those verses in parentheses). See comments by John J. Collins in *The Old Testament Pseudepigrapha*, ed. James H. Charlesworth (Garden City, N.Y.: Doubleday, 1983), 1.330.

11. Dio Chrysostom 46.8; Philostratus, *Life of Apollonius* 1.15.

12. Wright argues (136–38) that *since* Pseudo-Phocylides elsewhere shows his disapprobation of homosexual conduct, the term must here be a reference to homosexual conduct. Of course the second point does not proceed from the first.

13. I use the edition by Robert M. Grant: *Ad Autolycum* (Oxford: Clarendon, 1970). Wright's quotation of this passage (134–35) has a different order for the vices because he is relying on the Greek text of Gustave Bardy, *Théophile d'Antioche, Trois Livres a Autolycus; Sources chrétiennes* 20 (Paris: du Cerf, 1948). There seems to be no textual evidence for Bardy's version—at least he gives none in the apparatus, and no edition I have examined suggests any textual variation here among the manuscripts. Bardy admits he is mainly following the edition by J.C.T. Otto: *Theophili Episcopi Antiocheni, Ad Autolycum, libri tres. Corpus Apologetarum Christianorum Saeculi Secundi* 8 (Wiesbaden: Martin Sändig, 1969; reprint of 1861). It is not clear, therefore, why he gives a different order for the vice list than do Otto and the other modern editions. Perhaps Bardy altered the order to conform more nearly to that of 1 Cor. 6:9, or he carelessly placed *arsenokoitês* after *pornos* because he *assumed* it belonged with the "sexual sins." If the latter is the case, it provides interesting evidence that the order of vices in the lists is important.

14. The term *pornos* would have been understood most often to refer to a male prostitute. See Jeffrey Henderson, *The Maculate Muse: Obscene Language in Attic Comedy* (New Haven: Yale, 1975); Scroggs, *The New Testament and Homosexuality*, 40. Eva Cantarella takes it as such even in its occurrence in 1 Tim. 1:10 (*Bisexuality in the Ancient World* [New Haven: Yale, 1992], 192–94). *Pornos* also seems to have become, at least in Jewish and Christian circles, a more general term for all sorts of persons considered "sexually immoral."

15. This reading may find support even from the position of the term in 1 Tim. 1:10, if *pornoi* there is taken to be a reference to male prostitutes rather than "fornicators" or sexually immoral persons in general (see Scroggs, *The New Testament and Homosexuality*, 118–21). Since Cantarella *does* read *pornoi* in 1 Tim. 1:10 as referring to male prostitutes and the term following *arsenokoitês* as a reference to people who enslave other people in order to prostitute them (*andrapodistai*), I am puzzled by her insistence that *arsenokoitês* in the same passage cannot refer to prostitutes but must instead be a reference to male–male sex in general (see *Bisexuality*, 192–94). If, on the other hand, we read *pornoi* as referring to prostitutes, the list supports my reading of *arsenokoitês*, occurring as it does between two other terms that refer to sex and economic injustice.

16. *Preparation for the Gospel* 6.10.25; *Die Fragmenta der griechischen Historiker*, ed. Felix Jacoby (Leiden: Brill, 1969), vol. 3C fr. 719.

17. Ibid.; see also *Die Pseudoklementinen II Rekognitionen in Rufius Übersetzung*, rev. ed. Bernard Rehm, earlier ed. Georg Strecker (Berlin: Akademie, 1994), 284–87.

18. I do not discuss other occurrences of the term mentioned by Boswell and Wright because I see no possibility that they shed light on the first-century meaning of *arsenokoitês*. Its meaning in a ninth-century inscription, for example, is unclear, in spite of Wright's overconfident interpretation; besides, the usage is very late (*Greek Anthology* 9.686; see Boswell, 344, n. 22; Wright, 130). The meaning in the sixth-century "Penetential" of (perhaps) John the Faster (see Boswell, 363–65) is equally unclear. Though Wright accuses Boswell of "irrepressible resourcefulness" and "desperate reasoning" in this case (139–40), I find Wright's exegesis no less fanciful or strained. Such late and opaque uses of the term should be set aside until we have clearer evidence about their meaning and relation to first-century usage.

19. This is certainly true of the later translations of the Greek into other languages. But later translations provide little reliable evidence for the meaning of the term in a first-century Greek contest.

20. See my *The Corinthian Body* (New Haven: Yale, 1995), 32–34, 222, 230–31, 241–42.

21. Some scholars define *malakos* as simply a synonym for *kinaedos*, citing texts where the two terms occur together. See, for example, Gaston Vorberg, *Glossarium Eroticum* (Rome: "L'Erma," 1965), s.v. Vorberg's citations do not support his definition; in every such case, *kinaedos* is better interpreted as constituting a subcategory within the larger category of *malakoi* (Diogenes Laertius, *Lives* 7.173) or simply another vice in a list of vices (Plutarch, *Moralia* 88C; Vettius Valens, *Anthologiae* 2.37.54 [ed. David Pingree, p. 108, 1. 3]; Appendix 1.173 [p. 384, 1. 11]). I take *arrêtopoios* in Vettius Valens to be a reference not to homosexual sex but to oral sex—which could, of course, be performed on a man or a woman (see Artemidorus, *Dream Handbook* 1.79). No text I have found equates *malakos* with *kinaedos* or defines one term by the other. Note the list of terms for "fucked men" from Attic comedy: Henderson, *Maculate Muse* 209–15, 222; *malakos* is not among them.

22. Plutarch, *Gaius Gracchus* 4.4; *Cicero* 7.5; Athenaeus 565E. Scroggs (*The New Testament and Homosexuality*, 42, n. 45) misuses such references to argue that dressing like a *malakos* would signal that someone was a *kinaedos*, and therefore *malakos* meant an "effeminate call boy." This ignores the fact that *malakos* more often occurs where neither homosexual sex nor prostitution per se is involved.

23. *Hellenica* 3.4.19; 6.1.6; *Apology* 19; *Memorabilia* 1.2.2. Note that in this last case, the reference to *malakos* relates to work, and it follows a reference to sex *(aphrodisiôn akrateis)*; *malakos* here has nothing to do with sex.

24. Epictetus 3.6.9; 4.1.25; "Epistle of Crates" 19 (Malherbe, p. 68); "Epistle of Diogenes" 29 (Malherbe, p. 126): in both cases, sleeping and eating too much are important.

25. Dio Cassius 58.4.6; Plutarch, *Pericles* 27.4; Josephus, *War* 6.211, *Antiquities* 19.197.

26. Xenophon, *Hiero* 1.23; Plutarch, *Moralia* 831B; 136B; *Pericles* 27.4; Athenaeus, *Deipnosophistae* 12.536C; 543B. In one of Philo's condemnations of decadence, he includes remarks about penetrated men as being thus made effeminate (*On Abraham*, 133–36). The term *malakos*, however, is used of this entire process of degenerating decadence and effeminacy due to luxurious living—including the effeminacy of *heterosexual* sex; the aspects of homosexual sex play only one part.

27. In Dionysius Halicarnassus, *Roman Antiquities* 7.2.4, people cannot tell whether a ruler earned the sobriquet "Malakos" because he had allowed himself to be penetrated as a young man or because he possessed an exceptionally mild nature.

28. The "softness of the Lydians" *(ta Lydôn malaka)* is reflected in their luxurious living, gourmet food, use of too many *female* prostitutes, and lots of indiscriminate sex with men *and* women (Athenaeus, *Deipnosophistae* 12.540F). Plutarch relates the "Lydian mode" in music to softness and general decadence: *Moralia* 83F.

29. Note a similar assumption mentioned by Athenaeus; the Syracusans are reported as forbidding women to wear gold or colorful clothing unless they confess to being prostitutes; similarly, men were not allowed to "dress up" unless they admitted to being either adulterers or *kinaedoi* (*Deipnosophistae* 12.521b).

Dressing up was considered effeminate, but that could mean an attempt to attract either men or women.

30. The suitors of a young girl arrive at her door adorned with long hair styled prettily (Athenaeus, *Deipnosophistae* 528d, citing Agathon, *Thyestes*). This entire section of Athenaeus is instructive for the ancient concept of effeminacy; it usually is related to luxurious and decadent living in general and is expressed far more often here by heterosexual activities than homosexual. For example, the Lydians, according to Clearchus, expressed their effeminacy by laying out parks with lots of shade, gathering the wives and virgins of other men and raping them, and then finally adopting "the manner of life of women," whatever that means (*Deipnosophistae* 12.515e–516a). There is no mention here of homosexual sex.

31. This point was made by John Boswell (*Christianity, Social Tolerance, and Homosexuality*, 340) but generally ignored by biblical scholars, who continue naively to assume that any concern about effeminacy would involve at least an unconscious anxiety about homosexuality. Thus, Paul's concerns about long hair on men in 1 Corinthians 11 must harbor a concern about homosexuality. See Scroggs, "Paul and the Eschatological Woman," *The Text and the Times* (Minneapolis: Fortress, 1993), 88, n. 38; originally in *JAAR* 40 (1972):283–303; *The New Testament and Homosexuality* (Philadelphia: Fortress, 1983), 53–55, 62–65; Jerome Murphy-O'Connor, "Sex and Logic in I Corinthians 11:2–16," *CBQ* 42 (1980):482–500.

32. For a character in Achilles Tatius's novel *Clitophon and Leucippe*, male love is natural, frank, real, and lacking in any softness or effeminacy (2.38; *ou malthassei*). Even Dio Chrysostom, no advocate of male–male love, knows that love of a woman is liable to be thought excessively feminine (7.151–52).

33. Noted also by Scroggs, *The New Testament and Homosexuality*, 46–48.

34. The degradation of the female comes to be linked with asceticism in general, especially but not exclusively in Jewish and Christian writers. Philo praises women who give up sex entirely, thereby becoming "manly," and Thecla, through celibacy, becomes masculinized and saved (*On the Contemplative Life*, 40–64; see Richard A. Baer, Jr., *Philo's Use of the Categories Male and Female* [Leiden: Brill, 1970], 99–100; *Acts of Paul and Thecla*).

35. A common practice among New Testament scholars has been to define *malakos* as the "passive partner" due to its proximity to *arsenokoitês*, which is taken to be the "active partner" (see, e.g., Gordon Fee, *First Epistle to the Corinthians* [Grand Rapids: Eerdmans, 1987], 243–44). But this is circular reasoning. The meaning of *arsenokoitês* is famously problematic, and there is *no* evidence that it was a special term for the "active" partner in homosexual sex (even if one concedes, which I do not, that it is a reference to "men who sleep with men"). Furthermore, while there is no evidence that *malakos* was considered a special ("technical") term for the "passive" partner (as Fee admits), its general meaning as "effeminate" *independent of sexual position or object* is easily demonstrated. To define *malakos* by *arsenokoitês* is to define something already clear by something that is obscure.

36. Every text cited by Scroggs in support of this reading, in his terminology "effeminate call boy" (*The New Testament and Homosexuality*), is better read as I have—by being penetrated, a boy shows his effeminacy, but *malakos* refers to the effeminacy, not the penetration; there were many other signs, many heterosexual, that could also reveal "effeminacy."

37. The list, of course, could be expanded. This is taken mainly from H. Herter, "Effeminatus," *Reallexikon für Antike und Christentum* (Stuttgart: Hiersemann, 1959), 4.620–650; for the associations of hair with effeminacy and decadence, see also Pseudo-Phocylides, *Sentences* 210–12, and the commentary by P. W. van der Horst, *The Sentences of Pseudo-Phocylides* (Leiden: Brill, 1978), 250; Hubert Cancik, *Untersuchungen zur lyrischen Kunst des P. Papianus Statius, Spudasmata* 13 (Hildesheim: Olms, 1965), 58. For masturbation as evidence of *malakia*, see Vorberg, *Glossarium Eroticum* s.v.

38. I say this to forestall one possible objection to my method. One *might* argue that although *malakos* and *arsenokoitês* did not mean, in the common linguistic currency, the "passive" and "active" partners in homosexual sex, that was surely what Paul intended by his use of the terms. The goal of translation, however, is to translate the text, not some guessed-at authorial intention. See Ferdinand Deist, "Presuppositions and Contextual Bible Translation," *JNSL* 19 (1993): 13–23, esp. 19–20. Furthermore, contrary to some assumptions of modernist historiography, the *scripture* for the church is traditionally the text, not a historically reconstructed authorial intention. Thus we translate and interpret not what Paul meant to say but what he said.

9

Gentile Wheat and Homosexual Christians: New Testament Directions for the Heterosexual Church

Jeffrey S. Siker

As Christians we want to know what it means to be living faithfully before God and one another in all aspects of our lives. One significant aspect involves human sexuality. What does a Christlike life look like in terms of our human sexuality? We begin, quite naturally, with where we find ourselves—as Christians at the end of the twentieth century who stand in long streams of interweaving Christian traditions, all of which claim the Old and New Testament scriptures as foundational witnesses both to what God has done and is doing in our midst and to what it means for us to respond in faith to God and to one another alike. I hope to contribute to ongoing discussions about the relations between biblical ethics and human sexuality, and in particular, to the ongoing debate about the status and presence of gay and lesbian Christians within the church.[1]

Introduction: Defining Sin and Discerning the Spirit

The traditional Christian approach to "homosexuality" has been to view homosexual behavior as a sin, based on the biblical witness and on Christian tradition. About this surface observation there can be little debate. The Bible nowhere condones same sex relations and in a few places explicitly condemns them (see Leviticus 18, Romans 1). The question, though, is what *constitutes* the sin of same-sex relations. As we will see, when looking at the pertinent biblical texts, it appears that the sin lies in embracing pagan and hence idolatrous practices or in going against ancient notions of human nature. It is important to ask about the character of sin and what it is that makes homosexual practices sinful, rather than merely assuming the sinfulness of all homosexual expressions.

What does "sin" mean? I define sin as that which goes against our understanding of God's intentions for faithful human existence. While it is not difficult to define sin as a term, it is extremely difficult to describe its contours, for notions of sin have changed significantly over time. Jesus and

Paul both redefined the character of sin in their day. For example, in Jesus' day it was sinful to touch a leper—for one then became ritually impure and unable to participate in the religious cult that regulated the life of the Jewish people, including the ability to make sacrifice for sins. For Jesus, however, it appears that *not* to touch the leper is a sin of omission. To avoid the leper is to go against God's intentions for human relationality. So Jesus touches the leper and in so doing both sins and redefines sin at the same time. In Paul's day, to eat non-kosher food was a sin for faithful Jews. And yet for Paul, who continued to see himself as a faithful Jew even after his call/conversion experience, anyone who mandated the eating of kosher food or mandated the observance of circumcision for Gentiles was sinning (see, e.g., Galatians 2 and the incident with Cephas). The disputes in early Christianity over what was sinful and what was faithful were vigorous and extensive. Passions ran very deep—to the point that Paul sees as accursed those in Galatia who teach the need for circumcision (Gal. 1:8–9). We can only surmise that these rival teachers extended to Paul the same courtesy of being accursed. In short, for Paul, being truly faithful was for his opponents being truly sinful, whereas acting sinfully (from Paul's vantage—by mandating ritual food laws and circumcision) was for them the truest act of faithfulness to God.

So how do we go about defining and describing sin and faithfulness? What does God intend for us and how do we know it? How do we go about discerning the Spirit? Apparently only with much conflict and disagreement. We trust and believe that we can perceive the Spirit of God at work. At times we are moved and persuaded by the convictions, actions, and words of someone we esteem to be saintly. We attribute the power of their testimony to the Spirit of God. We lend authority collectively as believers to the testimony of what we deem to be prophetic and wise voices in our midst. And we stay or change courses accordingly.

Thus, according to Acts, were Christians in the early church moved and persuaded by the spirited testimony of Peter and Paul regarding God's inclusion of the Gentiles apart from law-observance: that is, as non-Jews? Thus, were Christians in the sixteenth century moved by Luther and Calvin as they testified amid great opposition to an understanding of the gospel that was different from what was commonplace in their day? Of course, still other Christians were persuaded by the spirited testimony of Pharisaic Christians in Paul's day (see Acts 11) and by the bishops at the Council of Trent in the days of Luther and Calvin.

In our time many of us have been moved by the witness of various women, among them Elizabeth Cady Stanton, Letty Russell, Rosemary Ruether, and Elisabeth Schüssler Fiorenza, who we believe have displayed God's prophetic spirit, and we have been convicted of the sinfulness of our sexism. (And we remember rival witnesses who persuaded other Christians differently, as in 1 Timothy 2.) Many have also been moved by the witness of such prophetic voices in the African-American Christian community as Martin Luther King Jr. and James Cone, to whom many of us attribute the power of God's spirit as we stand convicted of the sinfulness of our racism. In both cases, of course, there remain Christians who see the full inclusion of women (in our terms) as sinful and against God's intentions; and there are still those who see the full inclusion of African Americans as a betrayal of God's intentions for race relations.

In our time many of us who identify ourselves as Christians in the Reformed and Roman Catholic traditions have been moved and persuaded by the spirited testimony and prophetic lives of self-affirming gay and lesbian Christians to accept loving monogamous same-sex unions as a faithful expression of God's intentions for those people who are gay and lesbian, even though we used to consider such relationships inherently sinful and against God's purposes for all humanity. However, most of the church today still sees such relations as sinful, in much the same terms as the tradition has long held, so we are at a painful impasse. To those of us who accept the legitimacy of same-sex relations, to maintain a "neutral" (whatever that might be) or negative position vis-à-vis our gay and lesbian brothers and sisters in Christ would be sinful. It would be to avoid touching and embracing those the church and society have traditionally deemed not just lepers but sinful lepers, those we have come to know as fellow Christians empowered by God's Spirit as we are, whose sexual relations are neither scandal nor sin but rather another expression of human sexuality created by God.

Is there a way beyond this impasse? I both hope and despair. I have some hope because I believe that as more Christians experience the faithful testimony of gay and lesbian Christians, they will slowly come to realize that all same-sex relations are not inherently sinful. And yet I despair at times, seeing many gay and lesbian Christians abandon mainstream churches as hopeless places where they will receive only more bashing, some of it vicious and some of it polite. I worry as I wonder how long gay and lesbian Christians can wait to find vibrant communities of faith where they are accepted for who they are as God's children.

Listening to Scripture and Experience: A Journey

Let me turn to argue in more constructive ways, and particularly in relation to scripture, why we should fully include and embrace openly gay and lesbian Christians in the church, as well as ordain qualified gay and lesbian Christians to the ministry of word and sacrament. By way of introduction, I should state clearly that I am not writing on behalf of gay and lesbian Christians. I would not presume to do so. Rather, I am writing as a heterosexual white male Christian who has come to believe that it is time—indeed, long past time—for us as a church to welcome fully and openly our brothers and sisters in Christ who are gay and lesbian. I speak as one who used to believe otherwise.

While serving on the Presbytery of the Pacific's Committee on Preparation for Ministry several years ago, I began to wrestle seriously with the issue of the status of gays and lesbians in the church. As an ordained Presbyterian minister and a professor of biblical studies, I realized I was not sure what I thought. And so I began to study and to learn.

Beginning with scripture, since that is where the Reformed tradition in which I stand is accustomed to begin and since I was, and still am, a biblical scholar, I was struck by three things in analyzing the biblical texts.

First, I was surprised to learn that scripture says almost nothing about homosexuality. Only six biblical passages address same-sex relations in any direct way, three from the Hebrew scriptures and three from the New Testament: the story of Sodom and Gomorrah from Genesis 19, two passages from the Holiness Code in Leviticus 18 and 20, and three passages from the Pauline writings (in Romans 1, 1 Corinthians 6, and 1 Timothy 1).

Second, it became apparent that what we mean by the term "homosexuality" in the late twentieth century is for the most part rather different from what the biblical texts are discussing. Indeed, in order to prevent reading our own modern understandings of homosexuality anachronistically back into the biblical texts, I think we should stop talking about what the Bible has to say regarding "homosexuality." As has often been noted, the term "homosexuality" was coined only in the nineteenth century and in present-day parlance is used most often when talking about sexual *orientation*, which involves much more than sexual action. Since the ancients did not have our notions of "heterosexual" and "homosexual" sexual orientations, to persist in using these terms when discussing "biblical sexual ethics" (yet another artificial construct) is misleading at best. Hence I will use "homoeroticism" as a descriptive term when addressing same-sex relations in antiquity. (Admittedly this term is also a modern one, but I think it avoids the danger of lumping together all ancient expressions of same-sex relations with contemporary understandings of homosexuality.)

The relevant passages in the Bible address what I would consider exploitive forms of homoerotic sexual practice, whether it be homoerotic rape (as in Sodom and Gomorrah), homoerotic acts within idolatrous cultic prostitution (as in Leviticus), or, as in the Pauline letters, the Greco-Roman practices of male homoerotic prostitution and pederasty (an older active male with a prepubescent, passive boy; more on this later).

Thus I became convinced that in our eagerness to apply the Bible to our contemporary questions about homosexuality, we often fail to see that what the Bible was talking about and what we are talking about are not just

a little different but very different, to the point that I have come to conclude that the Bible offers almost no direct teaching about homosexuality
as we understand it. And let me be clear about what I mean, lest there be
any confusion. I am referring primarily to a mutually consensual, monogamous, loving, and committed relationship between an adult gay couple or
an adult lesbian couple. (There are other definitions of contemporary homosexuality, but this is the one I am using.) The homoerotic aspect of such
a relationship is just that, one aspect among many, just as heteroeroticism
is one aspect among many within heterosexual relationships. As best as I
can tell, nothing in the Bible directly addresses contemporary homosexual
relationships so defined.[2]

This leads to my third observation. In looking to the Bible for guidance
on contemporary homosexuality, it became clear to me that one has to sit-
uate any questions about homosexuality within the larger context of what
the Bible has to say about human sexuality overall. This means realizing
that different biblical authors from different periods of time said different
things in different situations, mostly related to sexuality within heterosexual marriages. Thus we move from tribal patriarchal households in ancient
Israel, where polygamy was not uncommon, to the period of kings with
multiple wives, to the time of earliest Christianity where Paul encourages
unmarried Christians to avoid marriage and remain celibate, to the time of
late-first-century Christianity, where the author of 1 Timothy encourages
women to marry and have children.

In the New Testament, Paul has the most to say about sexuality. Essentially, he encourages mutuality and reciprocity (1 Corinthians 7), and
he assumes that there is a committed monogamous relational context for
all sexual expressions. For Paul, especially in 1 Corinthians 7, the reason
for having sex is not procreation but mutual fulfillment and, with it, the
strengthening of the relationship. To be sure, Paul takes relations between
men and women as normative. But it is not so easy to take Paul's pre-
sumption of heterosexual relationships and move from there to advocating
such relationships as normative to the exclusion of all homosexual relationships. Perhaps this can best be demonstrated by turning to that work-
horse of debate over Paul's "position on homosexuality," Romans 1, especially verses 24–27, where Paul explicitly discusses homoerotic relations. I
begin by citing that passage:

> Therefore God gave them up in the lusts of their hearts to impu-
> rity, to the degrading of their bodies among themselves, because
> they exchanged the truth about God for a lie and worshiped and
> served the creature rather than the Creator, who is blessed forever!
> Amen.
> For this reason God gave them up to degrading passions. Their
> women exchanged natural intercourse for unnatural, and in the

same way also the men, giving up natural intercourse with women, were consumed with passion for one another. Men committed shameless acts with men and received in their own persons the due penalty for their error.

A couple of preliminary observations.[3] First, the literary context. The main topic of this passage is God's actions in revealing God's wrath within the Gentile world. In turn, Rom. 1:18–32 functions in the wider context of 1:18–3:20, where the topic is the human predicament and humanity's need for God's saving grace. Paul concludes this section in 3:23 with his well-known statement that all have sinned and fallen short of God's glory, Jew and Gentile alike. Paul indicts the Gentiles especially in 1:18–32; he goes on to indict the Jews in 2:17–3:20. The primary sin of the Gentiles is idolatry, as is clear from 1:25—"they exchanged the truth about God for a lie and worshiped and served the creature rather than the Creator"—on which account God gave them over to the consequences of their idolatry, including various forms of sexual immorality.

In his condemnation of Gentiles and their idolatrous behavior, Paul resembles his Hellenistic Jewish contemporaries, who accused Gentiles of the same things in much the same way, as a comparison of Paul with the Wisdom of Solomon and Philo demonstrates. Thus the cultural context of Paul's comments is important. Paul shared four presuppositions with other Hellenistic Jews regarding homoerotic actions among Gentiles.

First, it was supposed that anyone who sought same-sex intercourse was going against his or her "natural" desire for the opposite sex. This can be seen in Paul's language regarding Gentile women who "exchanged natural intercourse for unnatural" and Gentile men who abandoned "natural intercourse with women" to have sex with other men. There is no notion of sexual orientation in the sense that we think of it today. Rather, the presupposition is that same-sex intercourse is a free and deliberate choice against nature.

Second, it was commonly supposed that homoerotic acts were intrinsically lustful and that all who engaged in such actions had an insatiable sexual appetite. Again, the only forms of homoerotic activity for which we have clear evidence in Paul's day are pederasty (an active adult man with a passive early adolescent boy), male prostitution, and situations where masters forced their male slaves to play a receptive and passive sexual role. These forms of homoeroticism were widely seen as willful and overly lustful. Paul reflects this view in his description of women being "consumed with passion for one another."

Third, it was supposed that sexual intercourse required one partner to be active and the other to be passive, and that the active role naturally belonged to the man, whereas the passive role naturally belonged to the woman. Homoerotic activity, then, was believed to result in a confusion of sexual identities and roles, for it was seen as demeaning for an adult male to play the passive or receptive role and equally outrageous and presumptuous for the woman to play the active dominant role.

Fourth, and finally, there were fears that homoerotic practice could lead to the extinction of the human species, as Philo and others wrongly presumed that same-sex intercourse rendered sterile the men who engaged in this practice. These cultural contexts are crucial for understanding Paul's comments about homoeroticism, especially given that on the whole we do not share these presuppositions today.

In addition to the literary and cultural contexts, it is also important to look closely at the theological context of Paul's comments in Romans 1. Paul's main point in Rom. 1:26–27 is to demonstrate the reality of the human plight, couched here in terms of Gentile idolatry expressed particularly in exploitive Gentile homoerotic practices. Essentially, Paul wants to show the brokenness of life apart from God, the consequences of human sinfulness. The root of human sin is idolatry, not recognizing God as God, and so pretending we can live fully apart from God. This sin is the refusal to accept our own humanity before God. Further, Paul uses the description of the human sinful plight before God in Romans 1—3 to set up his proclamation of God's grace in Christ to Jew and Gentile alike in 3:21–8:39.

Overall, then, what can we say about the significance of Rom. 1:24–27 for our contemporary theologizing about same-sex relations? What stands out most are the contrasts between the presuppositions Paul and his contemporaries had about such relations with the presuppositions we have today. Paul saw homoerotic relations as a free choice against natural law. We see homosexual relations primarily in terms of sexual orientation, which one does not choose but of which one naturally becomes aware in the process of maturation. Paul knew only of exploitive forms of homoerotic expression—particularly pederasty and prostitution—and then probably indirectly. We know of forms of homosexuality where the relationship is one of mutuality, commitment, and care. Paul saw all forms of homoeroticism as expressions of insatiable lust. We know of homosexual relationships where the sexual aspect is no more or less obsessive than in comparable heterosexual relationships. Paul presumed that all homoerotic relations were a consequence of Gentile idolatry. We know of gay and lesbian Christians who truly worship and serve the one true God and yet still affirm in positive ways their identity as gay and lesbian people. Paul apparently knew of no homosexual Christians. We do. What we can affirm with Paul is his condemnation of exploitive forms of homoeroticism, which are the consequence of human sinfulness in refusing to acknowledge God as God. What we cannot and must not do is anachronistically to condemn gay and lesbian Christians in our age and with our understandings on the basis of what Paul says about non-Christian homoerotic activity in *his* age with *his* understandings.

In addition to the conclusions I have drawn on the basis of the biblical materials, another significant factor led to my change in heart and mind: the realization that in discussing the inclusion of gays and lesbians we are dealing not with an issue but with persons. And thus the first step in any discussion about gay and lesbian people in our church is to recognize that they are persons and not objects of study. Recognizing them as persons means that we listen to what they have to say and get to know them, first and foremost as persons and not as "homosexuals." That is often difficult for us to do, primarily because our own fears and presumptions (homophobia and heterosexism) get in the way, just as racism, for example, still may get in the way for most of us who are white in seeing African Americans as persons first and foremost.

Above all, I believe the Spirit of God has led me to see lesbian and gay Christians as sisters and brothers in Christ. When I witness something of the prophetic and healing ministry of gay and lesbian Christians as they reach out to people with whom most of us still feel uncomfortable, what can I do but praise God for God's Spirit at work in ministering to those most despised by our society and church? What can I do but recognize the risen Jesus embracing the least among us through their hands? And when I feel God's Spirit moving in worship at West Hollywood Presbyterian Church, what am I to say—that it can't be? That the words "gay" and "Christian" cannot go together?—or rather that God is at work in what to me are surprising ways and surprising places?

When I realize, then, that a gay or lesbian person does not become heterosexual when he or she becomes a Christian, I am faced with a decision. Either I say that homosexuality is a tragic sexual orientation that is a reflection of generic human sinfulness, so that homosexuals must refrain from and repent of homosexual desires and actions; or I say that homosexuality is *another* sexual orientation, certainly different from heterosexuality, certainly not the predominant sexual orientation, but no more sinful in nature or design than heterosexuality. What is sinful is when we exploit one another, when we fail to recognize one another as persons created by God, persons who glorify God as we seek the full humanity of one another, a humanity expressed most clearly in Jesus.

I understand that arguments on the basis of experience are not self-corroborating. But we dare not subordinate the role of experience in theological deliberation to the point that it takes least place in the quadrilateral that also includes scripture, tradition, and reason. Experience must be given an equal voice and not denigrated as a lesser authority in our decision-making process.

I find it unfortunate that Marion Soards, for example, tends to downplay the role of experience, as can be seen from the subtitle he has chosen, "The Ambiguity of Experience" (in his *Scripture and Homosexuality*). He states that "a theology of experience is dangerously subjective" (55), which can certainly be true. But in the case of most Christians, inclusive of gay and lesbian Christians, it is not experience alone that gives direction to theology but an understanding of the gospel message found in scripture, especially God's inclusion of outcasts over against prevailing cultural norms, especially when such norms have infected the so-called people of God (see, e.g., Luke 4:16–30).

Further, when we think of Paul we should not forget it was his experience of the risen Jesus, his experience of a revelation from God, that was the central motivating factor underlying all his theological articulations, an experience that led him to read scripture and tradition in radically new ways. Many of Paul's contemporaries apparently dismissed him precisely because of the seeming subjectivity of his revelatory experience, which ran counter to scripture and tradition. Others, however, were persuaded by the fruit of Paul's ministry that his experience and his consequent revisioning of scripture and tradition were valid and authoritative interpretations of God's actions in the world through Jesus. We should not forget that Paul's experience of God in Christ has become scripture for us. Thus while I agree that we should be wary of theological arguments made solely on the basis of experience without significant recourse to scripture, tradition, and reason, at the same time we need to pay close attention to the living reality of Christian experience, and especially to communal experience of God's Spirit at work in our midst.

Gentile Inclusion as a Model for Including Gay and Lesbian Christians

When I reflect upon the personal presence of gay and lesbian Christians in our midst, I cannot help but be reminded of a difficult struggle that the earliest Christians faced, already mentioned: On what basis can Gentiles be included in the community of faith?[4] By and large, the first generation of Christians, almost all of whom were Jewish Christians, viewed Gentiles in the same way that first-century Jews did: Gentiles were by definition sinful and unclean in the eyes of God. (Remember Paul's words from Gal. 2:15: "We ourselves are Jews by birth and not Gentile sinners.") The only way a Gentile could be part of the people of God was by converting, by becoming a Jew. This meant circumcision, abiding by the Jewish law, and renouncing and repenting of one's former life as a Gentile. The earliest Jewish Christians also assumed that no Gentiles *as Gentiles* could be part of the people of God. They first had to become Jews.

But much to the shock of Peter and his associates, God had poured out the Spirit on the Gentiles *as Gentiles*. "The circumcised believers who had come with Peter were astounded that the gift of the Holy Spirit had been poured out even on the Gentiles, for they heard them speaking in tongues and extolling God" (Acts 10:45–46). Peter and those with him bore witness to the outpouring of the Spirit upon the Gentiles, to their utter surprise. No one had expected such a scandalous thing. Indeed, the next thing Luke reports (Acts 11:1–3) is that, when the Jewish Christians in Jerusalem heard that Peter and those with him had gone to Gentiles, "the circumcised believers criticized him, saying, 'Why did you go to uncircumcised men and eat with them?'" Peter told them about his experience, and their response was one of great surprise: "When they heard this, they were silenced. And they praised God, saying, 'Then God has given even to the Gentiles the repentance that leads to life'" (Acts 11:18). There continued to be great opposition to the Gentile mission from a significant number of Jewish Christians, who were convinced that Gentiles as Gentiles could never be included among God's people, as Acts 15 and Galatians 2 richly attest. Paul fought this fight throughout his ministry.

Before I came to know various Christians who are also homosexual in their sexual orientation, I was like the hard-nosed doctrinaire circumcised Jewish Christians who denied that Gentiles could receive the Spirit of Christ. But just as Peter's experience of Cornelius in Acts 10 led him to realize that even Gentiles were receiving God's Spirit, so my experience of various gay and lesbian Christians led me to realize that these Christians have received God's Spirit as gays and lesbians and that the reception of the Spirit has nothing to do with sexual orientation. Indeed, the church has long honored as esteemed brothers and sisters in Christ many gays and lesbians who were simply never known as such. I once thought of gays and lesbians as Peter and Paul thought of "Gentile sinners," but now, with Peter, I am compelled to ask, " 'Can anyone withhold the water for baptizing these people who have received the Holy Spirit just as we have?' " (Acts 10:47).

While I can understand the sense of moral revulsion that many heterosexual Christians today may have when they contemplate homosexual relationships, is it in essence much different from the moral revulsion that early Jewish Christians apparently felt when contemplating association with impure and unclean Gentile Christians? Was not their sense of betraying the long-standing and sacred truth of ritual purity in the face of Gentile inclusion similar to the sense of some heterosexual Christians today that to welcome gays and lesbians into the church along with their homosexuality is to betray the long-standing tradition of heterosexuality as God's revealed truth? But it is one thing to understand such intolerance; it is another to condone it. Peter and Paul called the Jewish Christian church in their day to move beyond the marginal toleration of Gentile Christians and welcome their full inclusion. Similarly, in our day we in the heterosexual Christian church are being called by God to move beyond our marginal toleration of homosexual Christians and welcome their full inclusion.[5]

The Parable of the Wheat and the Tares
as a Model for the Church

Toleration is, in my view, a crucial issue in the debate over the presence of gay and lesbian Christians in the church. What are we in the church to do when we disagree over the wisdom of including openly gay and lesbian Christians? How are we to proceed? In addition to the analogy of Gentile inclusion just developed, I would suggest we pay careful attention to Jesus' parable in Matt. 13:24–30 of weeds among the wheat, known traditionally as the parable of the wheat and the tares. Let me begin by citing the parable in full:

> He [Jesus] put before them [the disciples] another parable: "The kingdom of heaven may be compared to someone who sowed good seed in his field; but while everybody was asleep, an enemy came and sowed weeds among the wheat, and then went away. So when the plants came up and bore grain, then the weeds appeared as well. And the slaves of the householder came and said to him, 'Master, did you not sow good seed in your field? Where, then, did these weeds come from?' He answered, 'An enemy has done this.' The slaves said to him, 'Then do you want us to go and gather them?' But he replied, 'No; for in gathering the weeds you would uproot the wheat along with them. Let both of them grow together until the harvest; and at harvest time I will tell the reapers, Collect the weeds first and bind them in bundles to be burned, but gather the wheat into my barn.'"

This parable occurs in the context of a whole series of parables Jesus tells in Matthew 13 about the kingdom of God (in Matthew the kingdom of heaven). What is the kingdom of God like? To what may it be compared? How does God rule? In the parable of the wheat and the weeds we learn that patience and tolerance with one another in the church should be the order of the day. We are quick to identify ourselves as wheaty faithful servants and others as noxious sinful weeds sprouting in our midst. And we are also quick to want to uproot the unwelcome growth, which in our view comes not from God but from the enemy. But we need to pay attention to the wishes of the householder: Should we try to pull out what we identify as weeds? "No; for in gathering the weeds you would uproot the wheat along with them" (13:29).

What should we do in situations where from our vantage we see sin making inroads among the faithful? From the perspective of church tradition and traditional readings of scripture, openly homosexual Christians should not be tolerated and should be actively discouraged. From the perspective of many others, gay and lesbian Christians are not sinning by engaging in loving relationships; indeed, the sin lies in the homophobia and heterosexism of the mainstream church and its exclusive intolerance. So what should we do? We should follow the command of the householder and not seek to uproot what appears to us to be weeds, lest in the process we also uproot the wheat that God has planted. What is wheat and what is weed? Ultimately that is for God to determine, for we are apt to mistake one for the other. What are we to do in the meantime? Be patient and be tolerant—on both sides. As J. R. Donahue has noted,

> The surprising element in the parable is that the householder allows the thorns to grow alongside the wheat. The central thrust of the parable is the contrast between the householder who waits until the harvest and the servants who are eager to root out the weeds at first sight. . . . In the kingdom proclamation of Jesus, this parable may have served as a defense of his association with sinners and his unwillingness to establish a "pure Messianic community." As the *Psalms of Solomon* (first century B.C.) attests, the arrival of God's kingdom was to be marked by the separation of the good from the evil and the purification of the land. Jesus does not deny that such a separation will take place but disassociates it from his proclamation of the kingdom. Now is the time for the offer of mercy and forgiveness to the sinner. Those who will be "blessed of my Father" (Matt. 25:34) will be known only at the final judgment.[6]

Of course, none of us wishes to be identified as the sinful weed, especially when we see ourselves as exercising our faithful response to God as wheat. Gay and lesbian Christians are tired of being told they are sinners, for they see their sexual orientation as given by God, just as heterosexual people see their sexuality as given by God. Those on the other side of the debate see themselves as defending the truth of the gospel by opposing full inclusion of gay and lesbian Christians, and yet to those affirming of gay and lesbian people, these others appear to be self-righteous and misguided sinners who are blind to God's inclusion of the traditionally outcast among us.

How then should we respond? Essentially, the parable instructs us to treat one another as wheat, that it is better to tolerate what we perceive as weeds among us than it is for us to be intolerant and risk accidentally pulling out some wheat along with the weeds. When in doubt, assume wheat and not weeds. Tolerance and patience are to be our guides. We must not rush to exclude and uproot one another.

So do we ever pull weeds? Do we ever cast out? Did not Paul counsel the Corinthians to cast out the sinful man from among them in 1 Corinthians 5? Did he not warn against the dangers of tolerating a little sinful yeast, saying it would corrupt the whole loaf? Yes, he did. With Jesus, however, he also admonished the Corinthians tempted to judge him not to "pronounce judgment before the time, before the Lord comes, who will bring to light the things now hidden in darkness and will disclose the purposes of the heart" (1 Cor. 4:5). Are we never to cast out? Never to name anything as sinful for fear of pulling out the wheat with the weeds?

Hardly. But we must be fully convinced as a community of faith that we are casting out bad fruit and not good fruit, to employ yet another agricultural metaphor. We must be very clear that there is no danger of accidentally confusing wheat with weeds. Jesus tells us we will know the tree by its fruit (Matt. 12:33; Luke 6:44). Jesus says, "I appointed you to go and bear fruit, fruit that will last" (John 15:16). As Christians we believe we will be able to discern over time what counts as good fruit and what is bad fruit. Sometimes we will disagree over what is what. In instances where we believe we have reached a broad consensus in the church, not a narrow one, we should act. For example, we believe now that it is sinful to treat women as inferior to men. We recognize the fruitful ministries of women.

In the case of homosexual Christians, the heterosexual church majority should act first and foremost with tolerance and inclusive patience. We should presume wheat. We should look at and recognize the fruitful ministries of gay and lesbian Christians among us. As for gay and lesbian Christians, I can only hope they will continue to be patient with those who sin against them, but that is not a decision I can make on their behalf.

Conclusion

What does a Christlike life look like in terms of our human sexuality? There are many heterosexual Christians who in their struggle to respond to the status of gay and lesbian Christians in the church have concluded— on the basis of scripture and tradition, and lacking clear guidance to the contrary—that the church should not rule in favor of accepting any homosexual practice.

I do not question the integrity of persons with this view, or their honorable intentions to approach this divisive question with pastoral care and concern for the gay and lesbian people to whom they are saying no. For example, Richard Hays, in his 1991 *Sojourners* article "Awaiting the Redemption of Our Bodies,"[7] concludes (p. 21):

> In view of the considerable uncertainty surrounding the scientific and experiential evidence, in view of our culture's present swirling confusion about gender roles, in view of our propensity for self-deception, I think it prudent and necessary to let the univocal testimony of scripture and the Christian tradition order the life of the church on this painfully controversial matter. We must affirm that the New Testament tells us the truth about ourselves as sinners and as God's sexual creatures: Marriage between man and woman is the normative form for human sexual fulfillment, and homosexuality is one among many tragic signs that we are a broken people, alienated from God's loving purpose.

But I would pose some questions for those who maintain this position. Is this not exactly what the law-observant Jewish-Christian opponents of Paul said when dealing with the question of Gentile inclusion? Could they not appeal to God's covenant with Abraham and point to circumcision and the full conversion to Judaism as normative for the inclusion of Gentiles within the covenant people of God, as it had always been (see Romans 4 and Galatians 3)? Could they not appeal to the sayings of Jesus himself to show that Jewish law had not been and could not be abrogated? Could they not complain that Paul was betraying the faith and was simply giving in to Gentile culture and making a mockery of the standards of Christian faith and practice? Could not these faithful, law-observant, Jewish Christians appeal to the preponderance of the testimony of scripture and tradition in response to these Gentiles who seemed to have the Spirit of God and say that they were welcome into the Christian community once they abstained from their former sinful Gentile practices (including not observing the Sabbath and eating unclean foods) and became converts to Judaism and only then to the true messianic faith?

Various law-observant Jewish Christians could do this, and they did do this. And if Galatians is any indication, many Gentiles were receptive to this message. But Paul saw things differently. Acts tells us that Peter saw things differently. Gentiles were not by definition sinners, for the Spirit of God had been poured out on them apart from law observance. The Spirit guided their lives, not the law. Just so, I would argue, the Spirit guides the lives of heterosexual and homosexual Christians alike, not their sexuality.

In conclusion, I would argue that the Bible does not give us clear guidance regarding inclusion of gays and lesbians in the Christian community, but it does give us clear guidance regarding treating one another as God's wheat. It does provide clear directions regarding the inclusion of those who, even to our surprise, have received the Spirit of God and join us in our Christian confession. In his own day Paul called upon the Galatians to pay attention to the experience of the Spirit. Did they recognize the Spirit through a doctrinal orthodoxy and orthopraxy called for by those Jewish Christians who insisted that the only good Gentile was a "Jewish Gentile"? Or did they recognize the Spirit through their faith? And so today we are called to ask an analogous question: Despite our experience, do we insist that homosexual Christians can have the Spirit of God only if they are "heterosexual homosexual" Christians? Or, with Peter and Paul, are we up to the challenge of recognizing, perhaps with surprise and with humility, that gay and lesbian Christians, *as* gays and lesbians and not as sinners, have received the Spirit in faith? If so, let us welcome our newfound brothers and sisters in Christ and get on with the tasks to which God has called us all.

NOTES

1. This chapter builds on and sometimes repeats portions of another essay I have written on this topic, "How to Decide? Homosexual Christians, the Bible, and

Gentile Inclusion," (*Theology Today* 51:2 [1994]: 219–34), which was reprinted with minor changes in *Homosexuality in the Church: Both Sides of the Debate*, ed. J. S. Siker (Louisville, Ky.: Westminster John Knox, 1994), 178–94.

2. Some scholars have sought to minimize the differences between ancient and modern understandings and expressions of homoerotic relations. See, for example, Marion L. Soards, *Scripture and Homosexuality: Biblical Authority and the Church Today* (Louisville, Ky.: Westminster John Knox, 1995), 46–50. To be sure, not every form of ancient homoeroticism was expressed in terms of pederasty. Still, I think Soards would be hard pressed to find significant examples in antiquity of what we would today consider mutual, reciprocal, loving, monogamous homosexual relationships. Part of what Soards overlooks is that the model of ancient homoeroticism emphasized the distinction between the active and the passive partner in homoerotic acts, regardless of the form of homoeroticism. To my knowledge, we have no evidence of ancient reciprocal loving relations where the notion of active and passive is unimportant. (This is not to say that such relations did not exist, but that ancient constructions of human sexuality did not honor such relations or preserve information about them.) The classic treatment of ancient Greco-Roman homoeroticism remains K. J. Dover, *Greek Homosexuality* (Cambridge: Harvard, 1978).

3. In my discussion of Romans 1, I am persuaded by the arguments of Victor P. Furnish ("The Bible and Homosexuality: Reading the Texts in Context," *Homosexuality in the Church: Both Sides of the Debate*, ed. J. S. Siker, 18–35), and Robin Scroggs (*The New Testament and Homosexuality: Contextual Background for Contemporary Debate* [Philadelphia: Fortress, 1983]). Hence I repeat many of their arguments here, especially those of Furnish.

4. On the use of Acts 10–15 in theological discussion, see especially Luke Johnson, *Decision Making in the Church: A Biblical Model* (Philadelphia: Fortress, 1983), 46–58, 67–87.

5. There are, of course, limitations to the analogy between Gentile Christians in the first century and gay and lesbian Christians in the present day. Gentile Christianity became the dominant form of Christianity by the end of the first century; it cannot be argued that the acceptance of homosexual Christians would result in the church's becoming predominantly homosexual, since persons with a homosexual orientation represent a small portion of the overall population, while Gentiles have always far outnumbered Jews. Further, whereas homosexuality is a category of sexual orientation, Gentile is a kind of ethnic description referring to anyone who is a non-Jew. The crux of the analogy, however, lies in the observation that early Jewish Christians viewed Gentiles as sinners because they were Gentiles, just as today most heterosexual Christians see openly homosexual persons as being sinners because they act according to their orientation.

6. John R. Donahue, *The Gospel in Parable* (Philadelphia: Fortress, 1988), 67. See also Daniel J. Harrington, *The Gospel According to Matthew* (Collegeville, Minn.: Liturgical, 1990), 200.

7. This article is reprinted in expanded form in Jeffrey S. Siker, ed., *Homosexuality in the Church*.

Epilogue: Ending without Closure

Diverse voices, many of which readers of this volume will never hear, mingled at the Consultation on Biblical Ethics and Human Sexuality at McCormick Theological Seminary, August 25–27, 1995. Each of the chapters in this volume provoked spirited discussion among the twenty-four biblical scholars in attendance. Their combined voices, like these chapters, expressed no view of biblical ethics or of human sexuality that holds together completely, let alone a consistent biblical ethics of human sexual behavior. An observer could charge the Consultation with vacillating, but in so doing would not express the mind of the participants. We have heard our own voices as a blend, not entirely harmonious to be sure, but a multiplicity of voices that together do say something.

One thing the multiplicity of these twenty-four voices expresses is a profound regard for one another's integrity and sincerity, even when our interpretations differ. We twenty-four affirm with deep respect for one another the value of our dialogue. Significantly, this profound respect comes not from avoiding our differences but through confronting them.

Some in our number would like to stake out grounds for at least three positions—one in support of the present position of the Presbyterian Church (U.S.A.) (that is, welcoming people who manifest homosexual behavior into the life of our Christian community but refusing to ordain those who do not discontinue their homosexual behavior); a second in support of ordaining persons who manifest homosexual behavior without requiring them to be heterosexual or celibate; and a third position espousing the evaluation of each candidate for ordination without a comprehensive decision in either of the first two directions.

But there are compelling reasons for us to let the entire range of voices continue to speak without self-selecting ourselves into three camps. One is the recognition of our limits. Choon-Leong Seow's chapter in this book is an effort to move beyond the present limits—inside which we usually discuss only a scattering of texts—to include portions of the Bible that have been neglected in the church's debate. This requires including experience and reason, inasmuch as experience and reason are warranted by the Bible itself. Further, we need to expand our limits because biblical study today embraces a wide variety of methods—historical, sociological, philological, and literary. Few scholars master more than a portion of these methods. Consequently, biblical interpretations are partial. There is not simply "one" position on the interpretation of the Bible, and so we need to hear what derives from a variety of methods. Further, though men of European descent form the largest portion of our number, our own social locations are varied—Asian, African American, Hispanic, female, male, homosexual, and heterosexual. We do not all look out the same windows. Moreover, the debate in the church today is set in the midst of a complex system of plays for power. Our society has been polarized by controversies that parade as diametrical opposites—Communism or democracy, socialism or free enterprise, affirmative action or racism, freedom of choice or right to life, feminism or male chauvinism, affirmation of gay and lesbian lifestyles or homophobia. Debates from such opposite extremes leave little room for negotiation. In the midst of varieties of methods, social locations, and plays for power, the multi-vocality of the dialogue in our Consultation has broadened the vision of us all.

Our stand for openness and dialogue means that one of our voices to and for the church is a caution against using the Bible piecemeal in support of absolute positions. Rarely does the Bible give final pronouncements. One value of the collection of books in the Bible is that it both preserves and gives us the basis for alternative positions. To give only one case in point, Ezra 9:1 opposes the marriage of people of Israel to foreigners, including explicitly the Moabites. The compelling story of Ruth shows how God works precisely through the marriage of the Israelite Boaz to the Moabite Ruth. The alternatives in the Bible, the deficiencies of our methods, our own social location, and the setting of the church's debate among plays for power lead most of the participants in our Consultation to agree that the biblical interpretation undergirding the current policy of the Presbyterian Church (U.S.A.) is inadequate. Thus, we are committed to openness and dialogue.

On another hand, this does not diminish the urgency of our ethical commitments. Even openness and dialogue can have grave consequences if they allow people to be wounded or the church to become fragmented. Further, in our commitment to broaden the boundaries of the discussion to include experience and reason, we continue to affirm the role of biblical interpretation in coming to decisions, and we resist the temptation to surrender the Presbyterian heritage of profiting from constant interpretation of the Bible.

In the discussion of our Consultation, we challenged the limitations of the interpretations represented in the chapters of this book. But in the very process of challenging the deficiencies of interpretations, we invested ourselves in the value of those very interpretations. Affirmations of the value of our biblical interpretations, challenges of their deficiencies, and profound regard for those who interpret the Bible differently from us are surely parts of the multiplicity of our voices to and for the church in its debate about human sexual behavior and orientation.

Jon L. Berquist, Westminister John Knox Press
Hans Dieter Betz, The Divinity School, University of Chicago
Robert L. Brawley, McCormick Theological Seminary
William P. Brown, Union Theological Seminary in Virginia
Edward F. Campbell, McCormick Theological Seminary
John T. Carroll, Union Theological Seminary in Virginia
Robert B. Coote, San Francisco Theological Seminary
David Cortés-Fuentes, McCormick Theological Seminary
Virgil A. Cruz, Louisville Presbyterian Theological Seminary
J. Andrew Dearman, Austin Presbyterian Theological Seminary
Lewis R. Donelson, Austin Presbyterian Theological Seminary
Elizabeth Gordon Edwards, Princeton Theological Seminary
W. Eugene March, Louisville Presbyterian Theological Seminary
Dale B. Martin, Duke University
Ulrich W. Mauser, Princeton Theological Seminary
Sarah J. Melcher, Emory University
Norman D. Pott, First Presbyterian Church, San Rafael, California
Katharine Doob Sakenfeld, Princeton Theological Seminary
Choon-Leong Seow, Princeton Theological Seminary
Jeffrey S. Siker, Loyola Marymount University
Herman C. Waetjen, San Francisco Theological Seminary
Paul W. Walaskay, Presbyterian School of Christian Education
Antoinette C. Wire, San Francisco Theological Seminary
Victor S. Yoon, Columbia Theological Seminary

Contributors

Robert L. Brawley is Albert G. McGaw Professor of New Testament at McCormick Theological Seminary.

J. Andrew Dearman is Professor of Old Testament at Austin Presbyterian Theological Seminary.

Elizabeth Gordon Edwards is Assistant Professor of New Testament at Princeton Theological Seminary.

Dale B. Martin is Associate Professor of Religion at Duke University.

Ulrich W. Mauser is Otto A. Piper Professor of Biblical Theology at Princeton Theological Seminary.

Sarah J. Melcher is a Ph.D. candidate at Emory University.

Choon-Leong Seow is Henry Snyder Gehman Professor of Old Testament Language and Literature at Princeton Theological Seminary.

Jeffrey S. Siker is Associate Professor of New Testament in the Department of Theological Studies at Loyola Marymount University.

Herman C. Waetjen is Robert S. Dollar Professor of New Testament at San Francisco Theological Seminary.

Scripture Index

New Testament